How the Slaves Saw the Civil War

Recollections of the War through the WPA Slave Narratives

Herbert C. Covey and Dwight Eisnach

 PRAEGER

AN IMPRINT OF ABC-CLIO, LLC
Santa Barbara, California • Denver, Colorado • Oxford, England

Library of Congress Cataloging-in-Publication Data

Covey, Herbert C.
  How the slaves saw the Civil War : recollections of the war through the WPA slave narratives / Herbert C. Covey and Dwight Eisnach.
    pages cm
  Includes bibliographical references and index.
  ISBN 978-1-4408-2823-2 (pbk. : alk. paper) — ISBN 978-1-4408-2824-9 (ebook)
  1. United States—History—Civil War, 1861–1865—African Americans.   2. Slaves—Southern States—History—19th century.   3. Slave narratives—United States.   4. United States—History—Civil War, 1861–1865—Social aspects.   I. Eisnach, Dwight.   II. Title.
  E453.C83   2014
  973.7'114—dc23   2013035030

ISBN: 978-1-4408-2823-2
EISBN: 978-1-4408-2824-9

18 17 16 15 14   1 2 3 4 5

This book is also available on the World Wide Web as an e-book.
Visit www.abc-clio.com for details.

Praeger
An Imprint of ABC-CLIO, LLC

ABC-CLIO, LLC
130 Cremona Drive, P.O. Box 1911
Santa Barbara, California 93116-1911

This book is printed on acid-free paper ∞
Manufactured in the United States of America

This book is dedicated to the two most important supporters of our work, our spouses, Marty Covey and Linda Eisnach. Without their support and encouragement, we would not be able to embark on projects such as this.

Contents

Preface

PURPOSE OF THE BOOK

Slightly more than 150 years ago, more than 3 million men fought in the American Civil War, and 620,000, or about 2 percent of the U.S. population, died during the conflict. An estimated 6 million fatalities resulted from the war (Faust 2008, xi). Although it has been a century and a half since this seismic shift in our nation's history, the war continues to draw our attention to its outcome. We continue to explore this almost incomprehensible American catharsis from every conceivable angle, trying to make sense of how neighbors, families, and fellow citizens could harm each other with such vigor and to what purpose.

The war dramatically affected every household on both sides and created a landscape where friends became foes and brothers became adversaries. It was a time of great controversy among Americans, as differences of opinion abounded on what the war meant and on its implications for the future of the United States. Divisions across American society had never been wider. Even President Abraham Lincoln's family was split on the issue, as he had in-laws who fought for the South. Even today, the war remains controversial and a subject of debate.

For many years, African Americans' contributions to and participation in the Civil War have been minimized (Shackel 2001). Historians and other shapers of the public memory have characterized the war as essentially a collection of great white heroes, North and South, fighting a series of battles but for shifting purposes as the war evolved. This effort created a legacy of the war as being something other than what it was mostly for: a war that was fought in uncommon times by mostly common people—African American, white, and indigenous. Numerous volumes of detailed research have covered the Civil War, and considerable information has been garnered regarding major personalities as well as battles and war strategies and their outcomes. However, as Marvin Cain (1982) has suggested, the human equation—that is, the daily lives and attitudes of the soldiers who fought the Civil War—has been neglected. We would add that the same neglect applies for the many slaves who also lived through, fought in, and survived the war.

What has received less attention has been the stories of many ex-slaves about how they perceived and experienced the war as well as what the war meant to them. It is important to acknowledge from the very beginning that it is wrong to assume that the war was experienced in any uniform manner by slaves, freedmen, or whites on either side. Rather, it was experienced in a multitude of ways. It would be serious injustice to the war's story to collapse the African American experience into simple categories and generalities. There were some commonalities, such as the great battles and personalities, but slaves and freedmen alike had their own personal experiences, interpretations, and observations. This book attempts to capture some of these individual experiences of ex-slaves in their own words or at least as close as we can interpret what they had to say.

We focus on the recollections of ex-slaves and their living experiences during that tumultuous time (Covey 2007; Covey and Eisnach 2009) and draw upon previous research on the Civil War, but we mostly rely on the Works Progress Administration (WPA) ex-slave narratives. The book also relies on selected earlier narratives (autobiographies), primary documents, and secondary sources when referencing the Civil War. The WPA narratives provide first-person accounts of the antebellum and war period. We believe that often the narratives speak for themselves and provide a rich and often moving record of how the ex-slaves experienced the extraordinary events of the war. The WPA respondents were witnesses to not only the major historical war-related events but also to the smaller daily affairs that were woven into the fabric of the war. Our objective was to determine how slaves experienced the war in their own words. Much of the information presented stems from direct quotations from the WPA narratives coupled with our own observations and those of others.

THE SOCIAL CONTEXT OF THE NARRATIVES

Most of the narratives were collected in the 1930s and 1940s during the Great Depression. The Depression was a difficult time for most people and was particularly hard for older African Americans (Wolters 1975). Even in the best of times, many African Americans lived in abject poverty

(Dollard 1957; Myrdal 1962), but during the Depression, African American incomes were exceptionally low. Census data from 1920 and 1930 on employment also indicate that African Americans were disproportionately employed in traditionally low-income jobs. In 1920 and 1930, 67.3 percent and 64.7 percent, respectively, of African Americans who were gainfully employed worked in low-income agricultural or domestic service occupational groups (U.S. Bureau of the Census 1923, 1933, 1975). After slavery, the legacy of sharecropping and tenant farming systems persisted well into the Depression, transforming many rural African Americans into debtors.

Because WPA interviewers conducted the interviews where the ex-slaves lived, the interviewers had direct exposure to the impoverished lives of the respondents. The WPA narratives, in comments by both the interviewers and interviewees, provide a sense of the extreme poverty faced by African Americans during the Depression in the rural South (Bailey 1980; Thomas 1995; Yetman 1984). Of the living conditions of the interviewees, the historian C. Vann Woodward (1974, 474) remarked that "After all, these were old and helpless people, often living alone in the worst years of the Great Depression, sometimes admitting they were hungry and not knowing where the next meal was coming from." Others survived the Depression satisfactorily as long as they performed needed tasks on their small farms and plots of land (Gordon 1979). The desire for the steady meals present under slavery, regardless of their adequacy, was expressed by some respondents (Escott 1979), and some even indicated that they were well fed under slavery (Joyner 1971). This claim is more evident in the WPA narratives than in earlier autobiographical narratives written before the Civil War (Bailey 1980). Respondents' living conditions at the time of the interviews affected how some recalled slavery, with some respondents saying that life was better under slavery.

The poverty experienced by the WPA respondents and their deplorable living conditions are expressed in a number of narratives. For example, one WPA interviewer (Rawick 1972, 1:44) described one woman, age 85, as living "in a dilapidated cabin which rests in a clump of trees by the side of the railroad. The sagged roof is patched with pieces of rusty tin." One WPA interviewer in Mississippi observed that "Uncle Gus Clark and his aged wife live in a poverty-stricken deserted village" (Rawick 1972, 9:22). Another former slave, Henry Gladney, age 82, lived with his wife, son, daughter-in-law, and seven children in a two-room house in South Carolina.

In addition to enduring poor living conditions, many of the WPA respondents had worked exceptionally hard their whole lives yet were unable
to support themselves due to poor health and disability. Being highly religious and having lost friends and family, some simply awaited death with
the belief of a reunion with their loved ones. The theme of approaching
death and a better afterlife surfaces repeatedly in the narratives. Alabaman
Simon Walker (Rawick 1972, 1:406) reflected the attitude held by many
older African Americans when he said, "But die ole nigger ain't no mo'
good fer hahd labor. . . . All mah white folks done gone on, an heah I is on
de Welfare, jist waitin' fer de good Lawd to call me up." The anticipation
of a better life after death characterized many of their comments.

We undertook this project with one simple but ambitious goal in mind:
to discover what slaves had to say about the Civil War. We realized from
the beginning that there is a voluminous amount that has been written
about the war. According to *The Library of Congress Civil War Desk Reference* (Wagner, Gallagher, and Finkelman 2002), approximately 70,000
books had been published on the Civil War as of 2002, and many more
have been written since. We readily acknowledge that some of this literature has incorporated comments directly attributed to slaves or ex-slaves.
We make no pretense that we have discovered anything that would lead to
a massive paradigm shift in our understanding of the slave experience of
the Civil War. We do believe, though, that the WPA narratives remain a
rich and relatively untapped source of information. Although some of what
is presented in this volume about slaves and ex-slaves has been addressed
by others, we believe that we have been successful in uncovering more
information as well as new information about slave perceptions of what
happened during the war. We hope this book adds to the body of knowledge and accurately captures what the war meant to those slaves directly
touched by this epic span in American history.

SLAVE DIALECT IN THE WPA NARRATIVES

The ex-slave dialect recorded in the WPA narratives reflects slang expressions, abbreviated words, misspelled words, and rough dialect that would
have been typical of ex-slaves during the 1930s and 1940s. The interviewers
recorded words such as "dis" (this), "nusin" (nothing), "chillums" (children),
"hab" (have), "I'se" (I am or I have), "tote" (carry or bear), "Buckra" (a white
man or owner), "cooter" (box turtle), "heered" (heard), "dem" (them), "ter"
(to), "dat" (that), "gwinter" (going to), and "neber" (never). This book makes

no effort to change any of the terms used by the ex-slaves to make them more socially acceptable, nor does it correct misspellings or other grammatical errors. Rather, it stays true to the narratives as they were recorded with an acknowledgment that the WPA interviewers may have edited some of the responses.

The terms "nigger," "nigga," "niggah," and various derivations of the same will be seen in this book and are from direct quotations in the WPA narratives and spoken by the ex-slaves themselves. These terms will appear in no other context within this manuscript. The authors realize that the N-word is a profoundly hurtful racial slur meant to stigmatize African Americans, yet we felt for the historical integrity of using the narratives that such quotations should not be altered or amended in any manner. We view it as part of the historical context of a time in which slaves referred to themselves as "niggers" even though by the early part of the 19th century the term had already become a familiar insult. Noted Harvard law professor Randall Kennedy, in his book *Nigger: The Strange Career of a Troublesome Word* (2002), traced the word's origins and examined its multifarious connotations. Later, in an online essay on the destructive impact of the N-word, Kennedy also observed that some blacks use "nigger" among themselves as a term of endearment but that it is typically done with a "sense of irony that is predicated upon the understanding of the term's racist origins" and a sensibility that is aware of African American history (Kennedy n.d.). Perhaps such was the case with slaves as well as with ex-slaves during the Great Depression. The purpose of this book is not to delve into the etymological history of the N-word or trace at what time it became associated with racism. Our purpose in discussing this term here is only to note that for the sake of historical truism, we have retained WPA narrative quotes untouched from how they were uttered or at least recorded.

Acknowledgments

We want to acknowledge our families for their support throughout this project. Special thanks to Marty Covey for her assistance in reviewing and assisting in so many ways with the preparation of this book. Her contributions are deeply appreciated. In addition, the patience and support of Linda Eisnach throughout the weeks, months, and years of research and writing cannot go unnoticed. Her constant inspiration and reassurance provided the necessary motivation to continue this project to completion. We also want to acknowledge the valuable and dedicated editorial and manuscript preparation staff at Praeger, most notably Michelle Scott. They are first-rate partners with whom to work. We also owe sincere thanks to Nicholle Lutz, production editor at BookComp, Inc.; her deft and amiable guidance and attention to detail throughout the production process are greatly appreciated. We give special thanks to Senior Editor Michael Millman for his interest in this project from the beginning. He was exceptionally supportive and helpful in every way imaginable in the publication and editorial processes. We are truly indebted to him.

Numerous individuals dedicated to the visual preservation of the Civil War stepped up in a significant way to ensure that the illustrations and photographs presented in this book were accurately identified and offered explicatory meaning to the text. Fundamental in providing assistance in finding an illustration where few exist was Kristi L. Finefield, reference librarian in the Prints and Photographs Division of the Library of Congress. Kristi's help went above and beyond in tracking down a wood engraving from 1864 showing the infamous Fort Pillow Massacre contained in Chapter 3. The illustration is all the more rare since it is not part of the library's online collection, and without Kristi's personal interest in this project, the illustration would have been left unfound.

We must also acknowledge the patience and perseverance of John Osborne, professor emeritus of history at Dickinson College, Carlisle, Pennsylvania, and codirector of the college's House Divided Project, which is a wonderful 21st-century digital resource for teaching the period from 1840 to 1880. Professor Osborne spent many hours trying to ensure that we had the highest possible resolution for two of the images in Chapter 4, and without his enthusiasm and cooperation the stories in Chapter 4 would be far less descriptive. Lisa Marine of the Photographic Reproductions Division and Sheri Dolfen of the digital lab, both with the Wisconsin Historical Society, were instrumental in locating and allowing us to use in Chapter 7, the arrival of a federal column at a Dixie plantation. Andrea Felder with the Permissions Department of the New York Public Library was most helpful in securing the rights to the illustration in Chapter 9, which depicts President Abraham Lincoln entering Richmond.

And last but certainly not least was the skillful guidance provided by Ann Drury Wellford of the Museum of the Confederacy, without whom we would not be able to reproduce the photograph of Marlboro Jones in Chapter 6, which is one of only a few existing photos of a slave dressed and posed in a Confederate uniform. Drury was most accommodating in helping to tell the story of slave involvement with the Confederacy.

And to the many others who influenced us, urged us, provoked our thinking, and otherwise unceasingly encouraged us to push forward, we thank you.

CHAPTER 1

The Works Progress Administration Narratives and the Civil War

Dey kept on fightin' first one place den anuther 'til dey has de battle ob Champion Hill, whar Pamberton was located, his force ob men was 'bout eighteen thousand men, de Yankees took 'bout twenty five hundred prisoners an' killed 'bout fourteen hundred men an' de res' ob de rebels fled towards Vicksburg. De Yankees den had 'nuther victory at a bridge ober de Big Black river whar Pamberton had five thousand soljers an' w'en he lost at dis place he retreated ter Vicksburg, an' de Yankees had command ob de Yazoo Ribber an' all no'th ob Vicksburg. Dey was now on de bluffs whar dey had been tryin' ter get fer so long wid de guns dey had taken an' de stores of ammunition de rebels had ter leave in dey hurry ter get away befo' dey taken prisoners.

Den de seige ob Vicksburg begun. General Grant's army was 'bout seventy thousand men; an' de rebels 'bout half so dey jes' held de city long as dey could an' de Yankees jes' starved dem out is de way hit cum down ter us from de folks dat was libin' ober close ter Vicksburg. De bluff ober de city had caves in hit an' de folks in de city moved inter dem, de bes' caves rented fer high rent, an' de food was so high dat folks was starvin' mos'. Flour sold fer ten dollars a pound an' bacon fer five dollars, an' dey eat mule meat, dey say "Mule tongue cold, a-la-Bray," an' named hit a french dish.

De folks dat libed in dem days say dat de newspapers would not gibe up hope an' dey say "De great General Grant intends ter celebrate de Fourth ob July by big dinner in de city, but he has ter ketch his rabbit 'fore he cooks hit." But de General caught his rabbit an' on de mornin' ob de Fourth ob July, dey was in de city. Dis meant dat de Mississippi was open ter de Yankees an' dey tell dat de merchant steamer Imperial dat lef' St. Louis on de eighth made hits way inter New Orleans on de sixteenth.

My ole Marster had already left Vicksburg but dey tell him 'bout hit atter de city taken. Hit was de same way in Richmon' w'en dey had de seige in de winter ob eighteen an' sixty-two, er three, coffee was four dollars a pound, tea eighteen ter twenty dollars, butter from a dollar an' a half ter two dollars 'er pound, lard fifty cents, corn fifteen dollars a barrel, calico a dollar an' seventy-five cents a yard, an' muslin dress goods was six ter eight dollars er yard. So de wimmen all used de homespun goods an' knitted dey own stockin's. An' de hats de ladies wore was de plaited out ob rye straw an' made wide brims an' fixed dem up like dey used ter buy from Paris befo' de Yankees shut off dey supplies.

We way off on de way ter Texas in Louisiana but we keep up wid w'at is happenin' an' den w'en de War is ober some ob de niggers dat stay in Richmon' cum an' tell us all 'bout hit. Dey tole us 'bout de blowing up ob de Labratory on Friday whar wimmen an' girls an' boys was workin' an' hit killin' some ob dem; an' de burnin' ob de Stuart home dat was named "Chantilly." Den dere was de death ob Stonewell Jackson dat eberybody lobed, dey say dat de funeral train was carried thro' de streets ob Richmon' an' den ter Lexington. De body was wrapped in er Confederate flag an' covered wid de lillies ob de valley an' udder spring flowers. He was buried, at his dyin' request, in de "Valley ob Virginny." Er w'ite lady wrote in de paper 'bout his death an' write er little verse dat go like dis:

"May his speerit forever wrap de dusky mountain,
An' his memory allers lib ergin,
As de smalles' boyou an' de bigges' ribber,
Rolls on dey way wid his name forever."

W'en de War ended an' few months atter-ward our ole Marster set his slaves free; he gave my pappy some money an' he started out fer himself, he went ter Milligan soon atter de ole Marster gave him his freedom an' rented lan' an' raised his fambly, I was one ob four chillun.

(Josh Miles, TX)

These observations about the Civil War by ex-slave Josh Miles (TX) are especially vivid and detailed, considering that they were drawn completely from his memory. Miles and many of his ex-slave cohorts had much to share about the war, at the outbreak of which slavery had existed in North America for more than 200 years. The war would jolt the norms of the institution of slavery at the everyday and macro societal levels. The war drew slaves and free black men into the governments of the North and South (see Berlin et al. 1987) and in doing so changed forever their relationships within American society.

This book identifies some of the ex-slave perceptions and reactions to the war. The former slaves' Works Progress Administration (WPA) narratives were collected during the Great Depression, when surviving former slaves were typically in their 80s and 90s. That the enslavement of African Americans had a devastating impact on communities and families was a foregone conclusion. This impact will be explored through the many comments made by those who experienced slavery before, during, and after the Civil War.

SCHOLARSHIP ON SLAVERY DURING THE WAR

It is difficult to describe everyday slave life without addressing the topics of the Civil War and the impact of the war on the lives of those who lived through the period. Several historical works refer to slavery and the war, including John W. Blassingame's *The Slave Community: Plantation Life in the Antebellum South* (1979); Eugene V. Genovese's *Roll, Jordon, Roll: The World the Slaves Made* (1976); George P. Rawick's edited volumes *The American Slave: A Composite Autobiography* (1972); Kenneth Stampp's *The Peculiar Institution: Slavery in the Antebellum South* (1956); Ira Berlin's *Many Thousands Gone: The First Two Centuries of Slavery in North America* (1998); and John Hope Franklin's *From Slavery to Freedom: A History of American Negroes* (1965). Charles L. Perdue Jr., Thomas E. Barden, and Robert K. Phillips's edited volume *Weevils in the Wheat: Interviews with Virginia Ex-slaves* (1976) made some references to Virginia slaves' experiences with the war. Andrew Ward's exceptional book *The Slaves' War: The Civil War in the Words of Former Slaves* (2008) comes the closest to the present volume by providing a comprehensive and accessible collection of narrative comments and context about the war.

Recently, there has been a surge of interest in African American involvement in the Union and Confederate militaries, with an emphasis on the former rather than on the latter. Historians have focused on the military contributions of African Americans on both sides, the creation of home or native guard units, local militias with African American membership, and other types of direct involvement of blacks in the war. Examples of notable books that have focused on African American participation in the Union

military include James M. McPherson's *The Negro's Civil War* (1965),
Battle Cry of Freedom (1988), and *Marching toward Freedom: The Negro
in the Civil War, 1861–1865* (1967); John David Smith's edited volume
Black Soldiers in Blue: African American Troops in the Civil War Era
(2002); Ira Berlin, Joseph P. Reidy, and Leslie S. Rowland's edited volume
Freedom's Soldiers: The Black Military Experience in the Civil War (1998);
Benjamin Quarles's *The Negro in the Civil War* (1968); William Wells
Brown's *The Negro in the American Rebellion* (2003, originally published
in 1867); and Keith P. Wilson's *Campfires of Freedom: The Camp Life of
Black Soldiers during the Civil War* (2002). For years, Dudley Taylor
Cornish's *The Sable Arm: Negro Troops in the Union Army, 1861–1865*
(1956) served as a critical and definitive reference on the role of African
American soldiers in the Union Army. Central themes in all of these books
are that blacks fought with valor to improve their status and gain their
freedom, were subjected to significant bigotry but continued to serve, and
played a critical role in the eventual Union victory.

Probably because of the dissonance that it generates, fewer scholarly
works have focused on African American voluntary or forced involvement
in the Confederate military. As difficult as it is today to understand and
accept, it is clear that some African Americans willfully fought and supported the Confederate cause. Few historians have been willing to acknowledge this notion, let alone seriously pursue the prospect as a research
topic. There have been a few exceptions, such as Charles Kelly Barrow,
J. H. Segars, and R. B. Rosenburg's edited volume *Black Confederates*
(2004) and J. H. Segars and Charles Kelly Barrow's edited volume *Black
Southerners in Confederate Armies: A Collection of Historical Accounts*
(2007). Central themes in these books are that African Americans did participate on the Confederate side in noncombat and combat roles, exhibited
loyalty not necessarily to the South but to individuals and personal relationships, and often fled to the North when the opportunity arose.

SOURCE MATERIALS AND APPROACH

Much of what is known today about the African American experience of
living under slavery has been handed down orally from generation to generation. During the antebellum period, a limited number of ex-enslaved
people wrote down or told their life stories under slavery. One of the earliest narratives was that of Olaudah Equiano titled *The Interesting Narrative
of the Life of Olaudah Equiano, or Gustavus Vassa, Written by Himself*

(1995, originally published in 1789). This book was instrumental in fueling public concern over slavery in England and the United States.

During the 1840s and 1850s, Frederick Douglass, Charles Ball (1859), Harriet Jacobs, Anthony Burns, Solomon Northup, and others who had escaped from slavery wrote down or told their stories. Most notable were two narratives written by Frederick Douglass. His autobiographies *Narrative of the Life of Frederick Douglass, an American Slave, Written by Himself* (1845) and *My Bondage and My Freedom* (1987, originally published in 1855) served to inform abolitionists and the general public of the horrors of slavery. Solomon Northup's *Twelve Years a Slave* (1968, originally published in 1853) noted the repression of slavery. Harriet Jacobs's *Incidents in the Life of a Slave Girl Written by Herself* (1987, originally published in 1857) provided readers with a female slave's point of view of the cruelty of life under slavery. Some of these autobiographical references and accounts have been incorporated into this study. These first narratives fueled the fires of abolitionists before the Civil War, but following the war, the general public and scholars showed little interest in these early narratives. These narratives had multiple purposes but always argued at their core for the abolition of slavery (Wallenstein 1998).

Following the Civil War, a second type of narrative emerged written by people such as Booker T. Washington. His *Up from Slavery: An Autobiography* (1901) sought to inspire African Americans to work hard and persevere against racism in American society (Wallenstein 1998). These narratives, or, more appropriately, autobiographical statements, provided personal views of life during and after slavery and then life under "freedom." This type of narrative was designed to counter the racism and prejudice confronting African Americans living in a racist society and reinforced the value of hard work and education. These narratives also made useful references to the war, although these references of life under slavery were largely ignored or neglected by mainstream scholars.

In the late 1920s, the neglected thoughts and views of ex-slaves changed when John B. Cade, Ophelia Settle Egypt, and others collected new narratives of ex-slaves in Louisiana. During the late 1920s, scholars and African American research staff at Fisk University in Tennessee made similar efforts by conducting 200 interviews of older ex-slave respondents in 1929 and 1930 in Tennessee and Kentucky that were published in 1945 (Fisk University 1945).

The largest collection of ex-slave narratives was assembled by the Federal Writers' Project during the late 1930s. During the middle of the Great

Depression, the federal government, through the WPA, created jobs for unemployed writers and researchers by paying them to interview former slaves. This massive project was an effort to capture the life experiences of older African Americans who had experienced slavery before their life stories were lost. Most of the respondents were elderly at the time of the interviews and not in excellent health, so gathering their recollections was urgent. Under the Federal Writers' Project, staff conducted interviews with ex-slaves wherever they could be located throughout the country but mostly in the South. Some states had more representation than others, with South Carolina (14 percent), Texas (12 percent), North Carolina (11 percent), and Georgia (11 percent) having the highest shares of the sample. The collection of narratives included accounts of interviewees from every state that condoned slavery and some Northern states. The narratives were organized by the states where the former slaves lived at the time they were interviewed, which were not necessarily the same states where they had lived under slavery.

A few books have been written using the WPA narratives almost totally as their source, including the Virginia Writers' Project's *The Negro in Virginia* (1940) and B. A. Botkin's edited volume *Lay My Burden Down: A Folk History of Slavery* (1945). The Virginia Writers' Project was created in 1935 as part of the WPA and used the same method as the Federal Writers' Project to record oral histories of Virginians who had lived through slavery and the Civil War. *Lay My Burden Down* used the WPA narratives to create a portrait of those whose lives were shaped by bondage in the feudal plantation economy. Ira Berlin, Marc Favreau, and Stephen F. Miller's *Remembering Slavery: African Americans Talk of Slavery and Emancipation* (2007) relied on the WPA narratives. Charles H. Nichols relied on the narratives for his book *Many Thousands Gone* (1963), as did others such as John Blassingame with his *The Slave Community: Plantation Life in the Antebellum South* (1979).

Other scholars have used the narratives to uncover such information as the experiences of women who were enslaved (Goodson 1979; Martin 2000), folk medicine (Covey 2007), childhood (Killion and Waller 1973; King 1995), old age (Close 1997; Covey and Lockman 1996), and general life under slavery (e.g., Baker 2000; Blassingame 1975, 1977; Clayton 1990; Escott 1979; Genovese 1976; Hurmence 1990; Rawick 1972). But after more than 70 years of scholarship, these WPA narratives remain a major and relatively unexploited source of information about everyday African American life during and after slavery.

Old Aunt Julia Ann Jackson, age 102, ca. 1937. This photograph was created for the Federal Writers' Project slave narratives collection. The Works Progress Administration interviewers frequently took photographs of WPA respondents, usually in or near their homes. Old Aunt Julia Ann Jackson, a WPA narrative participant, is seated near the chicken coop where she lived. She used the large tin can in the foreground as a stove, clearly illustrating the impoverished conditions many ex-slaves lived in during the time of the collection of the narratives in the Depression years. She reported to the WPA interviewer that she was grown up when the *Civil Wah* broke out. (Library of Congress)

CAUTIONS REGARDING THE USE OF WPA NARRATIVES

More than 2,200 ex-slaves from 17 states participated in the WPA slave narrative project during the 1930s (Rawick 1972). This is a sizable sample of respondents who lived under slavery and experienced the war. The interviews represent a large sample of rural, southern, older ex-slaves during the Depression (Bailey 1980). Several of the interviewees continued to live and work on the same plantations as they did when they were enslaved (Rawick 1972). The narratives provide a rare glimpse into the daily lives of ex-slaves and their lives under slavery and in the postwar South.

Scholars have debated the value of the narratives (Thomas 1995). Before the WPA narratives were collected, Ulrich Bonnell Phillips (1918) dismissed the earlier autobiographical narratives as having little value. Scholars have noted that the WPA narratives have limitations and shortcomings, such as the editing done by some of the interviewers (Berlin, Favreau, and Miller 2007; Clayton 1990). In addition, there was no effort on the part of the interviewers to select a systematic sample of ex-slaves (Escott 1979; Yetman 1984). Researcher Anne Yentsch (2007), while noting that the narratives are invaluable and insightful, also concluded that the stories lack specifics. In addition, Woodward (1974) warned that use of slave narratives to understand history must be approached with caution and discrimination.

Life in the Jim Crow South during the 1930s was also marked by continued discrimination and racism, which undoubtedly affected the perceptions and attitudes expressed by the WPA respondents in that region. Factors such as Ku Klux Klan lynchings, discriminatory labor contracts, and high debt all shaped the comments made by the ex-slaves (Archer 2009). African Americans living during this time would have had much to fear, and many would have guarded what they were willing to share with white strangers.

Living conditions during this time affected what some ex-slaves were willing to tell predominantly white interviewers. Some respondents undoubtedly avoided incriminating questions or told stories that were irrelevant (Escott 1979; Thomas 1995). Comments about white society and slavery often were guarded, because many of the former slaves resided in the same areas as their ex-masters' descendants and depended on them for help in obtaining old-age pensions (Baker 2000; Blassingame 1975, 1977). The WPA respondents occasionally painted a somewhat rosy picture of life under slavery because they had been conditioned not to say anything critical or uncomplimentary about plantation life (Genovese 1976). In contrast, the Fisk University interviews were conducted by African Americans and thus provide different perspectives on life under slavery and the Great Depression.

The gender, race, and educational backgrounds of the WPA interviewers varied, as did the interviewing techniques and questions used (Bailey 1980). Blassingame (1975) noted that the white interviewers lacked empathy with the former slaves and often phrased their questions to obtain the answers they wanted. Most of the WPA narratives were gathered from respondents who would have been very young at the time of slavery and the Civil War (Joyner 1991; Yetman 1967). Yetman noted that 67 percent of those interviewed were 15 years old or younger when emancipated. Therefore, they would have experienced slavery as children and not as adults. Specifically, more than 80 percent of the WPA interviewees were born after 1840 and thus would have been young children or adults during the war (Bailey 1980). Thomas (1995, 150) wrote that "Most slaves were emancipated in 1865, those still living in 1937 were 72 years removed from slavery, and many experienced it only as children." Given such a long time span, undoubtedly some of the respondents forgot details and may have had lapses of memory. In addition, some respondents relied on memories of stories they had been told rather than on actual personal experiences (Thomas 1995).

At times, the WPA interviewer may have misspelled, misreported, or misheard terms (Moore 1989). Another important concern is the ability to generalize from the WPA narratives to the full antebellum and Civil War periods. For example, slavery was more diversified in practice in the upper slave states than in the Deep South (Bailey 1980). This difference influenced some of the WPA experiences with slavery and the war. Caution must be exercised about relying solely on the narratives when writing about the antebellum South, because most of the respondents would not have been alive before the 1850s. Thus, the narratives, although somewhat reflective of the antebellum and neighboring periods, are restricted to the end of that historical span. In some narratives, references are made to times other than during slavery, and those may be difficult to unravel.

Caution should also be exercised regarding whether or not the war references found in the narratives actually are referring to the war or a time thereafter. Although the intent of the interviews was to capture information about life under slavery before it was lost, the respondents frequently drifted back and forth to times other than the period of the war. It is sometimes difficult to conclude whether their war references and knowledge apply to periods before, during, or after the Civil War. In some cases, however, respondents clearly linked their comments to the war. In summary, Blassingame (1979), who made extensive use of the WPA narratives, warned that they need to be read with a critical eye.

In spite of their shortcomings, the WPA narratives represent a valuable source of information about everyday slave life and should not be ignored (Berlin, Favreau, and Miller 2007; Woodward 1974; Yetman 1967). Without the WPA narratives, the largely neglected but important voices of those who experienced slavery and the war would remain unheard. As Paul D. Escott noted in *Slavery Remembered* (1979), the words of the slaves themselves constitute the best source on the African American experience under slavery. The WPA sample represents a broad spectrum of African Americans who lived under slavery and experienced the Civil War (Joyner 1984, 1991; Yetman 1984). These narratives, when used with supplementary documents, represent a valuable foundation about life during and following the war from the ex-slaves' viewpoint. Shackel (2001, 666) wrote that "While there is always a strong movement to remove subordinate memories from our national collective memory, minority groups continually struggle to have their histories remembered." The WPA ex-slave narratives help do just that.

Finally, as anyone who has studied the narratives will attest, there is richness to the storytelling and the expressions of the ex-slaves who participated in this WPA effort. The more one looks, the more one finds interesting human stories and accounts of what daily life was like. A case in point is an observation made by respondent Harriet Robinson (OK) who described in one paragraph what life was like for her under the cruel oppression of slavery and the changing times with the North's defeat of the South. Most important, she had triumphantly outlived all of the other slaves and her owners:

> One day whiles master was gone hunting, Mistress Julia told her brother to give Miss Harriett (me) a free whipping. She was a nigger killer. Master Colonel Sam come home and he said, "You infernal sons o' bitches don't you know there is 300 Yankees camped out here and iffen they knowed you'd whipped this nigger the way you done done, they'd kill all us. Iffen they find it out, I'll kill all you all." Old rich devils, I'm here, but they is gone.

POWERFUL AND LASTING IMPRESSIONS

The Civil War, more than any other span in American history including the American Revolution, the Great Depression, and World Wars I and II, dramatically molded and powerfully touched the lives of many Americans. Although lasting only four years, the Civil War and what followed cut deep scars into the American experience. When the healing began, a new and more modern nation had been born. The narratives contain many ex-slave accounts that suggest that although the war had ended more than 70 years earlier, people had vivid recollections of the events that had transpired. For some, the memories were as fresh as if they had happened the day before. As Candis Goodwin (VA) quipped, "Kin ah 'member de War? Yes, indeed! 'Member jes' lak 'twas yestidy." Ann J. Edwards (TX) had a similar lasting impression of the war: "I remember the beginning of the war well." She then said, "The conditions made a deep impression on my mind, and the atmosphere of Washington was charged with excitement and expectations."

Another ex-slave said, "I remember the Civil War better than I remember the World War" (Fisk University 1945, 9). Adeline Rose Lennox (IN) recalled hearing the distant roar of cannons "when they were fighting up near Shiloh, Tennessee." Margret Hulm (AR) had several memories about the war:

> Oh, yes, I remember lots about the war. I remember dark days what we called the black days. It would be so dark you couldn't see the sun even. That was from the smoke from the fighting. You could just hear the big guns going b-o-o-m, boom, all day.

Some respondents had personal reminders of the war. While most were very young, others were old enough to have fought in some of its conflicts. For example, William H. McCarty (MS) fought in many battles, such as the ones near Baton Rouge, Port Hudson, Vicksburg, Wolf River, Fort Williams, Memphis, Corinth, Spanish Fort Alabama, and Mobile. Altogether, he claimed to have fought in 36 battles and was wounded seven times. His WPA interviewer observed that he had a bullet scar over his right eye where a bullet had gone through his head.

Others were haunted by their war experiences. Louis Fowler (TX), well past the events of the war, was reminded of it every time he ate eggs:

> De missy am walkin' in de yard and den go in de house and out 'gain. She am a-twistin' her hands and cryin'. She keeps sayin', 'Dey sho' gits kilt, my poor babies.' De massa talk to her to quiet her. Dat help me, too, 'cause I sho' skeert. Nobody do much work dat dey, but stand round with quiverments and when dey talk, dey voice quiver. Why, even de buildin's quivered. Every once in de while, dere am an extry roar. Dat de cannon and every time I heered it, I jumps. I's sent to git de eggs and have 'bout five dozen in de basket, holdin' it in front of me with my two hands. All a sudden, one of dem extry shoots comes and down dis nigger kid go and my head hits into de basket. Dere I is, eggs cozin' all round me and I so skeert and fussed up I jus' lays and kicks. I wants to scream but I can't for de eggs in my mouth. To dis day I thinks of dat battle every time I eats eggs.

However, some of the WPA respondents were reluctant to relive the events of the war (Berlin, Favreau, and Miller 2007). Slavery was a terrible time that was replete with bad experiences for slaves, and some chose not to talk about those memories. Rhoda Hunt (MS) spoke only with much reluctance: "Yessum, I could tell you a heap about the Civil War and when the Yankees come but I'se been thinkin' 'bout it and my conscience tells me to keep my mouth shet, let de dead rest and don't bother trouble lessen trouble bothers you."

OBSERVATIONS

This book attempts to identify slave perceptions about the Civil War, how its progress affected their lives, and their involvement with the actual war effort through the use of the WPA narratives of former slaves. Although black involvement in the Union and Confederate militaries was long neglected in the decades after the war, during the second half of the 20th century historians began devoting much more scholarship to this topic even though much more emphasis was given to the African American contribution to the North. While blacks did participate both with voluntary and forced assistance to the Confederate cause, much less scholarship has been applied to document this side of the war.

Basically three different types of ex-slave narratives evolved over a 100-year period beginning in about 1840 to record the African American slave experience. The first type to emerge was the autobiographical narratives of former slaves, such as Frederick Douglass, who had escaped and in the 1840s and 1850s began to write or tell of their experiences, which largely fanned the fires of abolitionists. The second type was narratives that came to print around the turn of the 20th century by writers such as Booker T. Washington that were written to inspire African Americans to work hard and persevere against racism in America. A third type of narrative started in the late 1920s and early 1930s when some writers began to collect narratives of ex-slaves, first in Louisiana, and then did so more broadly during the 1930s. These types of narratives were greatly expanded through the WPA's Federal Writers' Project. Although many inherent methodological weaknesses have been pointed out in the WPA narratives, it can be argued that the narratives nevertheless provide a fascinating glimpse into the African American experience during the years that began their transformation from slaves to citizens.

CHAPTER 2

Civil War Living Conditions for Slaves

White folks was cruel in slavery times. You see I was free and could go where I wanted too, and I see'd a lot. Old Myer Green would take a Nigger and tie his feet to one side of a railroad track and tie his hands on the other side, and whip him till the blood ran. Then he would take him down to the smoke house and rub him down with lard and red pepper. "Rub plenty in," he would say, "Don't let him spoil."

(H. B. Holloway, AR)

There were several reasons for fighting the Civil War, including the preservation of the Union and the abolition of slavery. Northerners did not expect the rebellion to last very long, and most thought that the Union would be quickly restored. For the South, it was initially a war about preserving states' rights and of perpetuating a way of life that included the peculiar institution of slavery. Before the war, the Missouri Compromises of 1820 and 1850 and the Kansas-Nebraska Act of 1854 alternately pacified and antagonized both sides of the slavery issue. These political compromises delayed the seemingly inevitable conflict that had been building since the Constitutional Convention in 1787. At the convention, the South had successfully lobbied for every state to determine its own policy in the matter of slavery. The long-term issue of how to add new states, slave or nonslave, to the Union was deferred. The Constitutional Convention did nothing to address the question of what to do about new applicants for statehood, and these subsequent acts attempted to deal with slavery as the nation spread westward (MacDonald 2011).

Slaveholders became fearful that as the population increased in nonslaveholding states, and as these compromises began to place limits on the spread of slavery, the South increasingly grew anxious about the future of slavery. When Abraham Lincoln was elected president in 1860, it was without the support of a single Southern state. Lincoln had made it clear that he was personally opposed to slavery but had no intention of ending it. However, most slaveholding states were quick to respond negatively to his election.

On December 20, 1860, South Carolina was the first state to declare its separation from the Union. Alabama, Florida, Georgia, Louisiana, Mississippi, and Texas soon followed. In February 1861, these states formed the Confederate States of America. After Lincoln called for volunteers to suppress the secession and shots were fired on Fort Sumter, the states of Arkansas, North Carolina, Tennessee, and finally Virginia joined the Confederacy. In 1863, West Virginia separated from Virginia and rejoined the Union as a new state.

Lincoln's administration initially was more concerned about not losing border states to the Southern rebellion. The administration believed that the loss of slaveholding border states greatly strengthened the Confederacy and thus would confound the eventual outcome of the coming war. Furthermore, the border states served as a buffer zone separating the Northern industrial states from the South. The initial position of the new administration was to simply halt the expansion of slavery but not necessarily see it abolished. From the onset, Southern slaveholders did not believe that Lincoln intended to protect slavery where it existed. In addition, because of their deep-rooted racial prejudice and ignorance about the cultures of Western Africa from which many of their slaves came, Southern whites were convinced that African Americans were inferior and that if they were freed they would pose a significant threat to white society. To Southerners, whether slaveholder or not, slavery was necessary as a means of social, economic, and racial control. They believed that slavery helped maintain the natural order between whites and blacks. Furthermore, the economic role of slaves was important. Southern states were very dependent on agriculture, much more so than in the industrial North. Much of the wealth of secessionist states came from the crops generated from slave labor. Indeed, many white Southerners did not think that white men ought to do the backbreaking labor required to produce tobacco, cotton, rice, and indigo, the main cash crops of the region.

STATUS OF SLAVES AT THE OUTBREAK OF WAR

The social and legal status of African Americans in the United States, with few exceptions, was dismal in the years preceding the Civil War both above and below the Mason-Dixon Line. In the controversial *Dred Scott* case (1857), the U.S. Supreme Court struck down the Missouri Compromise

Sweet potato planting on the James Hopkinson plantation at Edisto Island, South Carolina, captured by Civil War photographer Henry P. Moore (1833–1911) on April 8, 1862. A discussion of whether or not the photo was staged can be found in *Soldiers, Sailors, Slaves, and Ships: The Civil War Photographs of Henry P. Moore* by W. Jeffrey Bolster and Hilary Anderson (Concord, New Hampshire: New Hampshire Historical Society), 1999, p. 78. This photo shows the fanner basket, probably of African origin, used for rice and other purposes, in the lower right corner. (Library of Congress)

and reinforced the notion that black Americans were viewed as inferior and that slaves were not persons but instead were property that could be taken wherever their owners wanted, even from free states or territories.

This lowly status transferred over to the living conditions and lifestyle experienced by slaves in the antebellum South. The *Dred Scott* decision, even more ironic in light of the three-fifths compromise reached at the Constitutional Convention 70 years earlier, further polarized the nation around slavery and set an irreversible course toward war. Although the three-fifths amendment recognized slaves as three-fifths of a person for purposes of taxation and apportioning members to the U.S. House of Representatives, the *Dred Scott* ruling disclaimed any notion that slaves were persons.

FAMILY DISRUPTION

To slaves, family and community were one and the same and the institution of slavery created much disruption in the lives of both. Slave laws had many mechanisms for the disruption of the slave family, including that slave marriages had no legal standing, masters could sell slave family members to other slave owners at any time, and slave parents had no rights to their children. In addition, masters expected loyalty from their slaves above any loyalty that slaves felt toward their own family members. Disobedient slaves risked being separated from their families. For example, slave masters dissolved an estimated 32.4 percent of known slave marriages (Blassingame 1979, 91). The narrative of Louis Fitzgerald (VA) is typical of the high degree of disruption experienced by many slave families. He commented on his grandmother's experience that "There were 4 or 5 of her children when they reached teen age were sold down south and she never saw them anymore."

The war provided even more opportunities for family disruption and separation. At any given time, slave family members could be transported (labeled refugees) deeper into the South, forced to join their masters in the war effort, forced to move because of military engagements, impressed into or captured by the military on both sides and forced to work, or killed. In addition, the draw of freedom was such that disruptions were often voluntary, with enslaved men escaping to the North to fight for their liberty. However, against these odds, many slave families persisted and flourished in spite of unwelcomed intrusions and disruptions by slave owners and the influence of the war (Douglas 1989).

REFERENCES TO HARD TIMES DURING THE WAR

The narratives reinforced that times were hard during the war. Jake Wilson (TX) said, "Us had putty hard time endurin' ob de war." William Kirk (AR) had a similar observation, "Them was turrible times." Then he added, "I don't never want to see no more war." Andrew Moss (TN) recalled, "Talk about hard times! We see'd em in dem days, durin' de war and most specially after de Surrender." Ike Derricotte (GA) said, "Times was hard durin' de war but from what I've heared de folks dat was old folks den say, dey warn't near as bad here as in lots of other places."

John Franklin (SC) thought that times were better before the war because his masters were good to the slaves. He noted that slaves had plenty to eat until the war came and the master went off to fight. Things were initially all right until either Yankee or Rebel troops would pass by and "take all they can carry." But Franklin noted a change in 1862 when food shortages hit and continued throughout the rest of the war: "That shortage begun in 1862, and it kept on gettin' worse all the time, and when Lincoln set all niggers free, there was such a shortage of food and clothes at our white folks houses, that we decided to move to a Dutch Fork plantation."

There is considerable evidence that during the antebellum period, slaves were never fed particularly well (Covey and Eisnach 2009; Genovese 1965, 1976; Kiple and King 1981; Kiple and Kiple 1977; Savitt 1978; Trinkley 2006). Slave rations primarily consisted of meager amounts of cornmeal and small amounts of low-grade pork. Rations were often slightly above subsistence level, forcing some slaves to look to other ways to supplement their meager diets through personal gardens, trade, foraging, hunting, fishing, and theft. Nourishment for slave children ranged from marginal to poor and was somewhat better for working adult slaves (Kiple and Kiple 1977; Steckel 1986a, 1986b; Sutch 1975, 1976).

The Civil War affected daily life and routines. There is little question that the war had a major impact on the Southern economy and corresponding foods available to both whites and slaves, severely limiting the availability of many foodstuffs. The Confederacy entered into the war without much thought as to how it would feed its civilian population, let alone its troops and slaves. A number of factors influenced the availability of food, such as the Union coastal blockade that limited shipping and thus food imports in the South. The blockade also severely hindered exports of cotton and other commodities from the South, which crippled the Confederacy and its ability to be recognized as a sovereign nation by foreign countries. Furthermore, the armies on both sides plundered local food sources and reserves whenever they could. Troops on both sides raided at will smokehouses, corncribs, fields, and livestock. When these raids occurred, slaves suffered the consequences along with their white owners.

The scarcity of food supplies during the war led to inflated food prices. For example, Williams (2005) reported that butter rose from 12 cents a pound at the beginning of the war to more than $1 dollar at the end. Corn that was $2 a bushel in 1863 was $14 by 1865. Bacon increased from 12 cents a pound to $4 at the end of the war. Ella Belle Ramsey (TX) noted the high costs of purchasing food during the war:

During de War things was so high dat you couldn't 'ford to buy nothing. I 'member one time Mis' Goldsmith fuss 'cause dey try to charge her five dollars for a little dab of sugar. I hear her say dat somebody tol' her dat dey sell potatoes an' carrots for a dollar each one. But people got to eat. Dey always bring us things to eat from de plantation. People use to take de Confederate money an' bury it

in dere yard an' in dere garden an' when de War was over it wasn'
even worth digging up.

Additionally, many stubborn cotton and tobacco farmers shortsightedly
refused to switch their fields to food crops that could have alleviated food
shortages. Williams (2008, 3) wrote that "To make matters worse, planters
devoted much of their land to cotton and tobacco, while soldiers and their
families went hungry." Planters placed a higher value on profit by growing
tobacco and cotton crops rather than on raising food for the war effort.
This agricultural practice touched the slaves but also hurt Southern whites
as well. Inflation hit the families and widows of Confederate soldiers
(Taylor 1982). Prisoners of war on both sides, especially Union soldiers in
Confederate camps, suffered the most. Some individual regions were hit
particularly hard by the war. For example, African Americans and some
whites as well who had migrated to southwestern Georgia toward the end
of the war starved to death for lack of food (Mohr 1986).

The nutritional status of slaves prior to the war has been the subject of
much controversy among scholars. Most would agree that the nutrition of
slaves was generally inadequate (Finkelman and Miller 1998; Hilliard
1972). Others suggest that while nutrition was poor for slave children, it
was relatively good for adult slaves who worked the fields and has been
linked to their value in slave markets (Steckel 1986b). Slaves suffered increasingly as the war progressed and experienced less and less meat in
their diets. Abolitionist Booker T. Washington (1901) even argued that
whites suffered more than slaves during the war. He suggested that slaves
were so accustomed to corn and pork with little else that when coffee,
sugar, tea, and other foods became scarce, they were relatively unaffected
by such shortages compared with Southern whites.

There is evidence that Southern meat supplies during the Civil War
were decimated. A case in point is General William Tecumseh Sherman's
March to the Sea in which his troops laid waste to everything in their path
from Atlanta to Savannah. But there is also evidence that the loss of livestock, draft animals, and corresponding meat supplies may not have been
as significant to slaves as once thought. Ransom and Sutch (1975) could
not find much evidence that Southern agriculture and meat supplies
were that significantly reduced during and following the war. They point to
the fact that the South recovered rapidly following the war, even with the
emancipation of the slaves. Ex-slave Frank Magwood (SC) might disagree
and recalled in his narrative that "Where Sherman's army stopped and

ate and fed their horses, the Negroes went and picked up the grains of corn they stowed there and parched and ate them."

What food was available through formal military channels was often unpalatable. Military rations were so bad that soldiers on both sides welcomed the culinary talents of free and enslaved African American women. African American women cooked for soldiers on both sides during the Civil War. Forbes (1998) wrote that a captured Union soldier shared his experiences of buying apple and blueberry turnover pies from African American vendors. Selling food on the side was a common practice among slaves during the war. For example, even though she received Union rations, to avoid suspicion Harriet Tubman worked at night making pies, gingerbread, and root beer to sell (Forbes 1998).

Besides selling and cooking for both armies, slaves sometimes became involved in providing provisions for war deserters. Although a boy during the Civil War, former slave Reverend Squire Dowd (NC) recalled:

The darkies also stole for deserters during the war. They paid us for it. I ate what I stole, such as sugar. I was not big enough to steal for the deserters. I was a house boy. I stole honey. I did not know I was free until five years after the war.

Demands for food and salt by the Confederate Army during the war severely affected the food supplies of Southern society, including slaves (Mohr 1986). The decline in the availability of salt had severe implications for the South because salt was critical for the preservation of pork and other meats that were served to the soldiers. After the Union destruction of the salt mining operations on Avery Island, Louisiana, in 1862, Southerners were restricted to salt licks, evaporation of seawater, and other inadequate sources of salt. When asked about the war, Adeline Willis (GA) indicated that times were much harder: "Why we didn't have no salt—jest plain salt, and couldn't get none them days." To obtain salt, she described how the slaves would filter dirt underneath the smokehouse. She then added, "Yes'm, times was sho' hard and our Marster was off in the War all four years and we had to do the best we could."

Many of the narratives make reference to the war and how it affected slave food supplies. It is evident that regardless of whether they were Union or Confederate, the day the soldiers arrived created lasting memories for the plantation owners and workers, generally in a negative way, with respect to food. Many of the Works Progress Administration (WPA) respondents had vivid recollections of the specific day the Yankees appeared (see Chapter 7) appeared. Many of these recollections included references to food, including cooking, pilfering, wasting, destroying, stealing, and plundering. Andrew Moss (TN) said, "You see, both armies fed off'n de white folks, and dey cleared out dey barns and cellars and smoke houses when dey come." Some of the respondents remembered being left without any food. Henry Warfield (MS) provided an account of how tough things were on his plantation during the war:

[E]atings were scarce in those days prior to July 4, 1862. We et mule meat, saltless pone bread, and drunk coffee made of oak and hickory bark without sugar. Often we et raw meat, hogs, calves, or anything that we could plunder and get and raw meat makes men mean. I have seen men after eating raw meat pick up little children and shove dem gin a tree and bust em into. We used to plunder and take things from men, but de Southern soldiers wouldn't harm a chicken belonging to a "widow woman" but would often steal things and take to her.

The hunger experienced by slaves surfaces in many of their narratives (Covey and Eisnach 2009; Genovese 1976). John Eubanks (IN) joined the Union Army when he was 21 years old, at a time when the North was losing the war and was involved in several battles. He said, "Most the time we's hungry, but we win the war." Emmett Augusta Byrd (AR) elaborated on the difficulties experienced regarding food:

Talking about hard times, war times is all the hard times I ever seen. No foolin'! It was really hard times. We had no bread, shoot down a cow and cut out what we wanted, take it on. We at it raw. Sometimes we would cook it but we at more raw than cooked.

For some slaves, the war meant reductions in their rations. Andy Anikeson (TX) reported that when his master went off to war, a cruel overseer cut rations and took to the whip. This made a big difference for Anikeson and the remaining slaves. He commented:

After dat, de hell start to pop, 'cause de first thing Delbridge do is cut de rations. He weighs out de meat, three pound for de week, and he measure a peck of meal. And 'twarn't enough. He half starve us niggers and he want no' work and he start de whippin's. I guesses he starts to educate 'em. I guess dat Delbridge go to hell when he died, but I don't see how de debbil could stand him.

Some of the WPA respondents saw the war being hard on whites and African Americans alike. Amy Perry (SC) recognized that all people, regardless of color, struggled to get enough to eat.

De white folks hab to live wherebber dey kin, and dey didn't hab enough to eat. I know whole families live on one goose a week, cook in greens. Sometimes they hab punkin and corn, red corn at dat. Times was haard, haard. De cullered people didn't hab nutting to eat neider. Dat why my auntie bring me to Charleston to lib.

Finally, sometimes as hard as it was there could be food windfalls for the slaves. Sarah Debro (NC) remembered when she and her brother were gathering acorns in the woods when:

We foun' sumpin' like a grave in de woods. I tole Dave dey was sumpin' buried in dat moun'. We got de grubbin hoe an' dug. Dey was a box wid eleven hams in dat grave. Somebody done hid it from de Yankees an' forget whare dey buried it. We covered it back up kaze if we took it home in de day time de Yankees an' niggers would take it away from us. So when night come we slipped out an' toted dem hams to de house an' hid dem in de loft.

Similar to food, slave clothing was minimal and inadequate for field hands and their families and only slightly better for house servants. Ill-fitting, worn-out, dirty, and ragged clothing was the norm (Savitt 1978). Many went barefoot, as shoes were a luxury unknown to some. Owners rationed clothing in such insufficient quantities that slaves suffered greatly from cold weather. Less than half of the WPA respondents thought their clothing was at least adequate (Bailey 1980). Some narratives mentioned how bad it could be for those without shoes. For example, John Eubanks (IN) recalled the toll it took on him to not have shoes in the winter:

Come the winter, it be so cold my feet were plumb numb most of the time, and many a time, when we got a chance, we drove hogs from out of the bogs an' put our feet in the warm, wet mud. They was cracked, and the skin on the bottoms and in the toes were cracked and bleedin' most of the time, with bloody scabs, but the summer healed them again.

Temple Wilson (MS) made a similar observation:

De winter times was powerful cole in dem war time days. De folks jes' nearly froze to death. De lakes all froze up an' de snow would fall so deep till everything would be civered fer days. Dem deseases broke out an caused a heap o' dyin' an' sufferin' an' food got scarce an' folks all had to go hungry. Everybody knowed dat was de way de war was won, de South was jes starved out.

As the war progressed, inadequate clothing for most field slaves worsened. Slaves typically received rations of clothes that often fell short of need. The growing number of Union victories, demand for military supplies, the relatively successful blockage of shipping, and the increasing Union control of the Mississippi River Valley all contributed to a shortage of clothing for the slaves. In addition, military forces from both sides raided supplies and food stores during the war. Amy Perry (SC) recalled that "De Yankees massicued de people, and burn dere houses, and stole de meat and aberyting dey could find." John Majors (TX) was very specific with his comments about the effect that the blockade had on everyone, white and African American:

I 'members w'en de blockade was on at New Orleans an' how all de folks had to git out dey spinnin' wheels to make de cloth dey called de Homespun for dey clothes, for dey could'nt git anything shipped into New Orleans or up to Memphis for de blockade.

Poor diet, inadequate clothing, exhausting work, and other factors contributed to illness among slave populations during the war. Disease and illnesses, such as smallpox, typhus, tetanus, flu, malaria, and the long-term chronic infection yaws, were rampant among slave communities. A variety of parasites, viruses, bacteria, and other microbes attacked and infected slave populations (Bankole 1998; Covey 2007; Kiple and King 1981; Savitt 1978). These maladies continued throughout the war years, exacerbated by the mass movement of populations. Child mortality rates were excessively high for slaves compared to whites (Kiple and King 1981).

Slave cabins on the Hermitage Savannah, Georgia plantation that were used to house slaves for market. This stereograph (ca. 1903) was originally published by Underwood & Underwood, New York, which at that time was the largest publisher of stereograph cards in the world. (Library of Congress)

Per capita income fell dramatically for Southern whites during the war and grew slowly thereafter. Ransom and Sutch (1975) suggest that the economic devastation of the war persisted in the following years but is probably overexaggerated. Any drop in Southern incomes would have affected slaves and freemen. Following the war, liberated slaves would continue to experience very low incomes for generations.

ESCAPE TO THE NORTH AND A BETTER LIFE

Escape to the North did not guarantee a better life for slaves, as times remained difficult for those who succeeded in escape and did not ensure economic security. The federal government initially did not know what to do with the migration of African Americans to the North, which in large part was amplified by the Underground Railroad in the years leading up to the war. The initial response was to intern migrants into contraband camps, such as the large camp in Washington, D.C. When slaves escaped to the North, they had very little in the way of possessions, clothing, or food. Most had no idea how they would survive, and most could not read or write. WPA respondent Ann J. Edwards (TX) described the plight of the new arrivals to the North when she said, "They came into the city without clothes or money and no idea of how to secure employment." Her father's church was a point of assembly for many of the new arrivals. She shared that helping them was a difficult task because "a large majority were illiterate and ignorant."

While many of the WPA respondents perceived dramatic declines in their standard of living during the war, others clearly did not. Some WPA respondents did not see much difference in their lives before and during the war. Annie Row (TX) shared that "Dere warnt any diffe'nce 'bout de wo'k or de food durin' de wah. De nigger gits 'bout de same, 'twarnt 'nough befo' de wah an' dere was no change." Tobe Zollicoffer (TX) did not remember any personal hardship but acknowledged that others suffered: "During the Civil War many people suffered for nourishment and clothes, but we had plenty of both; we raised our food at home, the only thing that we did not have was coffee."

NEWS ABOUT THE WAR

Just as food, clothing, and shelter were important to slaves during the war, information about the events of the war was also critical. Everyone hungered for information, and slaves were no exception. A. M. Moore (TX) commented that "We kept posted on the war all the time." News about the war was important to whites and blacks on both sides of the conflict. For slaves, news about the war was scarce, often outdated, and usually had a spin to it that supported either one side or the other. Whatever news African Americans were exposed to was most often by word of mouth, as most could not read. Much of the war news was nothing more than propaganda, as both governments had a major stake in controlling public opinion about how the conflict was going and who was winning. Southern whites made a significant effort to control what slaves and free African Americans knew about the war. Owners sometimes prohibited their slaves from even talking about the war. Others were only exposed to what the Southern whites wanted them to hear. Yet others learned from the many informal communications shared among Southern and Northern blacks through mechanisms such as the Underground Railroad. Finally, house servants were exposed to many of the conversations held within the confines of the big house or on plantation grounds. This placed them in a unique position of hearing private conversations among owners that they would later share with others.

A key aim of the Southerners' efforts to control the news was to keep abolitionist ideas out of the South (Mays 1984). If notions of freedom and equality could be kept out of the South, the institution of slavery could be maintained and the Southern way of life could be preserved, or so it was assumed. Masters assumed that ignorant slaves were more easily controlled. In spite of their efforts, Southerners were never fully successful in controlling all of the information that slaves were exposed to or shared with others.

In the absence of reliable and accurate information about the war, slaves sometimes took whatever measures they could to learn about war-related events. If whites would not share information, slaves would learn what they could from conversations occurring in the big house. As house servants, they were often privy to information and discussions not meant for slaves' ears. For example, Elizabeth Russell (IN) shared that as a little girl, she acted as a "spy" for her people:

> I was very small at the time of the Civil War yet I served my people as a secret service agent. I was kept in the big house during the day to rock and attend the babies and I would often pretend to be asleep and hear the folk at the big house were saying about the battles and which side was winning or losing and when the word came that the north had won and the slaves were free, it was I who carried the word to the hundreds of slaves in our section, having crawled to my mother's cabin to give the news and though only a little child, God used me as a bearer of good news to my people.

Squire Irvin's (MS) comments underscore how some slaves obtained a limited amount of information about the war. Slaves would transport private notes to and from whites and listen to conversations when the notes were being written or being read to garner what they could, because for the most part slaves could not read:

> We couldn't find out much about what was going on. When the white folks wrote notes to each other, who so ever carried the note, picked up all the news he could gather both going and coming. It was powerful little we heared even that way. If we got hold of a

newspaper, there wasn't none of us could read it, so that didn't do
us no good.

Noting how few slaves could read anyway, Temple Wilson (MS) spoke
of how owners prohibited their slaves from reading news about the war.
Instead, what many slaves knew was through oral communication:

Now everything was stirred up fer a long spell fo' de war to free us
come on. It was talked an' threatened an' all kinds o' bad signs
pinted to war, till at las' dey jes' knowed it was bound to come on.
De slaves wont allowed to read a thing rit on a piece o' paper. Of
course dey wont much danger o' dat as sich a few could read no
how. Dey wont allowed to talk to strangers for fear dey would be
tole things by de Yankees. De white folks was up sot over de fear o'
loosing all deir slaves. In spite o' everything it got floated 'round dat
de slaves was to be freed an' sometimes hear dat dey would git
home or land or mules an' de lak, but as things always go during
war times nobody knows jes' what to expect.

William Mathews (TX) also noted the oral dimension about war news:

Everybody know 'bout de War. All kind of War talk was floating
'round 'fore de Yankees come. Some say de North was going to
fight for freedom an' some say de Yankees going to kill all de
slaves. 'Tween dis an' dat you don' know what to do.

Mark Oliver (MS) also underscored the importance of word of mouth
among slaves. While observing that the owners did little to inform slaves,
African Americans did have an oral network in which war news flowed:

They didn't try to keep the war news from us. They didn't exactly
come out and tell us nothing but they didn't care if we heared it.
The children would hear them say the soldiers were near Petersburg;
they would tell it to us, and we pass it on to the next one, same as
they do now. We knowed pretty much what was going on. They was
fighting right at us, at Milligan's Bend.

A few slaves did know how to read. Cora Gillam (AR) indicated that her
master taught his slaves to read, which he concluded got him "in trouble"

because "Slaves was not allowed to read." If they read, they would know that "freedom was coming." Cora Gillam's Uncle Tom shared information about the war with other slaves. She described Uncle Tom's efforts to share the news and his punishment for doing so:

> He had a newspaper with latest war news and gathered a crowd of slaves to read them when peace was coming. White men say it done to get uprising among slaves. A crowd of white gather and take uncle Tom to jail. Twenty of them say they would beat him, each man, till they so tired they can't lay on one more lick. If he still alive, then they hang him. Wasn't that awful? Hang a man just because he could read? They had him in jail overnight. His young master got wind of it, and went to save his man. The Indian in uncle Tom rose. Strength big extra strength seemed to come to him. First man what opened that door, he leaped on him and laid him out. No white men could stand against him in that Indian fighting spirit. They was scared of him. He almost tore that jailhouse down, lady. Yes he did. His young master took him that night, but next day the white mob was after him and had him in jail. Then listen what happened. The Yankees took Helena, and opened up the jails. Everybody so scared they forgot all about hangings and things like that.

Other slaves had access to information about the war from the letters written from the front and sent home to their mistresses. A. M. Moore (TX) spoke of how the plantation mistress would read letters to her slaves from those in the army. Some information also came from those returning from the war:

> I remember Mistress reading letters from our folks that was in the war. She would read it and say, "They had a big battle yesterday." Sometimes they would say when they would be home on a visit. Sometimes they got to come and sometime they didn't.

SILENCE DURING THE WAR

Many owners prohibited their slaves from talking about the war and would spread fabrications about how the war was going for the Confederacy. Rhoda Hunt (MS) recalled how her mistress was silent about the war: "No, mam, my mistress nebber would talk 'bout dem happenings enduring the Civil War and you ain't gonna get me to talk about nothin' my white folks wouldn't talk 'bout." Mrs. Lydia Calhoun Starks (GA) also observed that slaves heard little about the war: "We didn't hear nothin' bout de war cept whut our white folks don read to us in de newspapers." She then noted that the war "Didn't 'fect us none." Pierce Cody (GA) recalled that "Knowledge of the war was kept from the slaves until long after its beginning." He then added that "Most of them had no idea what 'war' meant and any news that might have been spread, fell on deaf ears." Mary Jane Simmons (GA) remembered that her master never let the slaves discuss the war. She stated that "We never were allowed to listen to the conversations of the white folks and I never heard Master Watson discuss the war."

Bill Simms (KS) took a different angle. He had insight into the imposed silence and control of information. In his analysis, Simms said:

Slaves were never allowed to talk to white people other than their masters or someone their master knew, as they were afraid the white man might have the slave run away. The masters aimed to keep their slaves in ignorance and the ignorant slaves were all in favor of the Rebel army, only the more intelligent were in favor of the Union army.

The consequences could be severe for slaves caught discussing the war. W. L. Bost (NC) shared that slaves secretly prepared for the day they would be freed but did not dare discuss the progress of the war:

Most of the people get everything jes ready to run when the Yankee sojers come through the town. This was toward the las' of the war. Cose the niggers knew what all the fightin' was about, but they didn't dare say anything. The man who owned the slaves was too mad as it was, and if the niggers say anything they get shot right then and thar.

George Eason (GA) shared a similar account of the consequences for slaves being caught talking about the war. "At the beginning of the Civil War, all the slaves talked among themselves concerning the possible outcome of the war," he told his interviewer. Eason then added, "However, they never let the master or the overseer hear them because it meant a whipping."

MISINFORMATION ABOUT YANKEES

It was in the best interest of Southern plantation society to characterize Yankees as demons, villains, enslavers, and less than humane. Confederate propaganda regarding Yankees became an important tool in controlling slave populations. Plantation owners feared that their slaves would either rebel or escape to the North or join the Union forces. By instilling fear and misperception about the Yankees, the risk of a slave insurrection or losing slaves to the North was diminished. White Southerners thought that this was an effective strategy, and some of the narratives support its effectiveness. Masters told their slaves that Union soldiers had no mercy for them and that captured slaves would be put on front battle lines, used as horses, or sold to Cuba as slaves (Mays 1984). Owners also told slaves that Yankees would kill them. Caroline Richardson (NC) recalled that "We niggers has been teached dat de Yankees will kill us, men women an' chilluns." She added that the slaves reacted by hiding when the Yankees appeared. Jane Sutton (MS), when referring to the Yankees, summed up what many slaves must have felt: "We was all scairt of dem." Reverend Henry Clay Moorman (IN) described how some slaves responded to the arrival of Yankees and how slave owners had "poisoned" their minds. He told his interviewer:

> The slave owners had so poisoned the minds of the slaves, they were in constant fear of the soldiers. One day when the slaves were alone at the plantation they sighted the Union soldiers approaching, they all went to the woods and hid in the bushes. The smaller children were covered with leaves. There they remained all night, as the soldiers (about 200 in number) camped all night in the horse lot. These soldiers were very orderly; however, they appropriated for their own use all the food they could find.

Albert Cox (MS) referred to the slaves' fear of the Yankees and their confusion:

> Folks den come 'long an' stirred up de war. As us slaves couldnt read nuthing, we didn't know only what us heard an' was tole to believe. We was tole we would git land an' homes an sich lak, but we never did. We never did know all through de war 'zactly what to believe. I do know we was alwas' scared ob de Yankees an' would run when we seed 'em a marching through.

White Southerners characterized the Yankees as demons to their slaves and by doing so effectively dehumanized the Northern soldiers. Mollie Williams (MS) said, "Us all thought de Yankees was some kin' of debils an' were was skeered to death of 'em." Aunt Mittie Freeman (AR) spoke of the coming of the "horned" Yankees:

> One day I was a standing by the window and I seen smoke—blue
> smoke a rising over beyond a woods. I heerd cannons a-booming
> and axed her what was it. She say: "Run, Mittie, and hide yourself.
> It's the Yanks. Theys coming at last, Oh lordy!" I was all incited
> [excited] and told her I didn't want to hide, I wanted to see 'em.
> "No" she say, right firm. "Ain't I always told you Yankees has horns
> on their heads? They'll get you. Go on now, do like I tells you." So
> I runs out the room and went down by the big gate. A high wall was
> there end a tree put its branches right over the top. I clim up end hid
> under the leaves. They was coming, all a marching. The captain
> opened our big gate and marched them in. A soldier seen me and
> said "Come on down here; I want to see you." I told him I would, if
> he would take off his hat and show me his horns.

Aunt Mittie Freeman (AR) was not the only slave who was told that Yankees had horns. James Gill (AR) had been told the same story and talked about how slaves feared them:

> Us was skeered of dem Yankees though 'cause us chillun cose didn'
> know what dey was and de oberseer, Jim Lynch, dey done tole us
> little uns dat a Yankee was somepin what had one great big horn on
> he haid and just one eye and dat right in de middle of he breast and,
> boss, I sure was s'prized when I seen a sure 'nough Yankee and see
> he was a man just like any er de res' of de folks.

Besides learning to fear the Yankees, slaves were also taught to hate them. Some slaves learned to hate the soldiers in blue because of how they treated their masters and their seemingly constant looting during the war. Ida Rigley (AR) gave the following account:

> One time some Yankees come. I run hid around Miss Betty's long
> dress. She was crying. They was pulling her rings off her fingers. I
> told them to quit that. One of the mean things said, "Little nigger,

I shoot your head off." They took all her nice clothes. They said they took all niggers. I sassed them. They went in another room. I shot under Miss Betty's big skirt. They looked about for me but they thought I run off to my mama. She was gone but they didn't know it. I seen my best times then. We had a good time there. Miss Betty was good and kind to me. Good as I wanted. I wish I had that good now. The soldiers come and I knowed it was the Yankees I hated. They took all they could find and wasted a lot of it. I was scared.

OBSERVATIONS

Slavery in the antebellum South had a long history of being harsh and punitive. Those enslaved had virtually no rights or personal freedoms, and their movements were highly restricted. Slaves were not considered human beings; they were considered to be property and consequently had no rights. Legislative bodies and the U.S. Supreme Court reinforced the notion of slaves as personal property.

The secession of the first seven Southern states beginning in late 1860 followed more than two decades of political attempts to pacify the interests of both slaveholders and those opposed to slavery. The *Dred Scott* case reinforced the loathsome nature of slavery and the lowly status of those caught in its web.

Hard times abounded for both African Americans and whites, though some, including Booker T. Washington and others, postulated that on a relative basis, whites suffered more than blacks from hunger and food shortages during the war since slaves for generations were already accustomed to meager rations and little variety in their diets. The food shortages in the South were aggravated by the insistence by many cotton and tobacco planters on continuing to grow those crops during the war instead of converting to food crops that could have helped sustain the South, a stubbornness that continued even after Lincoln ordered the Union blockade of Southern ports on April 19, 1861. Many historians believe that this was a key factor in dooming the Confederate cause.

The control of information and the demonizing of Union soldiers and political leaders was a resolute feature of plantation owners' attempts to control their slaves and minimize any move toward insurrection that the owners feared from nearly the beginning of the war. However, slaves clearly talked about the war and sought whatever information they could gather about its progress. As mentioned, slaves transported private notes to and from whites and listened to conversations when these notes were being written or read. They garnered what information they could, later sharing such news with others in private.

Southern whites did what they could to ensure that what little information slaves learned about the war was biased against the Yankees. White Southern propaganda characterized Yankees as devils who should be feared, hated, and not trusted. The message was given that the North certainly would provide no answer to the issues faced by the slaves or their lot in life. We know that this propaganda was effective for some, but for many others this patterned strategy of disparaging the Federals did not stem their desire to escape to the North. According to the National Underground Railroad Freedom Center (2012), between 1810 and 1850 approximately 100,000 slaves were able to make their way from slavery to free states in the North, and hundreds more slipped away to freedom during the war. And with this movement, many African Americans began the long struggle toward citizenship and being recognized as persons instead of property.

CHAPTER 3

Ex-Slave Accounts of Battles

When de war finally broke loose an' kept a gwine on an' on, Marse den he had to go. Dat was sad news fer all ob us. Things was a lookin' bad 'nuf' wid out dat. De day come when he had to go, an' he say to me, "Simon I'se a gwine to take yo' wid me." I was glad an' scart too, but I went wid him as a servant an' stayed wid him 'till de War ended. I had a heap o 'sperences durin' dat time. I seed de men a marchin' an' drillin'. I seed 'em come foot sore an' mos' dead after de battle. I'se seed 'em go hungrey. I'se seed 'em kilt, an' die from sickness an exposure. Dey was finally jes' starved out. Dats' what won de War. Sometimes dey would camp close to de Union Army, one on one side ob a river an' one on de uder side. At night dey would swim across an' set wid each other 'round de camp fire, dey would tell jokes, wrestle an' swap tobacco an' food stuf. Dey would have fun an' joke lak nothin' was wrong, den dey would swim back across de river knowin' dey would be a killin' each other de nex day.

(Simon Durr, MS)

That terrible War Between the States took all the young boys and some of our best men that had families. No wonder the race of people is getting weak because war comes and takes out the very best men that we have both white and black and leaves the ones that are not fit for war service to raise some more soldiers, that is not right because our husbands are weak cripples and if them boys come back home they are not fit for husbands and fathers because they come home shell-shocked and gassed and their children are weaklings. Our home county was over run with soldiers and they shot up everything, treated our women wrong, burned and tore down houses and fences. Their damage never

will be overcome. Them guns popping and soldiers lying there
dead and wounded is enough to sicken the best of us.

(Rosa Pollard, TX)

The recollections of Simon Durr (MS) and Rosa Pollard (TX) capture
what many slaves must have felt about the war. It touched people, white
and black, in powerful and lasting ways. African Americans saw military
action in almost every battle of the Civil War (Franklin and Moss 2000).
They fought with honor in the battles at Port Hudson, Louisiana; Mobile,
Alabama; Milliken's Bend, Louisiana; Honey Springs, Oklahoma; Fort
Wagner, South Carolina; and other places. Three of these battles in
particular established in the minds of many Northerners and Southerners
alike that blacks acted bravely under the heat of fire. African American
casualties at all of these battles were high and lopsided. At the Second
Battle of Fort Wagner (July 18, 1863) alone, 1,515 Union troops suffered
casualties compared to 174 Confederate troops (Shackel 2001). Following
these critical battles, any doubt about the bravery of blacks on the battlefield
was erased.

A pivotal siege and battle occurred at Port Hudson, Louisiana
(May 21–July 9, 1863), that convinced many Northerners that African
Americans should be allowed and even encouraged to enlist in the Union
Army (Hewitt 2002). The battle not only persuaded many whites that black
soldiers performed well in heavy combat but also inspired many African
American men to enlist. Following the Emancipation Proclamation in
1862, its implementation in 1863, and the Union victory in 1863 at
Gettysburg, black men found a new purpose for joining the Union forces:
the pursuit of freedom. Over the course of the war, an estimated 180,000
African American men enlisted in the Union Army (Hewitt 2002).

The battle at Milliken's Bend on June 7, 1863, was another noteworthy
engagement involving African American soldiers (Grant 2000; Lowe
2002) because the Union commanders relied heavily on black infantry.
The Union's most important objective in the West was to control the
Mississippi River, and Milliken's Bend was located on the river near key
fortifications at Vicksburg. Controlling the bend allowed Union forces to
approach Vicksburg, which sat strategically on the river. The battle involved
hand-to-hand combat, and three African American regiments, although
they were relatively untrained and inexperienced, fought with distinction
(Lowe 2002). Milliken's Bend was a victory for the North but at a heavy
cost of black soldiers. African American units had casualty rates as high

as 45 percent during the battle, and the conclusion drawn by Northerners was that black soldiers fought with valor and exceptional distinction (Grant 2000).

Although they were active participants in many major battles of the war, there was a persistent reluctance within the army to acknowledge African American contributions to the war. They entered the war on inequitable terms relative to whites, and by war's end little had changed. Although fully emancipated and having contributed on the battlefield, some African American war veterans felt compelled to document their wartime contributions. For example, following the war, William Wells Brown (2003) published *The Negro in the American Rebellion* in 1867. Brown's purpose for the book was to illustrate examples of African American bravery and contributions to the Union's military efforts. Brown, formerly an escaped slave, wanted to firmly establish that black soldiers were courageous in the heat of battle. He focused on their masculinity and honorable acts on the battlefield. Although he wrote purposely and was biased in his accounts, Brown was a keen observer of the conditions leading up to the war and subsequent events. He included several eyewitness accounts of some of the major battles in which African American troops participated. The Works Progress Administration (WPA) narratives also include references to battles in which the ex-slave respondents either were witnesses or participants.

Historians, journalists, participants, and eyewitnesses have documented the battles and other military engagements of the war in great detail. It has been said that the Civil War was fought in more than 10,000 battles and seemingly across every state. Time lines and depictions of these battles and the war are abundant. Our understanding of the Civil War at this level becomes a history of major military leaders, significant battles, battlefield tactics, numbers of casualties, strategic military maneuvers, types of weapons, numbers of troops, and winners and losers. But the war was much more than major battles and historical figures. Individuals—white, black, and Native American—fought and experienced the war at a routine and daily level. The war was much larger than just a collection of battles. It was an inescapable reality of everyday life. The WPA narratives reveal details about how individuals and their families experienced the extraordinary and ordinary events of the war on a personal level. The Civil War on this level was more than numbers of casualties, body counts, historic figures, or military tactics. It became more intimate when viewed by those who experienced it on a daily basis. The narratives give us a sense of how this

Escaped slave Nick Biddle, an aide to Captain James Wren, Company B, 48th Pennsylvania Volunteers, became immortalized as being the first casualty of the Civil War. On April 18, 1861, less than a week after Fort Sumter, Biddle and other Pennsylvania volunteers moved through Baltimore en route to Washington, D.C., to defend the nation's capital. Southern sympathizers and pro-Confederates in Baltimore threw stones and bricks at the volunteers. Biddle, although 65 at the time, was unshakable and courageous in the face of a mob hurling a barrage of objects, and yelling racial slurs and threats. An object struck Biddle in the head causing a serious head wound. Once in Washington, the volunteers' reception was in sharp contrast and a grateful President Lincoln allegedly shook Biddle's hand after seeing his head wrapped in blood-soaked bandages. Biddle carried the scar for the rest of his life and died destitute in 1876 without even enough money to cover his burial expenses. (Library of Congress)

uncommon war was experienced by common people who survived as slaves or free people. Some of these experiences are included in the following sections, beginning with the war's early days.

THE BRAVADO OF GOING OFF TO WAR

A number of the slave accounts describe the bravado in which many white Southerners and Northerners went off to war. The exuberance of young white Southern men to teach the Yankees a lesson surfaces in many of the narratives. This excitement was also present among some African American men in the North who wanted the opportunity to fight for their rights. In the North, including in the Union slave states of Kentucky, Maryland, Delaware, and Missouri, many blacks, free and enslaved, also were eager to join the fight. However, the many optimistic young men on both sides soon discovered that the war was not the glorious opportunity they thought it would be. Those fortunate enough to have survived the many battlefields came back beaten and changed men. In the beginning, most people on both sides expected the war to be over in a few weeks. Following the early battles, such as First Bull Run/Manassas on July 21, 1861, it became quickly evident that the war would not be won quickly. Early on, President Lincoln only asked soldiers to enlist for 90-day commitments. His assumption, shared by many, proved terribly wrong.

Slaves witnessed the tragedy experienced by these young men and shared their memories of those men going off to war. For example, ex-slave John Moore (TX) spoke of his young master's ambition when he headed off: "Young marster say he gwine to war to kill a Yankee and bring he head back and he take a servant 'long." Moore then added that "He didn' bring no Yankee head back but he brung a shot up arm." Mary Williams (AR) shared a similar account of her young master's boasting. Her 18-year-old master Henry "say he goin' to take old Lincoln the first thing and swing him to a limb end let him play around awhile and then shoot his head off." She then added, "But I 'member the morning old mistress got a letter that told how young master Henry was in a pit with the soldiers and they begged him not to stick his head up but he did anyway and they shot it off." In a similar vein, Jennie Webb (MS) noted that her master had four sons go off to war. Everyone gathered to send the young men off. The young men then instructed the slaves. "Dey tole us to be good to our ole Missus dat dey was gwine to whip dem Yankees hell can scortch a feather." A short time thereafter, she observed that young master Tom had returned in a coffin. The return of fallen soldiers was a common occurrence and was mentioned in several of the narratives.

PERSONAL TRAGEDIES OF WAR

Slaves experienced the war on many levels. On one level, slaves saw the general carnage of the aftermath of some of the major battles. Hammett Dell (AR) expressed what many slaves must have thought about the war: "Lady it ain't nuthin' but hell on dis earth." This hell was likely felt when Ellen Betts (TX) detailed her return to the plantation from nearby woods where slaves had been sent to hide following a military engagement with the Yankees:

> When us driv back to de plantation, sech a sight I never seen. Law, de things I can tell. Dem Yanks have kilt men and women. I seed babies pick up from de road with dere brains bust right out. One

old man am drawin' water and a cannon ball shoots him right in de well. Dey draws him up with de fishin' line. Dey's a old sugar boat out on de bayou with blood and sugar runnin' long side de busted barrels. 'Lasses run in de bayou and blood run in de ditches. Marse have de great big orchard on de road and it wipe clean as de whistle. Bullets wipe up everythin' and bust dat sugar cane all to pieces. De house sot far back and 'scape de bullets, but, law, de time dey have!

Nelson Davis (TX) shared a similar account of the horrors of war. "Dar was times atter er big battle dat Ize seed de ditches plum full ob dead folkses." Anna Smith (OH), as related to her interviewer, experienced several tragedies. She lost many of her family members, including her husband:

Her oldest brother was 50 when he joined the Confederate army. Three other brothers were sent to the front. One was an ambulance attendant, one belonged to the cavalry, one an orderly sergeant and the other joined the infantry. All were killed in action. Anna Smith's husband later joined the war and was reported killed.

Another level of the war revealed by the narratives was in the many personal tragedies shared by the WPA respondents. The ex-slaves shared their observations of some of the personal losses they experienced or witnessed firsthand during the war, often as the consequence of major battles but also due to short-term encounters with forces from opposing sides. War was not something that happened to others; it was experienced and felt very directly by some of the slaves. Even though he was not directly involved, the war was all around Preston Tate (TN), who was playing with other children "with shot and shells flying thick and fast."

Aunt Jane Mickens Toombs (GA) did not remember much about the war but did recall how her mistress's husband wrote home and indicated that he would be returning. They then began to prepare for his return, but instead, according to Aunt Jane:

Den dey brung her er letter sayin' he had been kilt, an' she was in de yard when she read hit an' if dey hadn't er kotch her she'd ov fell. I 'members de women 'takin' her in de house an' gittin' her ter bed. She was so up sot an' took hit so hard. Dem was sho' hard times an' sad 'uns too.

The narrative of Charity Jones (MS) is a great example of how the war affected families. Her narrative begins with a reference about Jefferson Davis and his plans to whip the North, but as it continued, she described how the war was tragic for her master's family:

When I was a chile I could hear dem talkin' 'bout Mr. Jefferson Davis an' how he was gwineter whup de Yankees, an' how de white folks was gwineter win dat war. Old Marster didn' go ter de war but sont his two boys, an' Old Missus she jes cried an' cried when dey lef' ter j'in de regiment. Now, long afte' dey was gone dey got news dat young Marse Leonard was shot, an' right den dey sont my uncle ter dat army ter nuss young Marster. But Marster died an' 'fo my uncle could leave de battle fiel' a bullet done hit him side of de head, an' kilt him an' he never come home.

Tines Kendricks's (AR) account contains a vivid description of how the war turned tragic for his master, Sam. According to Kendricks, Master Sam enlisted with the goal of killing Yankees in Virginia and returning home as soon as possible. Sam wrote back, and apparently the content of his letters was either overheard by or read to Kendricks. The letters indicate that Sam was shot and sent to a field hospital for recovery. The letters he wrote indicate that he "say dey had a hard fight, dat a ball busted his gun, and another ball shoot his cooterments [accoutrements] off him; the third shot tear a big hole right through the side of his neck." Despite his serious wounds, he planned to return to his company, but from his letters, he shared that he was not getting better, possibly because the Yankees had put poison on their bullets. It should be noted that poison was not the likely cause of problems with his bullet wounds, but rather the problems were due to crude and unsanitary surgical practices that likely resulted in infection. Then Kendricks witnessed a "sign" that someone would die, and he said, "I just knowed it was Mars Sam." The next day they received word that Master Sam was dead.

Sometimes the respondents noted the general consequences of the war on local men. Emma Simpson (TX) felt sad for the loss of life and physical casualties resulting from the war. Perceiving how large were the casualties, she said that "The war between the states they get might near all the young men in the county" and added that "I'se begins to think they was gone get all them." She noted that a celebration was given to those sent off to war but with a sense of pending loss. "When it started they gives great big dance and supper in Huntsville to tell them good by, both white and black were there to tell the soldiers boy good by, cause they knew some would not come back no more." She concluded that "War is terrible cause lots of our boys come home sick cripple and one legged one armed and so on."

Most of the time for slaves, the war was in the background. Battles were not witnessed but instead were heard in the distance. Julia Ann James (OH) observed that "Us cud see de flash fum firin' en de smoke, en it was nothin' fer us ter hear de roar of de guns day en night." Parilee Daniels (TX) mentioned that "We could hear them guns popping and we put cotton in our ears so'es we wouldn't be so scared." She then said, "Them there guns sounded like they was gone to get you every minute." Johnson (1969, 36) cited an ex-slave who recalled the battle for Nashville: "When the Yankees on Capitol Hill gave the signal—God bless your soul—it sounded like the cannons would tear the world to pieces. I could hear the big shells humming as they came they cut off trees like a man cutting weeds with a scythe."

African Americans on both sides buried the dead and gathered remains from battlefields following engagements. They salvaged what they could, took care of the dead, and sometimes helped distinguish the wounded from those for whom there was no hope. Many of the soldiers, especially Confederates, near the end of the war were children. Ex-slave Elige Davison (TX) spoke of hearing the cries of wounded soldiers, many of whom he saw were children:

Yessir, I believe the war was terrible cause they shot them Kentucky hills flat. Master he killed in the war I'se cook for the soldiers, then the Yankees whilest General Grant, they captures everything that got in front of them. Boss I picked up purty white soldiers until it got to be terrible. I heard them white soldiers hollerin and cry until I'se plum crazy. I'se seen them every night after I go to sleep, and some of them were just children.

James Lucas (MS) provided a similar account of the many battlefields' wounded:

Law! It sho' was turrible times. Dese old eyes o' mine seen more people crippled an' dead. I'se even seen 'em sew off legs wid hacksaws. I tell you it aint right, Miss, what I seen. It aint right at all.

The scope of the carnage following a battle was incomprehensible. Bodies of the dead, their horses, and the wounded were scattered all over the battlefield. Survivors piled the bodies high, buried them where they fell, let them decay in situ, or tossed them in mass graves. Many of the bodies would remain where they fell until after the war or at least many months latter (Faust 2008). Laura Thornton (AR) remembered how "Aftuh de battle was ovah we would walk ovah de battle groun' an look at de daid bones, skellums ah think dey called em." Anna Washington (AR) had memories of rows and rows of dead men. "The men lay dead in rows and rows and rows." She added that "The dead men covered whole fields." Hardy Miller (AR) recalled that the battlefield dead had their uniforms removed by other soldiers and that it was difficult to tell Confederate from Union soldiers. Miller had heard that "the old folk what knowed say you could tell the Yankees from the Rebels comse the Yankees had blue veins on their bellies and the Rebels didn't."

Mary Johnson (TX), a child at the time, told what she saw of a Mississippi battlefield and the tragedy and horror of the war:

> I see lots of sojers in 'Sippi. Dey hab on sorter yaller clo'se. My
> daddy fit wid de Yankees. Dey had a big fight right close dere. Dey
> have a whole lots of dead bodies layin' 'roun' like so many logs.
> Dey didn' had no time to bury 'em so dey jis' stack' 'em up and sot
> fire to 'em. You could see 'em burnin' night and day. I's jis' a tot but
> I 'member dat. Dey had long fights w'en dey can't git nuthin' to eat
> or drink. Dey lay down and shoot and den dey jump up and stick
> 'em wid a ba'net. Dey say dey drink de blood out dey side w'en dey
> stick 'em wid a ba'net 'cause dey ain't got time to git no water.

Ned Thompson (OK) recalled what he witnessed as a child in the aftermath of a battle:

> We went through a battlefield where there were many dead persons.
> Some were white and some were Indians. It was six or seven miles
> east of High Spring. There was a house close and there were some
> who were living in the house but the wounded were in there on
> beds. One of my sisters had bad dreams and cried all night because
> of what she had seen. The dead were in the corn rows.

Control of the rail lines passing through Corinth in northeastern Mississippi meant access to the Confederate heartland as well as a means to reach its coastal ports. Defending Corinth was critical to the Southern effort. Doc Quinn (AR) remembered the aftermath of the 1862 Corinth battle:

> An' let me tell yo' somethin', whitefolks. Dere never was a war like dis war. Why I 'member dat after de battle of Corinth, Miss., a five acre field was so thickly covered wid de dead and wounded dat yo' couldn't touch de ground in walkin' across it. And de onliest way to bury dem was to cut a deep furrow wid a plow, lay de soldiers head to head, an' plow de dirt back on dem.

Martin Jackson (TX) followed his young master into the Confederate Texas 1st Cavalry. Although Jackson wanted the Yankees to win and suspected that they would, he held out hope that his Confederate unit would not be destroyed in the process. "I wanted them to win and lick us Southerners, but I hoped they was going to do it without wiping out our company," he said. As happened to some African Americans serving in the military on both sides, Jackson said that his commanding officer, a person he held in high esteem, died in his arms. Jackson said of Colonel Carl Augustus Buchel that he was "as fine a man and a soldier as you ever saw." Jackson described the day Buchel was shot:

> I was about three miles from the front, where I had pitched up a kind of first-aid station. I was all alone there. I watched the whole thing. I could hear the shooting and see the firing. I remember standing there and thinking the South didn't have a chance. All of a sudden I heard someone call. It was a soldier, who was half carrying Col. Buchel in. I didn't do nothing for the Colonel. He was too far gone. I just held him comfortable, and that was the position he was in when he stopped breathing. That was the worst hurt I got when anybody died. He was a friend of mine.

Although in his narrative Jackson said that Colonel Buchel died in the Battle of Marshall, Buchel actually died in April 1864 after being mortally wounded in the Battle of Mansfield/Pleasant Hill in Louisiana, which was a Confederate victory (National Humanities Center Resource Toolbox 2013). Perhaps Jackson incorrectly recalled the battle name after seven decades or the interviewer typed "Marshall" for "Mansfield." The Texas 1st Cavalry did not fight in the 1863 Battle of Marshall in Missouri. As another historical point of reference, according to the online handbook of the Texas State Historical Association (2013), Buchel's commanding officer, General Hamilton P. Bee, wrote in his official report of the battle that Buchel died from his wounds two days after the battle. It is unclear how this aligns with Jackson's narrative, but at the very least the ex-slave's narrative paints an exceptionally poignant picture of the emotion felt by slaves caught up in the horrors of battle.

Sam Kilgore (TX) lost his master after only two weeks of conflict. Sam grieved for a "long time" and took responsibility for the loss of his master's life. Sam said, "Ise always feel dat if Ise been wid him Ise could save his life."

All of the war's losses had personal implications for the survivors. Virtually no family was untouched by death. Survivors often wanted to know how their loved ones died. Did they die horribly, honorably, in pain? Where did they die? They also wanted to bring their fallen loved ones home for a proper send-off to the afterlife (Faust 2008). Caroline Bevis (SC) never got over the loss of the man she loved:

> He was very handsome. He had black eyes and black hair. I had seven curls on one side of my head and seven on the other. He was twenty-four when he joined the "Boys of Sixteen." He wanted to marry me then, but father would not let us marry. He kissed me good-bye and went off to Virginia. He was a picket and was killed while on duty at Mars Hill. Bill Harris was in a tent near-by and heard the shot. He brought Ben home. I went to the funeral. I have never been much in-love since then.

THE WOUNDED

The crude but damaging weapons used during the war left soldiers on both sides with significant and often disabling injuries. The heavy weight of minié and musket balls maimed, crushed bones, and ripped through tissue. Grapeshot, cannonballs, and other military ordnance crippled soldiers. Battle wounds frequently resulted in infections and amputations. The narratives describe some of these wounded survivors of the war. For example, Ellen Claibourn (GA) observed the wounded in great numbers:

> Oh my Gawd, I saw plenty wounded soldiers. We was right on the road to Wrightsboro, and plenty of 'em pass by. That Confed' rats War was the terriblest, awfullest thing.

Andrew Boone (NC) told of a chance encounter between a Rebel and a maimed Yankee soldier:

> One time a Rebel saw a Yankee wid one eye, one leg an' one arm. De Yankee wus beggin'. De Rebel went up to him an' give him a quarter. Den he backed off an' jes' stood a-lookin' at de Yankee, presently he went back an' give him anudder quarter, den anudder, den he said, "You take dis whole dollar, you is de first Yankee I eber seed trimmed up jes' to my notion, so take all dis, jes' take de whole dollar, you is trimmed up to my notion."

Martha Cunningham (OK) recalled the battlefield outside Knoxville, Tennessee, and the aftermath for the wounded:

> I went over the battlefield at Knoxville, Tennessee, two or three hours after the Yankees and the Rebels had a battle. It was about a mile from our house, and I walked over hundreds of dead men lying on the ground. Some were fatally wounded, and we carried about six or seven to our house. I saw the doctor pick the bullets out of their flesh.

TRAGIC ENCOUNTERS OFF THE BATTLEFIELD

Sometimes slaves were caught up in military events that were not major battles. The tremendous fatalities on the battlefields were accompanied by other casualties outside of the battlefields. Patrols, guerrilla warfare, skirmishes, raids, chance encounters, and other war-related incidents resulted in tragedies for many. Some of these off-the-battlefield encounters were noted in the narratives. In one case, ex-slave Preston Tate (IN) was surprised and frightened when soldiers, with shot and shells flying thick and fast, surrounded him and other slave children. Preston and the others avoided being hurt by hiding behind trees and crawling through the thicket.

The circumstances surrounding these encounters varied. An example of a tragedy resulting from defiance and pride was reported in the narrative of Fanny Cannady (NC). After detailing the arrogance of her owner and his two sons, Fanny described a tragedy involving one of the sons, Master Gregory, whom she characterized as a bully. She told of him being on furlough and strutting about the yard when he noticed a slave named Leonard Allen say under his breath, "Look at dat God damn sojer. He fightin' to keep us niggahs from bein' free." Gregory challenged the slave as to what he was talking about, and Leonard, unafraid, repeated, "Look at dat God dawn sojer. He fightin' to keep us niggahs from bein' free." This bold statement made Gregory red with anger, and he ordered that his shotgun be brought to him. Then, Fanny reported:

When Pappy come back Mis' Sally come wid him. De tears was streamin' down her face. She run up to Marse Jordan an' caught his arm. Ole Marse flung her off an' took de gun from Pappy. He leveled it on Leonard an' tole him to pull his shirt open. Leonard opened his shirt an stood dare big as er black giant sneerin' at Ole Marse. Den Mis' Sally run up again an' stood 'tween dat gun an' Leonard.

Ole Marse yell to pappy an' tole him to take dat woman out of de way, but nobody ain't moved to touch Mis' Sally, an' she didn' move neither, she jus' stood dare facin' Ole Marse. Den Ole Marse let down de gun. He reached over an' slapped Mis' Sally down, den picked up de gun an' shot er hole in Leonard's ches' big as yo' fis'. Den he took up Mis' Sally an' toted her in de house. But I was so skeered dat I run an' hid in de stable loft, an' even wid my eyes shut I could see Leonard layin' on de groun' wid dat bloody hole in his ches' an' dat sneer on his black mouf.

Much of the war consisted of small-scale conflicts between small units of Yankee and Confederate forces, some of which were witnessed by slaves. These encounters often turned tragic for those involved. For example, Claiborne Moss (AR) spoke of a lost Yankee soldier who found his way to the plantation. He asked for directions back to Louisville. Claiborne then described what happened. "The old boss pointed the way with his left hand and while the fellow was looking that way, he drug him off his horse and cut his throat and took his gun off'n him and killed him." In another example, Jack and Rosa Maddox (TX) reported how some Confederate soldiers came looking for an individual, probably a slave, named Bob Anderson. They asked his "maw" where he was, and she indicated that she did not know. They then threatened to burn her out, and he came out of her house. According to their narrative:

They tied him with a rope and tied the other end to the saddle of one of the men. They went off with him trotting behind the horse.

His maw sent me following along in the wagon. I followed thirteen miles. After a few miles I seen where he fell down and the drag signs on the groun'. Then when I come to Hornage Creek I seen they had gone through the water. I went across and after a while I found him. But you couldn't tell any of the front side of him. They had drug the face off him. I took him home.

ACCOUNTS OF MAJOR CIVIL WAR BATTLES

There are numerous references to Civil War battles in the narratives. Slaves fought side by side with their masters at Bull Run/Manassas in July 1861. The First Battle of Bull Run/Manassas was described by Henry Gladney (SC), who talked about how he chased down a Yankee soldier and choked him to death. George Jackson (OH) shared the following observation about the battle:

I heard shootin' and saw soldiers shot down. It was one of de worst fights of de war. It was right between Blue Ridge and Bull Run mountain. De smoke from de shootin' was just like a fog. I saw horses and men runin' to de fight and men shot off de horses. I heard de cannon rear and saw de locust tree cut off in de yard. Some of de bullets smashed de house. De apple tree where my massa was shot from was in de orchard not far from de house.

Some of these accounts include references to the Battle of Atlanta. Arrie Binn (GA) said that she "remembers the days of war, how when the battle of Atlanta was raging they heard the distant rumble of cannon, and how 'upsot' they all were." William Irving (TX) spoke of the Battle of Chattanooga and how the Yankees scaled Lookout Mountain and forced the Rebels to retreat.

De way de Yankees scaled old Lookout Mountain, and broke de rebels lines dat caused dem to start dey retreat, was one of de biggest things dey did. Dey own Generals was surprised dat dey goes on to de top, dey had orders, hit seemed to keep dem busy fightin whilst de Yanks in some other point was doin' dey part, but up dey went, an dey did'nt stop until dey gits to de top. I thinks hit was ole Joe Hooker dat took dis mountain, an' anyway w'en dey did, de people in de valley's thought hit was time to git out of de way of de Yankee's, an' dat is w'en Judge Easterlin' refugeed to Greensboro.

Irving (TX) also offered a brief description of his experience of the heavy fighting at the Battle of Chickamauga:

W'en de battle of Chickamauga was goin' on for three days, we could hear de poppin' of de guns, an' de sound of de canon as dey go, boom, boom, boom, wid a stop long enough to load again w'en dey is empty. Dey sounded like de tollin of de bells.

Richard Franklin (OK) described the aftermath of the battle at Fort Gibson in 1864. Although he did not fight in the battle, he went to the battlefield following the conflict. "I went down there and found lead bullets and saw big trees with the tops shot off by cannons." He added, "I also saw blood on the ground but did not see any dead men." Regarding the battle at Fort Hill, Henry Warfield (MS) said, "There was lots of blood, plenty of noise, big fires, and crowds of strange faces that he had not seen before." William Irving (GA) shared his memories of Sherman's March to the Sea: "Dey burned all de barns, an' took all de corn dey could carry and didn't leave de people anything." Lindsey Moore (GA) remembered the slaves on her plantation leaving with Sherman but only after his troops tore up the railroad tracks and station. Sallah White (TN) "Cud hear de roar of de cannons" being fired at the Battle of Lookout Mountain.

Hammett Dell (AR) noted that although he lived about 10 miles from Murfreesboro, Tennessee, the roar of the cannons during the battle shook his house, and the "earth quivered." In the aftermath of the battle, George W. Arnold (IN) remembered seeing many soldiers going to the pike road on their way to Murfreesboro. "Long lines of tired men passed through Guy's Gap on their way to Murfreesboro." He then said, "Older people said that they were sent out to pick up the dead from the battle fields after the bloody battle of Stone's river that had lately been fought at Murfreesboro."

Other battles mentioned include Petersburg, Virginia (Sim Younger, MO; Charlie Giles, SC), and Fort Pillow (William H. Cross, AR; James Lucas, MS). Fort Pillow took on special significance because of the wanton slaughter of captured African American Union troops by General Nathan Bedford Forrest. William H. Cross (AR) fought on the Union side and was at the Fort Pillow massacre (see Chapter 5). While he considered General Forrest the best Confederate general because he seemed to be everywhere, he was also guilty of ordering the massacre of Union troops at Fort Pillow, including many African American soldiers, and it "was the meanest thing he did." There is contradictory evidence of what actually happened at Fort Pillow (Cimprich 2002). There is consensus that Rebel troops were angry that the Union allowed blacks to be armed and to fight against them. After that, historians disagree about whether or not what followed the Confederate victory was premeditated and deliberate or whether events simply careened out of control, but all agree that a massacre took place and that many soldiers who had surrendered and even civilians were ruthlessly slaughtered. Both sides later embellished and exploited the event to further their cause (Cimprich 2002).

This wood engraving entitled *The War in Tennessee: Rebel Massacre of Union Troops After the Surrender at Fort Pillow* appeared in *Harper's Weekly*, date unknown. The battle at Fort Pillow was fought on April 12, 1864, and the ensuing massacre included the maiming and slaughter of many black soldiers. Southerners were outraged at the North's use of black soldiers and Confederate military leaders were faced with the question of whether to treat black soldiers captured in battle as slaves in insurrection or, as the Union insisted, as prisoners of war. In what proved the ugliest racial incident of the war, soldiers under Confederate General Nathan Bedford Forrest left no doubt they did not consider black soldiers prisoners of war. For the remainder of the war, black soldiers going into battle used the cry "Remember Fort Pillow!" to avenge their murdered brethren. (Library of Congress)

The Battle of Vicksburg was a long and drawn-out affair that was referenced many times in the narratives. The importance of Vicksburg was that with its capture and that of Port Hudson, the Union had complete control of the Mississippi River. General Ulysses S. Grant's troops encountered and fought armed black Confederates during this siege. Union troops were puzzled by why Southern blacks would fight against them and support their oppressors (Barrow, Segars, and Rosenburg 2004). Virginia Harris (MS) told of her father's experience in the Battle of Vicksburg:

> When the great battle of Vicksburg started up, we was close enough
> to hear all them guns and things shooting. Mr. Pennington, he
> walked out one day and he say, "Mr. Grant, do you recon you is ever
> going to see inside of Vicksburg." Mr. Grant say, "I don't know but
> I sure is going to try." That very night they took the city. My Lord!
> that was some fight. My pa was right in the thick of it. He said when
> the two armies got close up, they stopped shooting and went to
> jabbing each other with their swords and sharp things on their guns.
> The Yankees sure paid for taking that town with many a soul.

Tom Bones (MS) shared the following observation about the Battle of Vicksburg:

> At the Seige of Vicksburg some Negro boys were sent to a run near
> by to dip up water to make coffee for the soldiers and as they
> dipped the water they found the color so dark it was found later that
> this water was blood from the battlefield that they were about to
> make coffee with.

Henry Smith's (TX) narrative contains several detailed descriptions of battles and military life while serving in the Confederate Texas Brigade. His narrative represents the longest continuous reference to the war in the WPA narratives. It is very detailed about what he experienced, containing descriptions of what life was like in the army during and between numerous battles. Smith provides what seems like an endless stream of descriptions of one battle after another fought throughout the South. He spoke of the circumstances that led up to the battle at what he referred to as "Chickahominy." It is almost certain that he was referring to the series of battles labeled the Peninsula Campaign. The Battle of Gaines' Mill, also referred to as the First Battle of Cold Harbor and the Battle of the Chickahominy

River, occurred on June 27, 1862, in Hanover County, Virginia. The battle was fierce, with Union casualties estimated to be slightly over 6,800 and Confederate loses being close to 8,000 (Burton 2001; Salmon 2001; Sears 1992). The battle was a Confederate victory that helped save Richmond from Union occupation, at least for the time being. The Union defeat helped persuade Army of the Potomac commander Major General George B. McClellan not to advance to Richmond.

Smith also made reference to the Battle of Seven Pines, which was another segment of McClellan's Peninsula Campaign to capture Richmond (Sears 1992). The Battle of Seven Pines, also known as the Battle of Fair Oaks, was fought from May 31 to June 1, 1862. The battle, up to that point in the war, was the second largest after Shiloh. Casualties on both sides were high, and both sides claimed victory. Smith mentioned being under the command of Confederate general Joe Johnson, who was seriously wounded in the shoulder during the battle. Union forces were turned back about six miles from Richmond, and it would be two bloody years before they would take the city.

Smith described what happened:

'Bout de las' ob May, de Texas Brigade fit in de battle what dey called Seven Pines. Dar was er railroad 'long de York Ribber an' de Texas Brigade was stationed erlong dis railroad. But all de fightin' ob dis battle, an' hit sho was er bloody one, was erbout er mile away, ter de lef' ob whar us was.

Smith noted that African Americans were not permitted to have guns but did use other weapons (see Chapter 6 for more on arming slaves).

Us officers said ter go git dem Yanks but not ter fire er gun. Dey want me ter stay behime, but how I gwine look atter Marse Jim? No ma'am, us black boys didn't hab no guns, but I had my razor an' er big club.

Smith described transporting the wounded to field hospitals, including his master. Medical treatment of battle wounds was crude and often resulted in serious infection, leading to death. He said that:

One ob our boys in de Texas bunch he git shot in de head an' in de lef' arm, shatterin' de bone up nigh he shoulder. Us didn't know dis fer hours an' Marse Billy Dunklin found him an' tuk to de fiel' hospital in de back ob us troops. Dar was so many wounded dat de doctor didn't git to dis Marse B. L. Aycock an' he didn't git he hurts fixed up f'om Thursday till Sunday an' den dey put him in an army waggin wid er lot more dat had got wounded, an' sont 'em nine miles ter Richmon'. Dat was er pow'ful rocky, rough road fer wounded folks ter jolt ober in er waggin. Dey done make er hospital outten de First Baptist Church in Richmond. De cut Marse Aycock's jacket offen him an' fixed him up. An' den a few days later, a place on de back ob he head swole up an' de doctor he git dat odder bullet out. He say dat de bullet what knocked him ober. Marse Aycock kep' dat bullet er long time; hit was flat whar hit had hit he skull. De nex' December, Marse Aycock was in Waco an' he git er doctor ter hunt fer de ball in he arm an' dey got dat. Wuzn't no blood pison neidder.

Smith told of General Robert E. Lee and the Battle of the Wilderness, fought between Lee's Confederate Army of Northern Virginia and Union lieutenant general Ulysses S. Grant's forces between May 5 and May 7, 1864. The battle was thought to be inconclusive, as Grant withdrew his forces to find better ground and continued his campaign against Lee's troops at the Battle of Spotsylvania, which was the second major battle in Grant's 1864 Overland Campaign. Smith also made a reference to the Battle of Spotsylvania and spoke accurately of how his Confederate troops waited in Spotsylvania for Grant's army, noting that Lee arrived at the Spotsylvania Courthouse before Grant. Fighting occurred from May 8 to May 21, 1864. Grant tried various approaches to break the Confederate lines but failed to do so. Even though the battle was determined later to be inconclusive, it was the costliest battle of the Overland Campaign. Smith noted General Lee's leadership and bravery in the heat of the battle:

Marse Aycock he shouldered er musket an' us jined Ginniril Lee at de close ob de furst day ob de Battle of de Wilderness in May. Colonel Longstreet marched us at double quick march fer seberal miles. Ginniril Lee's men was all wore out w'en us git dar. Ginniril Lee come to de Texas Brigade an' he made a talk dat sho' roused our boys all up. Ginniril Gregg was de main man ober our boys in de Brigade den. An' Ginniril Gregg he tole us w'at Ginniril Lee done said. Den de boys went inter de battle line.

. . . Dey had one ob deir cannon in a dense thicket in front, and de Northern soljers seed hit an' dey seed Ginniril on he hoss Traveler right close to hit. One ob de Brigade boys seed whar Ginniril Lee wer gittin' right in plain view ob de Northern skirmishers so one ob de Texas boys he gits holt ob Ginniril bridle rain an' he say "Lee to de rear" an' dat's one time de Ginniril obeyed a private's command. An' allers de Texas boys say dat's what saved Ginniril Lee's life. He seemed to want ter lead de charge all de time, dat was somethin' he nebber had done an' he nebber was allowed to do, if he was er Ginniril.

It was common for slaves to take care of their fallen masters (see Chapter 4). Smith indicated that he faithfully buried his Master Jim, gathered his master's personal items, and returned them to his family. This was the end of Smith's involvement in the war. He recalled:

In dis battle on de Darbytown road, somehow Marse Jim, he git er gun an' gits inter de middle ob things. W'en dey go ergin' de Northern breastworks, er lot ob our boys didn't come back. Atter dark some ob 'em come back to whar us was behime de lines, but dar wuzn't no Marse Jim. I crawls out whar dey tell me dat dey think he is. I gits him up cross my shoulder, an' brings him back an' buries him, an' den dis boy git er mule an' er little grub an' some ob Marse Jim's things an' den I gits inter er awful time. I starts ter Texas. Dat was an awful trip but I finnerly gits ter de ole Marster an' tells what I has ter an' gibs what I could keep ob Marse Jim's things ter de folks. I'ze mos' dead but dis ole nigger got ter live er long time.

Given the number of battles that Smith referenced in his narrative, he and his master beat the odds for most of the Civil War. According to Smith's narrative, he was present during the Peninsular Campaign, Mechanicsville, the First Battle of Cold Harbor, Seven Pines, and the Wilderness, among others. Odds were that he and his master, given their many travels and battles, could have easily died from disease or from battle, and after several battles his master did. A Union soldier had a 1 in 8 chance of dying due to illness and a 1 in 18 chance of dying in battle (Weider History Group 2012). Correspondingly, a Confederate soldier had a 1 in 5 chance of succumbing to disease and a 1 in 8 chance of dying in combat. Although his master died from battle wounds, Henry Smith survived to old age.

NAVAL BATTLES

The narratives contain a few accounts of naval battles and encounters. During the war, Union vessels blockaded Confederate ports and were used to control the waterways and major rivers. References to ships and boats are present in other sources as well. For example, the famous abolitionist and slave liberator Harriet Tubman recalled being told by one escaped slave, "I see, 'peared to me a big house in de water, an' out of de big house came great big eggs, and de good eggs went on trou' de air, an' fell into de fort; an de bad eggs burst before dey got dar. Den I heard 'twas the Yankee ship [the *Wabash*] firin' out de big eggs, and dey had come to set us free" (McPherson 1993, 59).

From the narratives, we learn that Alex Huggins (NC) joined the Union Navy in 1864 and was assigned to be a cabin boy for the captain on the ship *Nereus*. His ship saw action at Fort Fisher and the West Indies. Ben Horry (SC) recalled seeing

> Two Yankee gun boats come up Waccamaw river! Come by us Plantation. One stop to Sandy Island, Montarena landing. One gone Watsaw [Wachesaw Landing]. Old Marse Josh and all the white buckra gone to Marlboro county to hide from Yankee. Gon up Waccamaw river and up Pee Dee river, to Marlboro county, in a boat by name Pilot Boy. Take Colonel Ward and all the Cap'n to hide, from gun boat till peace declare.

On some occasions, troops used boats to travel to battles. For instance, Sim Younger (MO) spoke of the landing at Fort Fisher:

> General Butler went down to Fort Fisher and failed, which was the last open port of the Confederacy. Another expedition was organized and General Terry given command. We embarked on the night of December 31, 1864; landed the morning of January 13, 1865, on the peninsula. On the night of January 15, 1865, we captured Fort Fisher.

In addition to references to battles, the narratives on rare occasions include references to prisoner-of-war camps. Henry Smith mentioned Libby Prison. Tines Kendricks's (AR) narrative described the conditions at one of the most notoriously deplorable camps at Andersonville. For captured black Union soldiers, Confederate prisons were even more difficult (see Chapter 5). Kendricks stated:

> Did you ever hear 'bout de Andersonville prison in Georgia? I tell you, Boss, dat was 'bout de worstest place dat ever I seen. Dat was where dey keep all de Yankees dat dey capture an' dey had so many there they couldn't nigh take care of them. Dey had them fenced up with a tall wire fence an' never had enough house room for all dem Yankees. They would just throw de grub to 'em. De mostest dat dey had for 'em to eat was peas an' the filth, it was terrible. De sickness, it broke out 'mongst 'em all de while, an' dey just die like rats what been pizened. De first thing dat de Yankees do when dey take de state 'way from de Confedrits was to free all dem what in de prison at Andersonville.

A small number of the narratives reference the surrender at Appomattox. James Lucas (MS) claimed to have been present when Lee surrendered his sword to Grant:

> I was on han' when Gin'l Lee handed his sword to Gin'l Grant. You see, Miss, dey had him all hemmed in an' he jus' natchelly had to give up. I seen him stick his sword up in de groun'.

Tom McAlpin (AL) spoke with admiration of the Confederate soldiers and his loyal support for the army. Tom transported wounded soldiers from Richmond because he was dependable and brave. He also claimed to be present at the Confederate surrender yet erroneously described the location as Richmond instead of Appomattox:

> I was in Richmond dat cold day dat Gen'l Lee handed his sword over to de yuther side, an' I seen Jeff Davis when he made a speech 'bout startin' over. I seen de niggers leavin' dere homes an' awanderin' off into de worl' to God knows whar, aeeyin' good-bye to dere white folks, an' atryin' to make dere way de bes' dey kin. But, white boss, it jee' seem lak you let a nigger go widout a boss an' he jes' no good. Dere ain't much he kin do, 'caze dere ain't nobody to tell him. Yaseuh, I was sont to Richmond to bring home some of our wounded Federates. Dey sont me 'caze dey knowed I was agoin' to do my bes', an' caze dey knowed I warn't afeered of nothin'. Dat's

de way I've always tried to be, white bose, lak my white people what raised me. God bless 'em.

OBSERVATIONS

The narratives provide another point of view of the battles that occurred during the Civil War. Much of the history of the war has been documented from written historical records, both official and unofficial, such as personal letters and diaries and eyewitness accounts of politicians, soldiers, and other combatants. What has been largely neglected are the eyewitness oral accounts of the slaves. These accounts, while not shedding earth-shattering new light on the well-documented descriptions of the war's battles, nevertheless provide some insight into how such battles and conflicts were experienced by those directly and indirectly involved. The narratives also verbally document some of the off-the-battlefield conflicts and tragedies that slaves experienced during the war. The calamity of the war as witnessed by slaves was clearly not limited to those in uniform but was also experienced by families, free and slave alike, as Slim Younger's (MO) narrative evokes:

I want to tell you of one of the tragic things that happened during the war, and I was there and saw it.

It was at the Southside railroad, at Petersburg, on September 27, 1865. I was put on picket duty. The "Rebs" had built a fire and the wind was driving it toward us. They began to holler and cheer, very happy over the fact.

All at once we could hear someone coming toward us. The pickets opened fire on what they thought were "Rebs," and found out to their distress that it was a bunch of recruits from our own lines. Many were killed.

At this, Younger's interviewer noted that after unburdening himself from the past horror of war, the ex-slave's mood brightened, and he said, "If I could choose my weapons for the next war, I would choose doughnuts, to be thrown at each other across the Atlantic."

Although one can sometimes find historical inaccuracies due to the memory lapse of age or the slippage of time or even based on the hearsay of oral tradition, it is inescapable that the narratives capture the raw emotion and poignant sentiment bottled up for decades in those whose condition became the substance of America's worst war.

CHAPTER 4

Taking Sides
Acts of Resistance and Loyalty during the Civil War

The Union soldiers came there often. They'd make out like they was hunting guns but they was hunting men that might be there. One day I happened to look out and saw some soldiers coming. The man was at home and I told him and he just barely had time to git away before they got there. They come in without knocking and told Young Miss that they was looking for guns and they looked in the drawers and under the beds and closets. Finally they said, "Little girl where is your Master?" I told them that I didn't know. They went on directly and I guess Young Miss's husband went back to his regiment. The first time I went there he hadn't enlisted. I stayed about two months that time. He had three men then and he sure was hard on them. He made them work like dogs and was always beating them for everything. One day I took their food to them and while they was eating they told me that they was going to run off the next day which was Sunday. I didn't say a word about it of course and the next morning we all got up and after the chores were done we went to church. Me and Aunt Callie and her little girl went to visit a family after church and didn't come home till kind of late in the evening. The men was there that morning but they didn't show up that night before we went to bed. The next morning their Master jumped up and called them. They always got right up and went to feeding and Master would go back to sleep till breakfast. He waked up again and didn't hear no sound so he called me and told me to go and wake them up. I got up and went to their cabin and come back and told him that they wasn't there and that their beds was still made up. He sure rolled out of there and got busy hunting them but he didn't catch them as they got away to the Union soldiers and

joined the army. Pretty soon he had to go, too, so he had to give
up hunting for them.

                                                    (Sina Banks, OK)

Sina Banks's (OK) narrative describes what was a common occurrence
before and during the war: the escape of slaves to freedom. The Civil War
for many on both sides was a time of twisted emotions and loyalties.
Slave reactions to the war were not uniform but instead were varied.
While many slaves rejoiced at the prospect of freedom, others resisted
and, it appears, remained loyal or at least civil to the very people who
oppressed them. It is inaccurate to depict the slaves' view of the war as
uniformly supportive; more accurately, it was mixed. As noted by Faust
(1980), this may have been due more to a sense of community and commitment to local interpersonal relationships than loyalty to masters or
indifference to freedom. A few slaves were devoted to their masters or to
their ways of life or perhaps feared the change that war would inevitably
bring to the extent that they willfully served in the Confederate Army.
Others remained at home and carried out their responsibilities on their
plantations and protected the women and children until the end of the
war. Yet others fled to the North as soon as they could to take up arms
against the South.

The Confederate era, according to some scholars, was a period of considerable cooperation between blacks and whites who remained loyal to
the South (Obatala and Maksel 1979). It is well documented that Southern
blacks on many fronts and in different capacities offered to help the Confederacy. For example, in 1861 a group of African Americans in Petersburg,
Virginia, volunteered to build fortifications in Norfolk and held a rally at
the courthouse square (Obatala and Maksel 1979). Free blacks offered
their services to the Confederate cause in Nashville in April 1861 (Lovett
1976; Williams 1968). Benjamin Quarles (1968) noted that in some communities, such as New Orleans, blacks organized into native guard units.
These groups were prepared to take arms in defense of the South. However, there is no evidence that these African American native guards played
any significant role during the war. Even Southern whites met these offers
of native guard assistance with skepticism (Obatala and Maksel 1979).
The prospect of arming blacks, in light of the many slaves who fled to the
Union and took up arms, was worrisome. Many Southern whites lived in
constant fear of slave revolts and feared the consequences of arming them
(Urwin 2004).

CONTRABANDS

Great numbers of slaves living on the borders of the Confederacy escaped to the North. An estimated 500,000 slaves escaped or otherwise came into Union lines during the war (Aptheker 1938). Beginning in 1861 and during the war, when Union troops were near and success of escape likely, slaves abandoned their plantations by the tens of thousands. The Union was ill-equipped to deal with the masses of escaped slaves who flooded over the Mason-Dixon Line and into Union-controlled areas. The escape often proved hazardous, as blacks fleeing to the North often succumbed to illness or other mishaps and died during their travel (Faust 2008).

At the beginning of the war, the Union did not have a policy on how to deal with escaped slaves (Mays 1984; Tomblin 2009). At the onset, Union generals Ulysses Grant and H. W. Halleck, the commander of the West, believed that the African American problem was of little to no concern to the military (Lovett 1976). As Union forces moved farther into the South and African Americans fled to the North in greater numbers, federal policies on what to do with this influx of population were vague or nonexistent (Franklin and Moss 2000). The Union had not anticipated the massive slave migrations to the North and had no plans about how to care for the many refugees and contrabands. Consequently, several escapees to the North found themselves in worse living conditions than they had known on the plantations. Many were forced to live in large camps. At one of these camps near Washington, escaped slaves were treated roughly and were inadequately housed and poorly fed (Jordan 1995). They suffered from disease, high mortality rates, poor sanitation, and a lack of medical care (Lovett 1976).

There were some positive aspects to the camps. For some escaped slaves, they were a better alternative than returning to the oppression of slavery. In addition, contraband camps, despite overcrowding and deplorable conditions, were where some slaves learned to read and write (Berlin et al. 1992). The North eventually used escaped slaves to build fortifications, breastworks, and other war-related construction projects. Whatever wages they earned were used to pay their living expenses. What is evident is that these contrabands provided much of the labor during the Civil War (Lofton 1949).

Initially, for political reasons President Abraham Lincoln was not interested in taking any action regarding escaped slaves. He wanted to add African Americans to his army and navy but faced resistance from racists in the North. His desire to maintain support from Northern-bordering slave states made him cautious in pressing blacks into the military for fear of alienating these border states (Ramold 2002; Valuska 1993). Lincoln did not want to lose the support of the slaveholding states that opposed secession. To change the status of slaves at that time would have jeopardized the delicate balance of the Union, which he tried desperately to preserve prior to the firing on Fort Sumter. In the absence of any clear guidance, the treatment of escaped slaves was left up to individual generals in the field.

Clarity of policy eventually came about through the field decisions of General Benjamin Butler. On May 23, 1861, Butler learned from three escaped slaves at Fortress Monroe, Virginia, that Confederates were using other slaves to construct Confederate defenses. Upon learning this, Butler declared that captured slaves should not be returned to their plantations but instead would be put to work on the Union side as "contrabands of war" (Ramold 2002, 38). Confederate major John B. Carey had requested that General Butler return the slaves to their owner under the Fugitive Slave Act. General Butler denied his request, not on moral grounds but because the slaves had been used as property against the Union, and he needed their labor. He viewed them as property, or contraband. Labeling runaway slaves as contraband rather than free men was more politically acceptable to Northerners (Mays 1984). The notion of humans as contraband caught on throughout the war. Butler was concerned that moving large numbers of contraband farther north would not be prudent and would alienate Northern whites who did not want their labor, so he took measure to keep them in the South. In the long run, he thought that their labor, following the conclusion of the war, would be needed for Southern agriculture and that the South would be better able to accommodate them. Soon Lincoln reluctantly approved Butler's contraband policy. Fortress Monroe became a major draw for escaped slaves. Although Northerners were not sure what the policy of returning slaves should be, the term "contraband" took hold following Butler's action.

On August 6, 1861, Lincoln would sign the First Confiscation Act proclaiming that slaves known to have worked on building Confederate defenses were considered contraband and were not to be returned to the South. The act indicated that any claims owners had for slaves were forfeited when the slaves had worked for the Confederate government. Contrabands were no longer slaves but were not free either, a political move in the act to appease the border states (Ramold 2002). When slaves were captured by Union forces, voluntarily joined the Union side,

Morning Mustering of the "Contraband" at Fortress Monroe, On Their Way to Their Day's Work, Under the Pay and Direction of the U.S. was the original title of this wood engraving, artist unknown, published in *Frank Leslie's Illustrated Newspaper* on November 2, 1861. This engraving shows contract laborers getting together to work on the fortifications at Fort Monroe. On May 27, 1861, Major General Benjamin Butler, under his own authority, decreed that slaves who escaped or were brought to Union lines, called "contrabands," were not subject to return to their masters. Although not the first to use the term "contraband" during the Civil War, Butler was the first to articulate the policy of not returning "contrabands." His declaration resulted in scores of escapes to Union lines around Fortress Monroe, General Butler's headquarters in Virginia. (Courtesy The House Divided Project at Dickinson College, Carlisle, PA.)

or simply escaped to the North, they were referred to as contrabands. Although the government still had no clear policy on how to handle contrabands, by 1862 most Union commanders had developed protocols for housing, feeding, and putting able-bodied individuals to work in the Union Army camps (McPherson 1993).

The first Confiscation Act did little to improve the legal status of slaves. As the war continued, a series of congressional actions eventually improved the plight of contrabands, although they were never fully welcomed or integrated into Northern society with full rights and privileges. In a letter dated November 20, 1862, probably written by George E. Stephens, an African American servant to an officer of the 26th Pennsylvania Infantry, the letter writer expressed concern about the plight of contrabands who followed Union forces. He also noted that differences were present between field slaves and house servants, the latter of whom he thought were pampered:

> As is ever the case when our troops fall back from the enemy's
> country, large numbers of contrabands or fugitive slaves follow in
> our wake. At the last battle of Bull Run [August 26–31, 1862] this
> whole region was depopulated of its slaves. None remain but the
> aged, infirm, young, and a few of that class of treacherous,
> pampered and petted slaves; known as house servants.
>
> (Redkey 1992, 22–23)

Contrabands proved to be a very useful source of labor for the Union forces. They made ideal spies because of their familiarity with local terrain and awareness of troop movements. They provided detailed information to Union troops on what they observed in the South, such as troop movements and fortifications. It is well established that many contrabands served as informants and spies for the North (Quarles 1968). Union forces found them to be an excellent source of information on Southern troop movements and other military operations. For example, near Jefferson City, Missouri, information that slaves provided to Union major Joseph A. Eppstein prevented a surprise attack on his unit (Wish 1938).

Those contrabands aiding Union forces did so at great risk. The lack of wearing a Union uniform did not prevent them from suffering at Confederate hands. Contrabands helping Union troops faced repercussions as much as black uniformed soldiers (Faust 2008). Contrabands could be executed, punished, or imprisoned for their pro-Union efforts.

However, the relationship between contrabands and the Union Army could be strained at times. Contrabands traveled with Union troops because they had no other place to go and were dependent on Union supplies. Contrabands frequently camped near and followed Union forces. When Union general William Tecumseh Sherman marched through Georgia, a very large group of contrabands followed his troops. Officers in the Union Army and the Union Navy were generally concerned about the large influx of contrabands into their camps or naval vessels (Tomblin 2009; Wilson 2002). The concern was for the impact that large numbers of refugees had on supplies, as large numbers of escaped slaves needed to be clothed, fed, and protected, all of which drained resources. For naval vessels, supplies could rapidly be exhausted.

Wayman Williams (TX) referenced contrabands in his narrative. He observed that some slaves who went to the North did not like it and returned

Fugitive Negroes Fording the Rappahannock Fleeing from Jackson's Army is half of a stereograph taken in August 1862, by Timothy H. O'Sullivan, an Irish photographer known for his images of the Civil War and Western United States. O'Sullivan worked for Mathew Brady before the war and for Alexander Gardner when he took this image. (Library of Congress)

to the South after freedom came. George Johnson (MN) gave an account of how his father smuggled his family north to Iowa. Johnson's story details the risks involved in the journey:

> Well, then when they was forming sides for the Civil War father got wind of it that they was going to send as many of the slaves as they could further south. I reckin 'twas cause they thought 'twould be too easy for most of 'em to get away, if they staid too near the border of the free state line. Well, my father and another one of the slaves on the place, each one of 'em had a horse of his own. So, early one morning they dumped all of us in the wagon. There was my father and mother, and brothers and sisters, an' the other man an' his wife an' family. Well they covered us up just like they would if we was a load of grit to keep it from gettin' wet when it rained. Well, when we got to the state line it was good day light. At the line there was a bunch of rebels standin' 'roun' an' all of 'em knowed father. Father said he got so nervous as he was drivin' through. One of the rebels said, "Nother load of grit, hey, Joe?"
>
> Yes suh, sed he and on he went. Well, when the ol' master discovered they had run off he come over in Iowa, after us but father had gone an' tole the Union men what he'd done, and when the ol'

master showed up, they told him he'd better get back cross that line. We landed in Mount Pleasant, Iowa.

George Johnson (MO) recalled how his father, Joe, packed up on a wagon and escaped to Iowa. In a similar vein, Ida Rigley (AR) also made an indirect reference to contrabands:

The slaves put their beds and clothes up on the wagons and went off behind them and some clumb up in the wagons. I heard Miss Betty say, "They need not follow them off, they are already free."

Willis Williams (SC) was taken by the Yankees and moved with them throughout much of the war. When the fighting stopped, the Yankees returned him to the South. For his own protection, they sent him back in Confederate clothing. He described his experience:

I been with the Yankee. I kin tell you bout the Yankee. They come home there to Rock Creek when the war was breaking up and carried me to Fayetteville [in North Carolina]. Kept me with 'em till Johnson surrendered in Raleigh,—then they kept me in Goldsboro and took me on to Petersburg. After everything over they give me free transportation back home. Free on train back to Fayetteville. They had put all the Yankee clothes on me,—all the blue shirt, blue coat and bumps on the shoulder,—and when they start me home took all the Yankee clothes way from me. Put gray clothes on me and sent me back.

CAPTURE BY THE OPPOSING SIDE

During the war, there were numerous cases when slaves would be captured by Union troops and taken to the North as contraband. While many stayed in the North as freed men, others escaped back to the South (Harper 2004). According to the March 21, 1865, edition of the *Raleigh Daily Conservative*, a squad of Union soldiers captured 19 slaves from Monroe, North Carolina. That evening, 13 of the captured slaves escaped and returned back to their homes (Harper 2004). John Smith (AL) reported on his capture by Union forces:

Us was fightin' on Blue Mountain when Marse Jim got kilt. I looked and looked for him but I never did find him. Atter I lost my marster

I didn't 'long to nobody and de Yankee's was takin' eve'y thing any-
how, so dey tuck me wid dem.

The prospect of capture by Union troops was a reality for some slaves. For
example, James Henry Nelson (AR) experienced the war from both sides.
He was first captured by the Yankees and later by the Confederates.
Although just a child of 10, he was put to work as a servant for both armies.
He indicated in his narrative that both sides treated him well:

> The Yankees taken me when I was a little fellow. About two years
> after the war started, young Marse Henry want to war and took a
> colored man with him but he ran away—he wouldn't stay with the
> Rebel army. So young Marse Henry took me. I reckon I was bout
> ten. I know I was big enough to saddle a cavalry hoss. We carried
> three horses—his hoss, my hoss and a pack hoss. You know chillun
> them days, they made em do a man's work. I studied bout my
> mother durin' the war, so they let me go home.
>
> One day I went to mill. They didn't low the chillun to lay around,
> and while I was at the mill a Yankee soldier ridin' a white hoss cap-
> tured me and took me to Pulaski, Tennessee, and then I was in the
> Yankee army. I wasn't no size and I don't think he would a took me
> if it hadn't been for the hoss.
>
> We come back to Athens and the Rebels captured the whole army.
> Colonel Camp was in charge and General Forrest captured us and I
> was carried south. We was marchin' along the line and a Rebel soldier
> said, "Don't you went to go home and stay with my wife?" And so I
> went there, to Millville, Alabama. Then he bound me to a friend of
> his and I stayed there till the war bout ended. I was getting along very
> well but a older boy 'suaded me to run away to Decatur, Alabama.
>
> Oh I seen lots of the war. Bof sides was good to me. I've seen
> many a scout. The captain would say "By G___, close the ranks."
> Captains is right crabbed. I stayed back with the hosses.

Bill Simms (KS), similar to James Henry Nelson, served both armies during the war. Simms was initially forced to serve the Confederate Army but
later voluntarily joined the Union Army to serve as a teamster:

> When the war started, my master sent me to work for the Confederate
> army. I worked most of the time for three years off and on, hauling

canons, driving mules, hauling ammunition, and provisions. The
Union army pressed in on us and the Rebel army moved back. I was
sent home. When the Union army came close enough I ran away
from home and joined the Union army. There I drove six-mule team
and worked at wagon work, driving ammunition and all kinds of
provisions until the war ended.

James Davis (AR) found the Yankees useful during his escape to the North.
Davis had already escaped when he was captured. At first he hid from the
Yankee troops but was discovered, and he decided to join them as they
headed North:

I runned away and I was in Mississippi makin' my way back home
to North Carolina. I was hidin' in a hollow log when twenty-five of
Sherman's Rough Riders come along. When they got close to me
the horses jumped sudden and they said, "Come out of there, we
know you're in there!" And when I come out, all twenty-five of
them guns was pointin' at that hole. They said they thought I was a
Revel and 'serted the army. That was on New Years day of the year
the war ended. The Yankees said, "We's freed you all this mornin',
do you want to go with us?" I said, "If you goin' North, I'll go." So
I stayed with em till I got back to North Carolina.

Finally, Andrew Moss (TN) described how slaves were captured and sent
off with the Yankees:

Sometimes dey takes and tie a rope round you, and they starts ridin'
off, but dey don't go too fast so you can walk behind. Sometimes
along comes another Yank on a horse and he ask, "Boy, ain't you
tired?" "Yes sir, Boss!" "Well, you get up here behind me and ride
some." Den he wrap de rope all round the saddle horn. Wraps and
wraps, but leaves some slack. But he keeps you tied, so's you won't
jump down and run away. And many's de time a prayin' Negro got
took off like dat and were't never seen no more.

OFF TO THE YANKEES

As noted, thousands of slaves fled to the North during the war to join the
Union Army. The magnitude of the migration and their joining the Union

effort helped secure a Union victory (Berlin, Favreau, and Miller 2007). Their escapes often occurred near the Union camps (Reid 1950). Crawford (2000, 108) reported that "Approximately 600,000 slaves abandoned their plantation and farm homes during the war and entered Union lines; nearly a quarter of the fugitives enlisted in the Federal army." For some slaveholders, the loss of their loyal house servants to the draw of freedom was particularly difficult to understand (Quarles 1968). When Yankee forces were near, the word was spread among slaves that escape was an option. For example, William Mathews (TX) said, "Only one time dey come in daylight, and some de slaves jine dem and go to war." John Smith (NC) shared that "I seed millions of Yankees, just like bees?" He went on to say that "When de war close I went wid 'em." Louis Thomas (MO) spoke of how some slaves went off to join the Yankees when they were near: "If de slaves could get as near as East St. Louis and Ohio with out getting caught, dey would join de Yankees and help fight for freedom."

However, being captured or voluntarily joining Union forces and being freed was no guarantee that life for slaves or their families would be satisfactory. Escape to the North and joining the army could have serious consequences for family members left behind (Berlin et al. 1987; Faust 2008). Berlin et al. (1987) reported that members of one Alabama slave family were sold by Union troops back into slavery to a new owner in the Union slave state of Kentucky. For those enslaved men from the Union slave states of Maryland, Kentucky, Missouri, and Delaware who served in the Union Army, consequences for their families could be significant. Slave owners in these states did what they could to deter their slaves from joining the Union Army, and those doing so risked retribution to their families.

Some escapees returned home after the war, but others were never heard from again. Ann May (MS) provide one such example:

> Most of the negro men on Mr. Alford's plantation ran away and went to Yankees. My husband went to them—he went on to Mobile and I never saw him for many years, when he come back and died in 1870 with small pox.

Mollie Williams (MS) provided another example:

> Some of de darkies went off wid de Yankees. My brudder Howard did, an' we ain't heerd tell of him since. I'll tell you 'bout it. You see, Mr. Davenpo't owned him an' when he heard 'bout de Yankees

comin' dis way, he sont his white driver an' Howard in de carri'ge wid all his valuables to de swamp to hide, an' while dey was thar de white driver, he went off to sleep an' Howard was prowlin' 'roun' an' we all jes reckin he went on off wid de Yankees.

William Nelson (OH) took off with the Yankees after selling them food. He later recalled:

How'd I cum North? Well, one day I run 'way from plantashun and hunted 'til I filled a bucket full turtl' eggs den I takes den ovah on river what I hears der's sum Yankee soljers and de soljers buyed my eggs and hepped me on board de boat. Den Marse Ben, he was Yankee ofser, tol 'em he take care me and he did.

Ella Belle Ramsey (TX) spoke of the fate of some field hands who ran off to the Yankees and were forced to enlist in the Union Army, an action according to Ramsey that some slaves did not like because of the manner in which they were treated:

I don' know 'bout any run'ways. I know some of de field hands run 'way to de Yankees when de War start, but de Yankees put 'em in de soldier Army an' put 'em to work fighting, so dey didn' like dat so much. Most of 'em stay wit' Mr. Goldsmith. I 'member hearing 'em talk 'bout de colored soldiers rising up somewhere an' killing all de white men officers. Den dey say dat in de town where de colored Federals was, dey come in de white folks' house an' take what dey wan' an' treat de women bad. Lots of de Federals didn' like colored soldiers theirself.

Escape to the Yankees was wrought with danger, as patrollers were on constant watch to capture runaway slaves. But for those runaways reaching Union lines, safety was often the outcome. The narrative of Squire Irvin (MS) describes how patrollers would chase after runaway slaves to little avail once they reached the Yankee forces:

Plenty of the slaves ran off to the North. They didn't get them back cause when they got out of reach the Yankee soldiers was near enough to protect them. Course they had Patrollers to go after them with the dogs, but that didn't do no good against them Yankee soldiers. Them soldiers is been known to come right on the white folks places and take all the slaves that wanted to go with them.

Some slaves, such as Andy Anderson (TX), were worried about being captured by patrollers. This fear was powerful enough that he and others did not attempt to escape:

[D]e war am started den for 'bout a year, or somethin' like dat, and de Fed'rals am north of us. I hears de niggers talk 'bout it, and 'bout runnin' 'way to freedom. I thinks and thinks 'bout gittin' freedom, and I's gwine run off. Den I thinks of de patter rollers and what happen if dey cotches me off de place without a pass.

Charles Grandy (VA) offered a detailed account of how he and another slave escaped to join the Yankees. Grandy's story is one of travel by night and the risk of capture by Confederate forces and possible return to the plantation. He and his colleague had several close calls of being captured. Grandy's hope was to join the Yankee soldiers and fight for his freedom. The following is the Works Progress Administration (WPA) interviewer's summation of Grandy's story:

The news of war, and the possibility of Negroes enlisting as soldiers was truly a step closer to the answering of their prayers for freedom. Upon hearing of this good news Grandy joined a few of the others in this break for freedom. One night, he and a close friend packed a small quantity of food in a cloth and set out about midnight to join the northern army. Traveling at night most of the time, they were constantly confronted with the danger of being recaptured. Successfully including their followers, they reached Portsmouth after many narrow escapes. From Portsmouth they moved to Norfolk.

Arriving in Norfolk, Grandy and his friend decided to take different roads of travel. Several days and nights found Grandy wandering about the outskirts of Norfolk, feeding on wild berries. While picking berries along a ditch bank, he was hailed by a Yankee soldier who, having come in contact with runaway slaves before, greeted him friendly and questioned him about his home and his knowledge of work. Grandy was taken to camp and assigned as a cook. At first he was not very successful in his job, but gradually improvement was shown. He was asked what wages he would accept. It was such a pleasure to know that he had escaped the clutches of slavery that he did not ask for wages; instead, he was willing to work for anything they would give him, no matter how small, as long as he didn't have to return to slavery.

Within a short period Grandy was given a uniform and a gun. He was fully enlisted as a soldier in the 19th Regiment of Wisconsin, Company E. There he remained in service until November 1862, after which time he returned to Norfolk to spend some time with his mother, who was still living. While sitting in the doorway one day with his mother, he was again confronted with the proposition of reenlisting. He agreed to do so for one year, to serve as guard at Fortress Monroe. He remained there until the close of the war, offering brave and faithful service.

It is well documented in the literature that slaves were viewed and treated as property and as such had value to their owners. There is considerable evidence that the loss of slaves was seen as a financial loss to owners. The prospect of financial loss did not stop some Rebel forces from killing slaves under certain circumstances. The narratives document that Confederates would shoot slaves to keep them from going over to the Northern side. Barney Stone (IN) shared how he hid from being shot by Rebel soldiers, was saved by the Yankees, and eventually joined their army:

> At the out-break of the Civil War and when the Northern army was marching into the Southland, hundreds of male slaves were shot down by the Rebels, rather than see them join with the Yankees. One day when I learned that the Northern troops were very close to our plantation, I ran away and hid in a culvert, but was found and I would have been shot had the Yankee troops not scattered them and that saved me. I joined that Union army and served one year, eight months and twenty-two days, and fought with them in the battle of Fort Wagner, and also in the battle of Millikin's Bend.

At the end of the war, some ex-slaves who had served in the Union Army returned to the South and their former plantations and families. Following the end of the war, former masters frequently mistreated ex-slaves who fought for the Union and then returned to their families (Berlin et al. 1987). Plantation owners and former masters resented the role that these triumphant African American troops had played in the war.

CONFEDERATE REFUGEES

Union victories at Gettysburg and Vicksburg, the latter of which resulted in the control of the Mississippi River Valley and both of which occurred in July 1863, marked the turning point in the war. These and other battles resulted in many slave owners moving their slaves to what they believed would be safer locations. Slave owners transported them deeper into the Southern interior and to the West rather than risk them to Yankee liberation. Owners also moved slaves who were difficult to control (Berlin, Favreau, and Miller 2007). Owners "refuged" their most valuable slaves away from the war zone (Berlin et al. 1992). Slaves who were transferred to the Deep South and Texas were called "refugees." Depending on where Union forces were operating, some slaves could also be refuged from the Deep South to northern Confederate states, such as from Mississippi to North Carolina. Some of the narratives suggest that owners believed that if they moved their slaves to Texas, they would never be freed. Such was the example of Ned Broadus (TX), who suggested that his owner believed that going to Texas ensured that his slaves would never be free. Said Ned, "Marse thought dere would nebber be no free niggers in Texas." Southern planters labeled the practice of refuging slaves to halt their wholesale exodus to the North or their capture by Union forces as "running the Negroes" (Franklin and Moss 2000). Numerous narratives refer to this practice.

Seabe Tuttle (AR), although a child during the war, provided this account of how slaves were refuged from the Tuttle property from stories her mother told her. Tuttle said that "all went in carriages and wagons down south following the Confederate army." Then she added that "my mother and me and the other darkies, men and women and children, followed them with the cattle and horses and food." Aunt Adeline (AR) reported a similar experience: "During the Civil War, Mr. Parks took all his slaves and all of his fine stock, horses, and cattle and went south to Louisiana following the Southern army for protection." Clarice Jackson (AR) was raised in Arkansas and lived there except when the owners "put us in wagons and carried us to Wolf Creek in Texas and then they carried us to Red River." Jackson concluded that it was "because it would be longer 'fore we found out we was free and they would get more work out a us." Temple Wilson (MS) told of how some masters "would git scart an' refuge 'em to Alabama or Lusiana." Squire Irvin (MS) recalled being refuged to Alabama. About his master, Squire said that "he put them in covered wagons and carried them to Selma, Alabama, to Mr. Ramsey's plantation." Irvin and the other slaves stayed there until the war was over.

Travel as refugees was challenging and could be perilous. For example, Elizabeth Russell's (IN) narrative included a depiction of some of the risks that refugees experienced. She made a reference to the Ku Klux Klan in relation to wartime refugees, though it is unlikely that the Klan was involved since it did not form until after the Civil War. This reference was likely a group of patrollers, forerunners of the Klan, who stole and then sold slaves. Russell recalled:

Finally the Civil War broke out and many of the southerners had to leave their slaves to go and fight. They loaded their slaves in wagons. When they started they had 15 mule teams and 15 yoke of oxen. Each wagon had its own group of slaves and they were all headed for San Antonio, Texas. It so happened that in this wagon train, Lizzie met up with her mother. The wagons were rolling along one evening, when about dusk they decided to pitch camp near a large wood which they were approaching. They started to pitch camp when one of the children saw a white head raise up out of the brush, then another and another. It was a group of the Ku Klux Klan, who immediately started catching up the slave children. All excaped except two who were never heard of again.

The caravan continued, finally reaching a town called Roslin in Mississippi. There they had word that the Yanks were coming from San Antonio and were meeting them. They couldn't turn back as the Yanks were both before and behind, so they kept moving. One day they heard the drums of the Yanks, so they draped their wagons in white, the sign of surrender. The Yanks told them the war was over and that they were free and all who wanted to go back to their old masters could do so. So little Lizzie and her mother returned to Atlanta, to their old master.

Jane Cotton (TX) mentioned how escaped slaves caught by patrollers suffered dire consequences:

I'se seen one or two slaves run off to the north, when the war started, and the soldiers they kill every one of them they could. We carry news with pass if we got off the plantation without pass the patter roller would get negro. Yessir, when he get negro, it was too bad.

Anna Smith (OH) remembered the sounds of slaves escaping to the North throughout the evening and how patrollers pursued them. She remembered

This wood engraving, artist unknown, entitled *"Negroes Driven South by the Rebel Officers"* was published in *Harper's Weekly* on November 8, 1862, pp. 712–713. The illustration shows refugee slaves being forcibly driven farther south by Confederate soldiers. The horse soldier on the left is whipping people as they travel. Being forced to move would have been a traumatic experience for many slaves because of the major disruption it posed for their families, individuals, communities, and lifestyles. (Courtesy The House Divided Project at Dickinson College, Carlisle, PA.)

the baying of bloodhounds in the evenings along the Ohio River tracking the scent of escaping slaves and the sound of firearms as white people employed by the owners tried to halt the slaves from crossing the Ohio River into Ohio or joining the Union Army.

A consequence of refuging slaves was that it broke some slave families up, as some slaves would remain behind to continue working. Similar to losing family members at the slave market, families might have members that were divided when some were left behind and others were refuged to far away locations. Some of these families were separated and were never reunited. For example, the narrative of Jim Threat (OK) mentioned how he and other slaves remained back while others were refuged. He said that "we never saw or heard of them anymore." These were major life-altering events in the lives of slaves.

Not all slaves cooperated with their masters in being refugees. William Mathews (TX) spoke of how he was forced to transport slaves from his master's plantation to Texas where the Yankees could not get them. The draw of returning home to their communities and families was so strong for some that they risked their lives to return home. Mathews indicated that some of the slaves he transported returned home, even under the threat of punishment or being shot by their owners:

> All de talk 'bout freedom git so bad on de plantation de massa make me upt de men in a big wagon and drive 'em to Winfield. He say in Texas dere never be no freedom. I driv 'am fast till night and it take 'bout two days. But dey come back home, but massa say if he cotch any of 'em he gwine shoot 'em. Dey hang round de woods and dodge round and round till de freedom man come by.

SOUTHERN RESISTANCE TO THE WAR

The Civil War occurred within a context of reluctance, reservation, and resistance from many on both sides, whether it was the Irish immigrants who participated in the draft riot in New York City or Southern nonslave-holding whites. The New York draft riot of July 1863 focused on two central issues. One issue was that conscription targeted the poor, as the wealthy could purchase their way out of military service; the second issue was that Northerners were fighting and dying for the freedom of slaves whom they believed would eventually become rivals for jobs. These and other factors, such as racism, destruction, and the cost of the war, fueled resistance to the war in the North. In all, the draft riot in New York resulted in 100 deaths, of which 11 African American men were lynched by white mobs (Faust 2008).

Similar resistance to the war was present in the South. David Williams (2008) made a strong case that the South was very much internally conflicted by the prospects of secession and the resulting Civil War. Southern blacks and many whites were actively opposed to secession and the Confederate cause. In many respects, it was a class conflict between wealthy slaveholding plantation owners and poor nonslaveholding whites who had no economic investment in perpetuating the institution of slavery. There was notable support for the Union and resistance to secession in Kentucky, Tennessee, and Virginia (Varhola 2011; Williams 2008). Some nonslaveholding whites even took up arms in open rebellion; others deserted or otherwise evaded military service, protested, sabotaged, escaped to the North, joined Union forces, assisted Union forces, and took other measures to undermine Confederate operations before, during, and after the war. In some cases, slaves took up arms and fired on their masters and Confederate forces. For example, near Richmond, Louisiana, in 1863, slaves fired at a Confederate company making battlefield preparations (Wish 1938).

Some Southerners did not view the war as their war. A major reason was that most white farmers in the South did not own slaves and viewed the conflict as a "rich man's war" and not their fight (Varhola 2011). Disagreement and dissension in the South was such that, according to Williams (2008, 11), "the Civil War did not begin at Fort Sumter. It did not even begin as a war between the North and South. It began, and continued throughout, as a war between southerners themselves."

As the war progressed, desertion and draft evasion became increasingly problematic for the Confederacy. Southern defeats at Gettysburg and Vicksburg damaged the morale of Confederate forces, and the South lost hope of gaining support from Europe. By 1864, about two-thirds of the Confederate Army was absent with or without leave (Williams 2008). Other reasons why some Southerners did not want to go off to war were related to economic and family circumstances. White and slave resistance to the war surfaces in the narratives. For instance, the narrative of Ben Lawson (OK) illustrates how his owner was reluctant to serve in the war because his business was thriving during the war and because he had a young family:

> Then the soldiers come 'round and got a lot of the white men and took them off to the War even if they didn't want to go. Master Bill never did want to go 'cause he had his wife and two little children, and anyways he was gitting all the work he could do fixing wagons and shoeing hosses, with all the traffic on de road at that time. Master Bill had jest two hosses, for him and his wife to ride and to work to the busy, and he Ned one old yoke of oxen and some near Seattle. He got some kind of a paper in town and he kept it with him all the time, and when the soldiers would come to git his hosses or his cattle he would jest draw that paper on 'em and they let 'en clone.

Some slave owners, unwilling to fight, simply migrated to other regions that were located away from the conflict. Ex-slave Josh Miles (TX) indicated that his master fled the war by going to Texas, a place where he perceived that he could maintain control over his slaves and avoid military service:

> So my ole Marster saw dat he would be in de war, an' he decided ter cum ter Texas, ter 'scape hit. He took several hundred ob his slaves

an' his folks an' horses an' cattle an' his house hol' things an' in a
covered wagon driving de mules, horses, an oxen, he started fer
Texas. Dey walk long by de wagon an' drive dem wid de long
whips. Dey took dere time an' started in time ter stop along de way
all dey want an' went befo' de battles at some ob de places. Hit took
two years ter make de trip. He stay a whole winter on de way at
one place.

Slaves were known to help Confederate deserters and draft evaders, and
the narratives contain examples of this. Williams (2008, 5) wrote that "Deserters escaping the Confederate army could rely on slaves to give them
food and shelter on the journey back home." Confederate deserters would
often hide in the swamps and countryside, where slaves would secretly
bring them food and supplies throughout the war. Reverend Squire Dowd
(NC) recalled that slaves "stole for deserters during the war" and were paid
for what they brought to them. Dowd was a houseboy and stole honey for
this purpose. Jennie Webb (MS) supplied food to her master, who was hiding in the woods to keep from going to war. Lorenza Ezell (TX) reported a
similar experience: "My old massa run off and stay is de woods a whole
week when Sherman men come through." Tobe Zollicoffer (TX) protected
his master even though ironically he felt the whip on occasion for disobe-
dience. Tobe said that his owner was not well enough to fight, so he hid
him in a cave "from curious passers-by." Tobe faithfully cut the brush to
hide the cave and every day would carry food and other things to his cruel
master. Jeff Rayford (MS) elaborated more on how he supported those
who did not want to fight:

My master was good to me. When the war (Civil War) came on it
was bad times. I remember how the men would hide out to keep
from going to war. I cooked and carried many a pan of food to these
men in Pearl River swamp. This I did for one man regularly. All I
had to do was to carry the food down after dark, and I was so scared
I was trembling, and while walking along the path in the swamp,
pretty soon he would step out from behind a tree and say: "Here
Jeff" and then I would hand it to him and run back to the house.

Aunt Ellen Godfrey (SC) told about what it was like for her master and the
slaves, stating that "Massa been hide." She added that he "Been in swamp."
According to the comments by Godfrey's WPA interviewer, this may have

been common practice in the region. The practice was troubling for family members because older men, such as grandfathers, were forced to hide in snake-infested swamps until the Yankees passed. The women recalled how these older men suffered while hiding. Jennie Webb (MS) told how her master hid in the woods to evade serving in the Confederate Army. She reported that "During de war ole Marse hid out in de thick woods to keep from gwine." Then she added that "We had to slip him food out dier an' de cavalerymen would come a hunting him."

The consequences for captured deserters could be drastic. Confederate forces sent groups out to locate deserters and evaders and on occasion would find and capture them. Nancy King (TX) described what happened to her master following his capture. She first noted that he did not feel that the war was right and that he would rather free his slaves than fight. With these beliefs, he deserted and ran off to the river bottoms, only to be run down by Confederate troops. Then, according to King:

> One of them says, "Jackson, we ain't gwine take you with us now, but we'll fix you so you can't run off till we git back." They put red pepper in his eyes and left. Missie cried. They come back for him in a day or two and made my father saddle up Hawk-eye, massa' best hoss. Then they rode away and we never seed massa 'gain. One day my brother, Alex, hollers out, "Oh, Missie, yonder is the hoss, at the gate, and ain't nobody ridin' him." Missie threw up her hands and says, "O, Lawdy, my husban' am dead!" She knowed somehow when he left he wasn't comin' back.

STAYING ON THE PLANTATION

Most slaves did not escape to the North, nor did they join the Union Army; rather, they remained on the plantations and farms and in the cities of the South in bondage throughout the war (Reid 1950). "Local patriotism, freedom after the war, fear, and loyalty were some of the motivating factors that at first kept most blacks working peacefully on the plantations" (Mays 1984, 6). Some slaves even reported that they worked harder when their masters went off to war (Ward 2008). The former slaves indicated other reasons for why they stayed on. In some cases, escape was not an option. Berlin, Favreau, and Miller (2007, 259) noted that "For some, particularly the very old and very young, the physical rigors of flight were too daunting." For others, they stayed to protect family, as did Prince Johnson (MS), who stayed on to protect the "women folks."

Some slaves were not interested in leaving their families and going to war. Union Army recruiter James T. Ayers wrote about his experiences and difficulties in recruiting blacks for the army. On April 30, 1864, he wrote from Huntsville, Alabama: "Poor ignorant Devils they would rather stay behind and geather up boxes of oald shoes and oald shirts and pants our boys have left than be soldiers." He would later write that "I have often been toald by them when trying to Coax them to inlist why say they I don't want to be a soaldier" (Reid 1950, 271, 273).

The narrative of Martin Jackson (TX) represents one example of a slave rationale for not escaping to the North. Jackson believed that he was treated well on his plantation, but he still pondered escape. Although he thought about it, he was encouraged not to run by his father:

> Even with my good treatment, I spent most of my time planning and thinking of running away. I could have done it easy, but my old father used to say. "He use running from bad to worse, hunting better." Lots of colered boys did escape and joined the Union army, and there are plenty of them drawing a pension today. My father was always counseling me. He said, "Every man has to serve God under his own vine and fig tree." He kept pointing out that the War wasn't going to last forever, but that our forever was going to be spent living among the Southerners, after they got licked. He'd cite examples of how the whites would stand flatfooted and fight for the blacks the same as for members of their own family. I knew that all was true, but still I rebelled, from inside of me. I think I really was afraid to run away, because I thought my conscience would haunt me. My father knew I felt this way and he'd rub my fears in deeper. One of his remarks still rings in my ears: "A clear conscience opens bowels, and when you have a guilty soul it ties you up and death will not for long desert you."

The fact that many slaves stayed on in their slave roles was not lost on Southerners. Slave contributions to the Southern cause were noted by Confederate leadership and exaggerated by Southern propagandists. President Jefferson Davis noted that much of the Southern success during the war could be attributed to slaves faithfully remaining on the plantations and otherwise supporting the war effort (Quarles 1968). Undoubtedly, slaves working in the Southern factories and fields freed whites to serve in the military (Wade 1964).

But Southern industry could not keep up with the demand for war-related goods. Thus, a variety of supplies and goods were produced on plantations to support the war effort. Mariah Calloway (GA) reported that her mistress's home became a sewing center for different women in the neighborhood. There, Calloway indicated, the women made vests, coats, shirts, and capes for the soldiers. In the same vein, Jane Smith Hill Harmon (GA) recalled how her mother spun for the soldiers: "I 'members dat, her er spinnin' an' dey say hit was fer de soldiers." Although a child, Mary Flagg (AR) was old enough to knit for the Confederate soldiers.

Others grew and prepared food for the troops. Rivana Boyton (FL) noted that during the war, "I used to turn the big corn sheller and sack the shelled corn for the Confederate soldiers." William Neighten (FL) also shelled and sacked corn for troops. Cora Gillam's (AR) mother helped cook for those building Confederate forts. David Goodman Gullins (GA) identified a variety of functions that slaves performed to support the Confederacy. He indicated that slaves prepared food, made clothing, dug ditches, and did manual labor for those who went to war.

SLAVE RESISTANCE ON THE PLANTATIONS

In the South and to a degree in the North as well, one of the preoccupations of whites was the question of whether slaves would rebel. Initially, Northerners were as uneasy about the possibility as were Southerners. For the North, the initial goal of the war was to preserve the Union, not eliminate slavery. The Union recognized that eliminating slavery would make reunification difficult. In the beginning, Union generals were ordered to defeat the Confederate Army and prevent slave rebellions and insurrections. At the beginning of the war, captured slaves and those escaping to the North were returned to their owners according to the Fugitive Slave Act of 1850. This fear of rebellion would prove to be unfounded, as slaves contributed in a number of ways other than insurrection to gain their freedom.

When given the choice, most slaves wanted freedom, and large numbers of them escaped to the North. But as noted previously, the overwhelming majority of slaves stayed on their plantations. Although most slaves remained in bondage, they still resisted. Many of them found ways to work toward freedom and undermine the Confederate cause. Initially to many slaves the war was not about freedom or emancipation, but as it evolved the prospect of freedom became more of a possibility. When given the choice, most slaves wanted emancipation. They did not halt working, but they did considerably less work than they had before the war. They organized work slowdowns and feigned illness or ignorance (Davis 2007). They sabotaged or destroyed equipment or used the threat of such action as a bargaining tool for better treatment. If they failed to get it, suicide was common (Williams 2008).

Plantation slaves were known to disobey their masters to aid Union forces. The slaves provided maps and directions to Union armies and helped destroy Confederate facilities (Franklin and Moss 2000). When Union troops were near, many slaves simply walked away from their plantations and sought protection behind Union forces (Franklin and Moss 2000). Even Confederate president Jefferson Davis was not immune from slaves escaping. Contrary to the image of Davis being benevolent and fatherly to his slaves, in May 1862 some of his slaves escaped from his Brierfield Plantation in Mississippi. Before they escaped, they took items from his house.

Prior to and during the war, some slaves were active in the Underground Railroad (Public Broadcast System 2012). They also harbored escaped slaves from other plantations and regions. For example, John C. Bectom (NC) spoke of sheltering an escaped slave named Mat Holmes:

> Mat Holmes, a slave, was wearing a ball and chain as a punishment for running away. Marster Ezekial King put it on him. He has slept in the bed with me, wearing that ball and chain. The cuff had imbedded in his leg, it was swollen so. This was right after the Yankees came through. It was March, the 9th of March, when the Yankees come through. Mat Holmes had run away with the ball and chain on him and was in the woods then. He hid out staying with us at night until August. Then my mother took him to the Yankee garrison at Fayetteville. A Yankee officer then took him to a black smith shop and had the ball and chain cut off his leg.

SLAVES AIDED RESISTERS AND UNION ESCAPEES

It is well established that slaves helped Union soldiers who had escaped from Confederate prisons (Quarles 1968). African Americans capitalized on their expertise and assisted Union soldiers in escaping from Andersonville Prison through the Underground Railroad (Davis 2007).

Personal accounts of hiding Union soldiers and spies have been recorded (Armstrong 1924). Escaped Union soldiers assumed that slave cabins always were safe havens. Slaves were in a great position to help escapees traverse unfamiliar areas and could be counted on to share their limited provisions. Blacks also assisted Union soldiers foraging for food (Tomblin 2009) and fed and cared for escaped soldiers for weeks at a time. The narrative of Sarah Ann Green (NC) described how her owners as well as slaves secretly provided care and protection to a young Yankee soldier at great personal risk:

> She tole her 'bout de Yankee. "He's jus' er boy, Hannah," she say, "he ain't no older den Marse Gaston, an' he's hurt. We got to do somethin' an' we can't tell nobody." Den she sen' mammy to de house for er pan of hot water, de scissors an' er ole sheet. Mis' Roby cut off de bloody ran an' wash dat sojer boy's head den she tied up de cut places. Den she went to de house an' made mammy slip him er big milk toddy. 'Bout dat time she seed some ho'seman comin' down de road. When dey got closer she seed dey was 'Federate sojers. Dey rode up in de yard an' Marse Billy went out to meet dem. Dey tole him dat dey was lookin' for er Yankee prisoner dat done got away from dey camp.

SLAVE SUPPORT FOR THE CONFEDERACY

In modern times, slave loyalty to the South and the Confederate cause can be difficult to understand. A case in point can be found in some of the documents of the time. For example, according to Wish (1938), the *Richmond Enquirer* on September 13, 1861, commented on local free African Americans' willingness to work on Confederate fortifications. In Tennessee, free blacks offered their services to the Confederate cause in Nashville in April 1861 (Lovett 1976; Williams 1968). In Atlanta, Harrison Berry, a shoemaker and slave of S. W. Price, published a pamphlet urging slaves to be submissive to their owners. Berry's *Slavery and Abolitionism, as Viewed by a Georgia Slave* was published immediately following Lincoln's election but before South Carolina's secession (Jordan 1995). In the document, Berry argued that being free in the North resulted in impoverishment, in contrast to being a protected and cared-for slave in the South (Berry 1969). But Berry's sentiments and beliefs were in no way reflective of the majority of slaves. Such pro-Confederate sentiment was difficult for Yankee troops to understand. According to Ward (2008, 262), "The feature of the slave south that most puzzled and disappointed the more idealistic Yankees was the diligence with which so many of the slaves they encountered protected and sustained their rebel masters' plantations." The contradiction of fighting and dying for those who were perceived as not wanting their freedom was difficult for Union troops to comprehend.

Quarles (1968, 262) noted that on the plantation, some house servants sympathized with their white masters, perhaps because of closer personal relationships, and were sometimes concerned with the plight of the stricken Southern "white folks." Clearly, there are documented instances of house slaves remaining loyal to their masters even when hoping for freedom. Many house servants adhered to the deeply instilled servile code of honor (Ward 2008). They almost always never deserted (Quarles 1968). The same cannot be concluded for field slaves, who were not as close to their masters and thus less inclined to remain loyal. Rather, they often waited for the outcome of the war, escaped to the North before its conclusion, or took subversive measures to undercut the efforts of the Confederacy.

Slave loyalty to owners and staying on the plantation was more pronounced in the interior Southern states. Mrs. C. B. Howard, who remained on the plantation with 200 slaves in central Georgia, praised her slaves' loyalty and service:

Can history produce such a parallel. Women and children left alone on an isolated plantation for years with Negroes whose faithful services continued as unchanged as if the lurid cloud of war had not risen above our once peaceful horizon. Such was my case, yet never a disrespectful word or look did I observe.

(Quarles 1968, 263)

Free and enslaved African Americans worked in the factories, coal mines, fields, shipyards, and salt mines as well as in transportation, often replacing whites who had gone off to fight in the war (Reid 1950). McPherson (1993, 24) wrote that "During the war, slaves and free Negroes not only raised most of the food and fiber for the Confederate army, but they did much of the work on rebel fortifications and entrenchments as well." Some even donated goods and money to the Confederate Army (Obatala and Maksel 1979). African Americans on both sides of the conflict made major contributions to the war effort. Free blacks and slaves, male and female, worked in factories, on farms, on plantations, and in the military to support the war effort (Berlin, Reidy, and Rowland 1998). Confederate forces relied on civilian support for food, clothing, and shelter. For example, Caroline Bevis (SC) helped make clothing for Confederate troops: "I made socks, gloves and sweaters for the Confederate soldiers and also knitted for the World War soldiers." Another example of black loyalty to the South was Horace King, who was born a slave and was freed in 1846 by special act of the Alabama legislature. King was a respected craftsman who built several bridges and supplied lumber for the construction of the Confederate ironclad battleship *Jackson* (Turner 1988).

There are examples of slave loyalty to owners and their families spread throughout the narratives. Louis Pettis (AR) spoke of his slave father saving his young mistress and baby from a burning house:

> Papa saved his young mistress' life. His master was gone to war. He had promised with others to take care of her. The Yankees come and didn't find meat. It was buried. They couldn't find much. They got mad and burned the house. Pa was a boy. He run up there and begged folks not to burn the house; they promised to take care of everything. Papa bagged to let him get his mistress and three-day-old baby. They cursed him but he run in and got her and the baby. The house fell in before they got out of the yard. He took her to the quarters. Papa was overstrained carrying a log and limped as long as he lived.

Rivana Boyton (FL) begged that her mistress not be killed or harmed and that the Union troops not plunder their food supplies. The Yankees granted part of her wish but burned some of the buildings on the property and looted the food stocks:

> So we begged, an' we say, "our missus is good. Don't you kill her. Don't you take our meat away from us. Don't you hurt her. Don't you burn her house down." So they burned the stable and some of the other buildings, but they did not burn the house nor hurt us any. We saw the rest of the yanks comin'. They never stopped for nothin'. Their horses would jump the worm rail fences and they come 'cross fields 'n everthing. They bound our missus upstairs so she couldn't go away, then they came to the sheds and we begged

and begged for her. Then they loosed her, but they took some of us for refugees and some of the slaves went off with them of their own will. They took all the things that were buried all the hams and everything they wanted. But they did not burn the house and our missus was saved.

While the cruelty of owners is an undisputed fact, some slaves believed, as did Rivana Boyton, that they were treated well by their masters. Julia Cox's (MS) narrative reflects how some slaves worried about their masters who had gone off to fight in the war. Julia and other slaves rejoiced when their masters came home on furlough:

Anuder worry us had was when mar's son had to go to de war. We loved him, he was kind to us, we had played wid him all our lives. After he lef' an' jined de Army, eber time a troop ob soldiers would happen to march near Mar's plantation wid deir canteens on deir backs an' a toteing deir long guns, if dey was grey boys we would climb up on de fence to watch an' see if we could see John. When he would have a furlow and come home fer a few day, Mars would go to de back ob de house, coop he's hands over he's mouth and yell, "All my little niggers come see my little boy." We went a running, swarmin' in lack bees and climb all over him. He would play wid us an' swing us 'round till us would be a staggering all ober de yard. After us git over de excitement ob a seeing him den he would tell us tales ob de war, ob how dey would fight, camp and march. Now us set 'round an' took in eber word.

Another example of slave loyalty can be found in the narrative of William Neighten (FL), who indicated that the slaves where he lived begged the Yankees for the life of their mistress and not to burn her house down. They "begged so hard" that the Yankees let her go, but some of the other slaves left with them as refugees. He did not choose to leave but stayed with his mistress.

In preparation for when the Yankees came, owners and their slaves would hide their food and valuables. Usually their most prized possessions were gold and silver. House servants were often privy to where these valuables were buried or otherwise hidden. Rather than tell the Yankees, some slaves would remain loyal and not disclose the location of valuable items. It is difficult to ascertain whether they did so out of loyalty or fear of reprisal. Emmeline Trott (MS) told of how she helped hide valuables from the Yankees:

> Soon after the Yankees invaded Pontotoc they stormed into Emmeline's cabin, commanded her to get up so they could search the bed. Emmeline saw the General looking in a window. She mutely held up her new-born baby, and the General ordered his men out of the house. "I sure was glad too," she chuckles today. "I was lying on rolls and rolls of silver, gold, guns, and other things Miz Adeline Bell had hid under me."

The obituary of George Washington Brooks (MO) from the *St. Louis Post-Dispatch* of January 18, 1937, described how as a little boy Brooks helped hide valuables from the troops and did not disclose their location:

> On one occasion during the war, George Brooks, then nine years old, rode a horse from French Village to Brooks Place in Jefferson County, through woods in which guerrillas were reported, with $1,000 in gold hidden in his boots. Later when troops were approaching French Village, he buried family valuables in the orchard and helped Mrs. Au Buchon (his owner) to conceal her personal jewelry in a ball of yarn. Soldiers ransacked the house and threw the ball of yarn across a room, cracking a mosaic pin, now an heirloom.

Beverly Pullin (GA) shared an account of how she stepped in front of her mistress to protect her from the Yankees:

> At the close of the Civil War during "Sherman's March to the Sea," some "Stragglers" came through Mr. Peeples' plantation. Sissy, Beverly's granddaughter, was churning; one of the men demanded a glass of buttermilk, which was given him warm from the churn. While drinking this he demanded Mr. Peeples to get up and turn over to him the family silver and jewelry. Mrs. Peeples told him that as they knew they were coming, all the silver and jewelry had been gathered up several days before and taken away and hid and even she did not know where it was. Evidently the soldier did not believe this for he drew his pistol, evidently to frighten her into telling him. Beverly stepped in front of his mistress and said, "If you have to shoot, shoot me, not my mistress." Where upon the soldier lowered

his pistol and threw the glass, from which he had finished the buttermilk, down breaking it. This, with the above incident, made Beverly so mad that if it had not been for the restraining hand and kind words of his mistress, he would have gone after the soldier.

Communication was essential on both sides of the conflict. Slaves were sometimes given the responsibility of conveying information about troop movements to Confederate forces. For example, Dave Harper (MO) served as a courier who shared information about the presence of Yankee troop movements in the area. He could have purposely failed to share the communication and in doing so would have helped the Union troops. Rather, he carried out his responsibility and delivered the warning according to instructions:

One time I saved his life. Dey was going to kill him, 'bout 75 or 100 men on horses. I warned de Colonel two hours before dey got dere. Dis is how it happened. Col. Harper gave me de first day of Christmas to go to see my mother. Us children want out in de woods playing and when we come back de yard was all cut up with horses hoofs. Dr. Sharp put me on my horse and told me to tell Col. Harper dis message, dat "dere was so many soldiers dat you might get hurt, you can come again some other time." I told Col. Harper and he left. I didn't see him again until I was cutting wheat.

The fact that most slaves who escaped to the North and to freedom and remained there is well documented. In stark contrast, however, were those slaves who escaped from either Union forces or the North and returned to the South. Frank Childress (MS) was one who voluntarily returned to the South after having been captured by the Federals. There were several reasons why slaves would return to the South, including the desire to return to families, a lack of survival options, a return to home communities, a familiar way of life, and in some cases slave loyalty to masters. Some undoubtedly were concerned that their families might be at risk of harm unless they returned. Frank Childress was a trusted slave who followed his master, Colonel Mark Childress, to the front lines as a body servant and dispatch carrier. Frank Childress was captured at Richmond and managed to get back to his master and then accompanied the colonel to Helena, Arkansas. Childress was 84 in 1936 when he was interviewed as part of the WPA narratives project and was living in the Confederate Soldiers' Home in Beauvoir, Mississippi, with his longtime friend, ex-slave Nathan Best, age 92, who corroborated his story. In his narrative, Childress claimed to have been captured by General Grant at Clayton, Mississippi. His interviewer is unknown, but the interviewer's narrative of Childress also says that he was captured by the Yankees at Helena, perhaps in a different skirmish. In his own words, Childress said of his involvement with the Federals that

> I was captured by Grant at Clayton Mississippi wen I was 14, and to keep fum feein' us He was goin' ter kill us, but Sherman said No, dont kill him. He served de south, now let him serve de north, den he sed to me "Load dat cannon or I kill you." an' I loaded it. I put four buckets of powder, put de flap back, den put de ball in, and pull de crank, it rolled right on back and nearly jarred me ter death.

Childress served with the Yankees for two and a half years and was released at the end of the war. He proudly told his interviewer, "Yassuh, I'se the one what fought on both sides, but I neber fought for de Yankees till dey captured me and put me in a corral."

Ora M. Flagg (NC) spoke of her mother's loyalty to her owners by not revealing the location of the family's silver. Flagg said, "The Yankees went through everything, and when mother wouldn't tell them where the silver wus hid they threw her things in the well." Susan High (NC) told of a broken promise made to her mother who protected her master:

> She heard 'em talkin', and she busted through de crowd and told 'em dat de stuff belonged to anudder man and dat her marster wus not lyin', an' not to hurt 'im. De Yankees said, "You have saved dis ole son of a bitch, we won't kill 'em den." Dey took all de meat, whiskey, an' everything dey wanted. Marster promised mother a cow, and calf, a sow, and pigs for what she had done for him an' to stay on an' finish de crop. When de fall o' de year come he did not give her de wrappin's o' her finger.

Rachel Cruze (OH) offered another account of how she, as a slave, remained loyal to her owner, keeping a joint secret with him throughout the war:

> If the Rebels had won the war ole Major would have been wealthy. At the beginning of the war he had put the bulk of his money into a seegar box, and he took out a couple of small stones from the foundation of the house and said, "Now, Baby, look sharp and dig a hole

inside there large enough to hide this box, and never tell anybody about this money." I was rather afraid to crawl into the darkness under the house but I did as I was told, and nobody ever knew anything about that money but ole Major and I. When the soldiers would say, "Where's the Major's money?" I'd always point to the big iron safe and say, "All the Johnny money is in there." Well, they were not looking for Johnny money, so they never bothered to open it. After the war was over, ole Major had me crawl under the house again and bring out the seegar box filled with money, but it wasn't worth anything. I used to play house with it.

SLAVE LOYALTY TO MASTERS?

It has been said that most slaves were faithful during the four years of the Civil War and did not betray their owners' confidence (Reid 1950). Tennesseans believed that blacks were lazy, stupid, and unfortunate beings who were loyal to their white masters (Lovett 1976). Some of the narratives seem to support the assumption that slaves were loyal. The narratives contain examples of ex-slaves expressing loyalty to their masters. According to Ward (2008), at first slaves identified more with their masters than they did with the Yankee "devils" who were invading their homeland. Wesley (1919, 241) summed it up this way: "To the majority of Negroes, as to all the South, the invading armies of the Union seemed to be ruthlessly attacking independent States, invading the beloved homeland and trampling upon all that these men held dear." Eventually this would change as the war progressed, and whether these expressions of loyalty were genuine, manifestations of fear, or perhaps engendered through intimidation was only known to the WPA respondents themselves.

Some of the respondents expressed loyalty to their masters by staying with them until they died. James Cornelius (MS) reported how he stayed with his master until he could be transported home. Cornelius said, "Marse Murry was shot an' I stayed wid him 'til day could git him home." Martin Jackson (TX) expressed compassion for a fallen Confederate colonel whom he knew before the war. Although admitting that he could do little for the colonel, Jackson acknowledged that he did "comfort" his "friend" in dying:

It was in the Battle of Marshall, in Louisiana, that Col. Buchell got shot. I was about three miles from the front, where I had pitched up a kind of first-aid station. I was all alone there. I watched the whole thing. I could hear the shooting and see the firing. I remember standing there and thinking the South didn't have a chance. All of a sudden I heard someone call. It was a soldier, who was half carrying Col. Buchell in. I didn't do nothing for the Colonel. He was too far gone. I just held him comfortable, and that was the position he was in when he stopped breathing. That was the worst hurt I got when anybody died. He was a friend of mine. He had had a lot of soldiering before and fought in the Indian War.

Many slaves were happy to see their cruel and oppressive masters go off to war, but some were not happy because they feared that their masters would not return. Samuel Smith's (TX) feelings were an example of this:

I 'member Marster went to war once, and when he told us, we all cried, 'cause we knew he would be killed. I begged him to let me go too but he said no. He said we could do his work, but he would do his own fightin'. He said he would never let one that he was 'sponsible for take any chances for him, I cried but it wouldn't do no good. Miss told him when he left that it was no use 'cause dere was too much agin' him. He say that its his place and he would be a man about it. He was gone less'n two years, and when he come back we was done free. Dey was nearly all dere when he come back, but some had left. I wouldn't go 'way while he was gone, and I was de proudest nigger you ever saw. He asked me why I stayed and I told him my pappy had stayed and I had no where to go and I loved him and Miss, so I wouldn't go. He say he could not keep us without payin' us and he had no money, so we would have to go.

Following battles, slaves would search the battlefields for their wounded or dead masters (Faust 2008). Slaves also accompanied the bodies of their masters home for proper burial:

The applications for Confederate pension contain touching references to the devotion many servants had to their masters. Anthony Watts from Laurens served until his master had died from battle wounds, and then arranged to have the body transported back home.

Zack Brown of Fairfield was a body servant to Robert F. Coleman, until Coleman was injured, whereupon Brown "stayed with him in hospital til it was captured."

(Barrow, Segars, and Rosenburg 2004, 110–111)

Other examples abound in the narratives. Richard Jones (SC) described how a slave named Uncle Wylie Smith accompanied his master's body back to be buried. Frank Range (SC) helped save his master from injury and death. While accompanying his master, a heavy bombardment buried the owner, and Range, out of fear for his safety, frantically dug him out and was able to drag him to safety. Although shells were falling "all around him," he avoided injury. There are also accounts of slaves remaining with their captured masters and continuing to serve them in Union prison camps (Barrow, Segars, and Rosenburg 2004, 24).

Lieutenant L. B. Mitchell, believed to be the company commander, wrote a letter in regard to the death of one of his troops, Zeb Williams. In his letter to Zeb's family, Mitchell mentioned a common practice of loyal slaves accompanying their slain masters' bodies back home:

It pains me much to record to you the death of your beloved son Zeb. He deposed of this life on Sunday nite at half after two in the morning. His illness was short after he was taken bad. I will start him home as soon as I can get him ready. John has been a faithful servant to Zeb. I put confidence in him getting Zeb home.

(Barrow, Segars, and Rosenburg 2004, 32)

Harvey Wish (1938, 449) concluded that "The extent of slave disloyalty to the Confederacy can only be inferred, rather than stated with precision. Memoirs of various former Confederates insist that the slave was loyal to his master during the Civil war, as undoubtedly a great number were." However, Wish suggested this might more accurately be interpreted as "civilized constraint." That is, for some slaves, living under slavery might have been a more acceptable alternative to fighting for the Union Army or moving North to uncertainty. As appalling as slavery was, it provided some slaves with a routine that they were familiar with as well as a predictable day-to-day existence. It may also be that many of the slaves had a sense of civility more than loyalty, a sense of respect that was not returned by their masters.

SELLING OUT MASTERS

Sometimes slaves turned on their owners and cooperated with both Union and Confederate forces. For example, Levi Ashley (MS) did not disclose who the men seeking her owner were but did indicate that she revealed his hiding location:

> When de War come, Marse John hid out in de woods. Men come 'round huntin' fer him but dey couldn' fin' him. One day two men caught me an' said, "Whar you been, boy?" An' I said, "To take Marse John his dinner." Dey said, "Whar is Marse John?" An' I said, "He is back of de cow pen." Dey sho' got him an' made him go wid 'em. I got a whuppin'.

Owners and slaves frequently hid valuables and supplies from both Union and Confederate troops. Sometimes, as mentioned previously, slaves' participation in this activity was out of a sense of loyalty to their owners. In other circumstances, revealing the locations of valuables to the Federals became an act of retribution toward an owner. In these instances, slaves might take this a step further by not only exposing where owners' valuables were hidden but also feeding Union soldiers, helping Union escapees head north, and providing companionship otherwise abetting the enemy against the Rebels (Reid 1950). These were ways to take revenge against cruel and unjust owners. Mary Reynolds (TX) provided an account of slaves who were eager to show Yankee troops where things were hidden. After a boat dropped off some Union troops, soldiers swarmed all over looking for items to plunder:

> Next day them Yankees is swarmin' the place. Some the niggers wants to show then somethin'. I follows to the woods. The niggers shows them sojers a big pit in the ground, bigger'n a big house. It is got wooden doors that lifts up, but the top am sodded and grass growin' on it, so you couldn't tell it. In that pit is stock, hosses and cows and mules and money and chinaware and silver and a mess of stuff them sojers takes.

OWNER LOYALTY TO SLAVES

It is documented that slaves could display loyalty to their masters on the battlefield, but the opposite was also true. Jim Polk Hightower (MS) told how an old Rebel soldier came to the rescue of a slave named Jim who had served him during the war:

> I will jest here name some of the instance where some of the old Soldiers have put himself between the old slave that followed him through the bloody war and death, to save the life of that faithful servant. Some years after the Surrender my old friend Jim Irby have some trouble in Sardis with some white men and they not knowing Jim would have shot him but for the timely arivel of the old soldier that he carried on his back when wounded out on some battle field. He saved the life of Jim but got the Ball through the top of his hat, and that was my old rebel friend J. M. Anderson.

Slaveholder and Confederate general Nathan Bedford Forrest, who is credited with the massacre of surrendered Union troops at Fort Pillow and later helped found the Ku Klux Klan, in his testimony before a Joint Congressional Committee in 1872 stated that

> I said to forty-five colored fellows on my plantation that it was a war upon slavery, and that I was going into the army; that if they would go with me, if we got whipped they would be free anyhow, and that if we succeeded and slavery was perpetuated, if they would act faithfully to me to the end of the war, I would set them free. . . . No finer Confederates rode with me.
>
> (Forrest 1872)

It was also the case that some masters encouraged their slaves to "refugee" to the North because they could no longer feed and care for them (Tomblin 2009).

SHIFTING ALLEGIANCES AND LOYALTY

The narratives contain a few references to Southerners shifting their loyalties depending on what side was approaching. These changes in allegiance, whether real or not, helped minimize the impact of the war on local residents as battle lines shifted and troops from both sides roamed about the countryside throughout the duration of the conflict. Rachel Cruze (OH) described how her white owner, "Ole Major," played it safe throughout the war. She noted that he had both Rebel and Union suits and depending on which side was approaching "wore whichever seemed to be most fitting at the time." Rachel also described how they provided food to both sides as well:

> Ole Major and Miss Nancy gave freely to both sides. Time and again they gave a corn field to the army who happened to be in the neighborhood—and there always seemed to be soldiers around us during those times. One time, after Miss Nancy had given a corn field to the Union boys, some of them went into another field and stole some roastin' ears from that field. The Union officers learned of it and the next morning, on parade, the one who had stolen the corn had the roastin' ears tied to his wrists and arms, and forced to march along with the other men. I was standing on the porch with ole Major, and he said, "See the one who is decorated? That's the one who stole our roastin' ears."

In some contested areas of the country, it made sense to owners to change their loyalties over the course of events, perhaps as a way to just survive a conflict that they wanted no part in. One claimed to be a Rebel when the Confederates were in the area and claimed to be a Yankee when the Federals were at the door. Wes Lee (MO) shared how it worked with his owner and noted the benefits of doing so:

> I was just a little feller during de war, but I can remember dat when de Rebel sojers come by our place old mastuh had de table set for 'em, and treat 'em fine—'cause he's a rebel—den when de "Yankees" come along he give dem de bes' he had, and treat 'em fine 'cause he's a "Yankee." Old Judge Ranney live on de next place and he and old mastuh was good friends—but he was such a hot southerner he couldn't stand old mastuh to act like dat. In a way I guess old mastuh was right for none of de sojers never bother nuthin' on de place.

Sometimes slaves would visit enemy troops without their owners' knowledge. Van Moore (TX) described how he and other slaves would visit Union forces and get what handouts they could from them. They would slip down to the Union camp, where soldiers would give them sugar and coffee, two scarce commodities during the war. In Moore's account, slave children were treated well by the troops.

According to one newspaper story, Charlie Hicks of Vidalia, Georgia, served in both the Confederate Army and the Union Army long enough to receive pensions from both (Barrow, Segars, and Rosenburg 2004). Hicks served his owner until captured by the Union Army, where he then served as a cook.

OBSERVATIONS

There was nothing inevitable about African Americans' loyalty to either side during the war years, and their loyalty to both sides was tested by the events of war (Wesley 1962). Many of the slaves who risked their lives by imposing themselves on Union forces at Fort Monroe and elsewhere remained uncertain as to whether their status as contraband would translate into real freedom. During the war, slaves had a variety of ways in which they demonstrated loyalty or commitment to either side, to families, masters, communities, and values. Slave loyalty to the Union or Confederacy was expressed in a variety of ways. The most widely known act of loyalty by slaves to the Northern cause was the well-documented large number of them escaping as contrabands, many of whom eventually joined the Union Army.

But slave loyalty was a much broader and more complex issue than simply escaping to the North or fighting with the Union Army. It took on other forms as well, such as those who stayed on their plantations continuing to work as they always had. Some Southerners at the time interpreted this as evidence of loyalty to the South. But it is also true that unknown numbers of slaves resisted and hampered plantation operations in subtle and sometimes concealed ways in an effort to slow the Confederate cause and help slaves gain their freedom.

For the duration of the war, Southern authorities were concerned that African Americans serving the Confederacy were actually more loyal to the Union, and indeed many did escape to the North at their first opportunity and joined forces with the Federals. Some states even passed legislation that remanded free African Americans to slavery to help with labor shortages during the war. In effect, this also served to control Southern free African Americans while meeting the needs of the war.

The narratives suggest that for some slaves, expressions of loyalty occurred at an interpersonal level. House servants who were treated well before the war were more loyal to their owners (Wiley 1938). We find examples of slaves accompanying their masters' bodies back home to ensure proper burial. Other slaves stood by their masters in the heat of battle and on occasion took up arms to defend their masters. Still others kept secrets from the Yankees to protect their masters, such as where the masters' hiding places were or where their valuables were hidden. In contrast, others dropped their loyalties in the presence of Yankee soldiers and revealed the locations of valuables to Union troops.

Other slaves were disloyal to their masters but remained committed to their communities and families. Some clearly went to great efforts to return to their families and communities during and after the war. Even for some who served in the Union Army, the pull of family and community was stronger than the unclear future they faced in either a defeated South or a victorious North.

The conclusion we reach is that one cannot paint slave loyalty with a single brushstroke. Slaves did not react in a monolithic manner to the war but instead reacted on an interpersonal level. At times they seemed surprisingly loyal to their oppressors, and at other times they seemed very disloyal. Slaves were on both sides of the war but only to a limited extent in the Confederacy (Wesley 1962).

According to Shackel (2001, 657), "There is the perception that the Civil War is all about loyalty to a cause, a sentiment that developed in the late nineteenth century that excluded African Americans from the Civil War story." Shackel noted that as the Southern revisionist movement gained momentum, whites gained considerable power over the story of the war and African American involvement. This led to a bias that the war was evidence of Southern commitment to an honorable and just cause. Slaves were mostly excluded from this story, and when they were included, they were depicted as being faithful to the old regime and loyal to their masters (Aaron 1973).

On the issue of slave loyalty to the South, Levine (2006) concluded that there were plenty of Southern apologists who rationalized and suggested that slave owners were benign and caring individuals who took good care of their slaves and were gradually moving many toward emancipation. Thus, slaves would be supportive of the kind, humane, and supportive system of slavery that cared for them until they were ready to make it on their own. Another Southern view held that slaves were basically satisfied with their inferior position in society and thus were not attracted to the promise of emancipation advanced by the North, and they therefore stayed loyal to the South. For others, their seeming loyalty to the South may have been simply a way to seek shelter from a changing world in which their futures were still very much in doubt. These rationalizations for slave loyalty to the South find very little support in the narratives. In reality, slavery was not the benevolent institution suggested by its supporters. While some Southern blacks, free and slave, did work to support the Confederacy, their numbers were relatively small, especially compared to those who escaped and supported the Union.

Following the war, there was no shortage of Southern loyalists who wasted little time in promoting the view that there were multitudes of slaves and Southern free African Americans who would have willingly fought for the Confederacy even when it was a lost cause. The proslavery journalist James D. B. DeBow, publisher of the popular *DeBow's Review*, incorporated stories of slaves who demonstrated loyalty by fighting cheerfully side by side with their white masters (Levine 2006). The narratives support this view to some degree but only in rare instances. The illusion of significant numbers of African Americans expressing loyalty to the South was truly that, a false impression. Had Southern leaders truly believed in their propaganda about loyal slaves, they would not have hesitated in arming a significant portion of them much earlier in the conflict.

CHAPTER 5

Slave Involvement with the Union Military

I was 23 years old when I was mustered into the Union Army at the
old Washington Court House. I was sent to Camp Dennison where
the Ohio men were assembled. I saw action in 12 battles, among
them the battle of the Creed and the battle of Sham. I was in Sherman's march to the sea and the battle of Gettysburg. In that battle,
I could have walked backwards for five miles and never stepped on
the ground—there were that many dead men all the way.

(Jack Riley, TX)

Since the American Revolution, African Americans have volunteered to
serve their country in times of war. Records of the American Revolution
and the War of 1812 have references to service by African Americans in
the military. The papers of the Continental Congress further support the
participation of slaves in the military. The Civil War was no exception, but
African American involvement was slow to be officially authorized. Once
it was sanctioned, African Americans fought in every major campaign of
the war.

Jack Riley's (TX) reference to his service in the Union Army follows
this long tradition. When interviewed in the 1930s for collection of the
Works Progress Administration (WPA) slave narratives, he recalled serving
as a soldier in 12 major battles, including Gettysburg and General William
Tecumseh Sherman's March to the Sea. Riley may in fact have served at
Gettysburg, but there is no record of him or other blacks serving with Sher-
man. Sherman was vehemently opposed to blacks serving in combat roles.
Nonetheless, as many as 10,000 slaves fled their plantations and followed
Sherman's troops during the march and welcomed him as a liberator.

In the North, there was not much initial support for blacks serving in the
Union Army. In the autumn of 1862, with a Union victory still not inevitable and the preliminary Emancipation Proclamation already announced,

President Abraham Lincoln yielded to pressure and authorized the formation of the first black army units. As the war progressed and with the North facing declining enlistments, an unpopular draft, and growing combat casualties, Congress passed the Militia Act of 1862 authorizing Lincoln to employ African Americans in military service (Winsboro 2007). African Americans were offered a step toward emancipation not because the white North wanted their freedom; it was because the North desperately needed manpower for the war effort.

African American troops distinguished themselves and were instrumental in the North's victory. When blacks were finally permitted to participate in the Union Army, many willingly jumped at the opportunity (Franklin and Moss 2000). They were especially proud to wear the Union uniform because it represented a dramatic change in their social status (Wilson 2002). The North became committed to enlisting African Americans into its war effort and held rallies devoted to recruiting them for service. Although discrimination was rampant in the North, many African Americans were still willing to serve. Lower pay, inferior equipment, disrespect, fewer rations, and insults were not enough to deter African Americans from putting on the uniform and actively working for their freedom. Ironically, Northern free blacks were often literate and could write as well as most whites (Redkey 1992), yet they had inferior military provisions and rights. The differential treatment was obvious from the beginning. As John Ogee (TX) noted in his narrative, one of the differences between a black soldier and his white counterpart was that "The nigger troops was mix with the others but they wasn't no nigger officers."

Attitudes of white soldiers toward blacks in uniform could be caustic. Wiley (1952) provided examples of anti–African American attitudes in some of the personal correspondence of white Union soldiers. One Union Ohioan named Artemas Cook wrote on January 3, 1864, that "I don't think enough of the Niggar to go and fight for them. I would rather fight them" (Cook 1864). A. Davenport of the 5th New York Regiment wrote in 1861 that "I think that the best way to settle the question of what to do with the darkies would be to shoot them" (Davenport 1861). Union soldiers were sometimes averse to putting blacks in uniform because they saw it as a threat to white control and supremacy (Wiley 1952).

In all, African Americans made significant contributions to the Union war effort. They fought in 449 engagements, of which 39 were considered major battles. Approximately 37,300 African American soldiers lost their lives to the Union war effort (Mays 1984; Varhola 2011). Their valor on

The 27 soldiers in this photograph are from Company E, 4th United States Colored Infantry at Fort Lincoln, District of Columbia. Taken between 1862 and 1865 by Civil War photographer William Morris Smith, who worked for Brady contemporary Alexander Gardner, this photo shows the soldiers in two lines with rifles resting on the ground. The regiment saw action in Virginia and North Carolina; taking part in the Richmond-Petersburg Campaign; the capture of Fort Fisher and Wilmington, North Carolina; and the Carolinas Campaign. Their detachment was assigned to guard the nation's capital. The regiment was also involved in the Second Battle of Petersburg from June 15 to June 18, 1864, and the Battle of the Crater outside of Petersburg on July 30. At the Battle of the Crater, Union troops suffered massive losses when they exploded a huge bomb that created a crater in the Confederate defenses. Unit after unit of Union troops charged into and around the crater, where they milled about in confusion. Confederate units recovered and fired at will into the confused mass, killing many Union soldiers. General Grant considered the assault "The saddest affair I have witnessed in the war." Brig. Gen. Edward Ferrero's division of African American soldiers was badly mauled. Following the Battle of the Crater, the 4th was involved in other major battles such as Dutch Gap, Chaffin's Farm, and Fair Oaks, and by the end of the war the regiment had produced three Medal of Honor winners, Alfred B. Hilton, Christian Fleetwood, and Charles Veale. (Library of Congress)

the battlefields was recognized by 25 African American soldiers being awarded the Medal of Honor. They contributed in a variety of ways, all important to the Union effort. Besides their well-known battlefield contributions and sacrifices to the war effort, they were of great value as scouts and spies because they knew the geography of the land and could move about posing as slaves (Franklin and Moss 2000).

ESTIMATED NUMBER OF AFRICAN AMERICAN UNION TROOPS

The compiled military service records of the men who served with the U.S. Colored Troops during the Civil War number approximately 180,000 plus 18,000 in the Union Navy (Bailey 2006; Berlin, Reidy, and Rowland 1998; Hewitt 2002; Mays 1984; Redkey 1992; Shannon 1965; Williams 2008; Winsboro 2007). Faust (2008, 44) estimated that 10 percent of the Union Army consisted of African American soldiers. Other estimates place the numbers of blacks serving in the military higher. Ramold (2002) estimated the number of black recruits to be in a range from 8 percent to 25 percent, noting that it was difficult to ascertain an exact percentage since race was not recorded by the navy. Nearly 200,000 freedmen worked as laborers, cooks, teamsters, scouts, and construction workers for the Union forces (McPherson 1993).

By the beginning of August 1863 there were 14 African American regiments and 24 more being developed in the Union Army, and by October the number had grown to 58 (McPherson 1967). Of these black troops, Williams (2008) estimated that three-fourths were native Southerners and that in total, almost half a million or one-fourth of Union troops, black and white, were from the South. Mays (1984) estimated that about 25 percent of Union Navy personnel were African American. In the end, regardless of the actual number of African American troops or sailors, the fact is that their participation was sufficient enough to hasten the defeat of the Confederacy (Hewitt 2002).

WHY JOIN THE UNION MILITARY?

When war became apparent, many Northern blacks and escaped slaves wanted to serve in the Union Army. The Civil War for African Americans was clearly a conflict about liberation (Warfield 1925; Wilson 2002). Of all the Union troops, black soldiers were fighting for the most significant of causes: freedom for themselves and their people. The Emancipation Proclamation crystallized their motivation by making the ending of slavery a goal of the war.

William Wells Brown (2003, 75) wrote that "Slaves and free Blacks alike entered the army committed to fight for 'God and liberty.'" But it was more than God and liberty, according to Faust (2008, 48): "Blacks fought to define and claim their humanity, which seemed to many inseparable from avenging the wrongs of the slave system that had rendered them property rather than men."

Proving manhood was one of the motivations for African American men joining the Union Army. David Bustill Bowser (1820–1900) was an African American ornamental artist and portraitist and a cousin of Frederick Douglass. He created this image sometime between 1860 and 1870 for use on a regimental flag for the 127th Regiment, U.S. Colored Troops. It depicts an armed and uniformed soldier heading off to fight while saluting Columbia, symbol of the Union. (Library of Congress)

Many African Americans, slave and free, were eager to enter into military service at the outbreak of the war. For example, on April 23, 1861, only days after Fort Sumter, Jacob Dobson, a resident of Washington, wrote to the secretary of war: "Sir: I desire to inform you that I know of some three hundred of reliable colored free citizens of this

City, who desire to enter the service for the defense of the City" (McPherson 1993, 19). In Pittsburgh, the Hannibal Guards offered their service to the state militia. John Eubanks (IN) was encouraged by his Kentucky master to join the Union Army, which he did, rather than simply escape like the other slaves. Eubanks recalled that his master's advice was "You-all don't need to run 'way if'n you-all want to join up with the army." He then said, "Enlist in the army, but don't run off" (Baker 2000, 124).

In spite of racism and oppression in the North, many African Americans wanted to help preserve the Union, strike a blow to slavery, and prove their worth as human beings on equal footing with whites. They joined the Union Army with great enthusiasm (Mays 1984). According to William Wells Brown (2003, 76), an African American chronicler who wrote during the period, African Americans entered the war similar to their white counterparts with a "deep religious zeal." In addition, some of them joined to settle scores with their white masters, while others sought to liberate slaves collectively (Berlin, Reidy, and Rowland 1998). Still others, such as Sidney Joyner, joined the Union forces for the more personal reason of freeing his enslaved family (Wilson 2002). In a similar vein, another black soldier stated that "I fought to free my mammy and her children all through Nashville and Franklin and Columbia, Tennessee, and all down through Alabama and Georgia" (Fisk University 1945, 218).

Frederick Douglass, in an 1863 speech titled "Why a Colored Man Should Enlist," identified several reasons why African Americans should volunteer:

> He who looks upon a conflict between right and wrong, and does not help the right against the wrong, despises and insults his own nature, and invites the contempt of mankind. As between North and South, the North is clearly in the right, and the South is flagrantly in the wrong. You should, therefore, simply as a matter of right and wrong, give your utmost aid to the North. There is, in presence of such a contest, no neutrality for any man. You are either for the Government, or against the Government. Manhood requires you to take sides, and you are mean or noble, according to how you choose between action and inaction. There is, if you are of sound body and mind, nothing in your color to excuse you from enlisting in the service of the Republic against its enemies.
>
> (Douglass 1863, 1)

To Douglass, it was a question of righting a wrong and validating one's manhood. He would also allude to taking up arms to fight for liberty. His thoughts would be shared by many other African Americans who enlisted.

Among the reasons for enlisting, American citizenship came first (Redkey 1992). Blacks wanted to demonstrate that they were worthy of full citizenship, including voting rights. They offered to enlist in the Union Army to prove their patriotism and morally obligate the nation to grant them first-class citizenship (McPherson 1965; Warfield 1925). African Americans serving for the Union viewed their military service as a passport to full citizenship (Mays 1984).

It should be noted that the Union Army paid blacks, both freemen and escaped slaves, about $7 a month. This was a considerable amount of money and allowed them to support themselves and their families (Wilson 2002). But in whatever capacity they served, the pay of African Americans was roughly half of what white soldiers were paid. Even before the war was over, black soldiers were fighting for their rights by taking on the U.S. government for equal pay. This required some to make the ultimate sacrifice in the crusade for equal wages. Sergeant William Walker of the 21st U.S. Colored Infantry was tried in court in January 1864 for inciting a mutiny after he refused to perform military duties because the government was discriminating against black soldiers on the issue of pay. He was executed before President Lincoln could review the case (Wagner, Gallagher, and Finkelman 2002, 434). Massachusetts governor John A. Andrew later said of the case that "The Government which found no law to pay him except as a nondescript and a contraband, nevertheless found law enough to shoot him as a soldier" (Wagner, Gallagher, and Finkelman 2002, 434). Walker's death spurred others to take up the cause for equal pay in the military. On April 2, 1864, an African American soldier with the initials "E.D.W" wrote a letter to the editor of the *Christian Recorder* of Philadelphia, a leading African American newspaper:

> Do we not fill the same ranks? Do we not cover the same space of ground? Do we not take up the same length of ground in the graveyard that others do? The ball does not miss the black man and strike the white, nor the white and strike the black. But sir, at that time there is no distinction made, they strike one as much as another.
>
> (E.D.W. 1864)

For some African Americans, the wages and benefits offered by the army were higher than they had ever experienced. Arnold Gragston (KY)

This chromolithograph was an uncut sheet of twelve illustrated cards presenting the journey of a slave from plantation life to the struggle for liberty, for which he gives his life as a Union soldier during the Civil War. It was created in 1863 by Philadelphia artist and lithographer James Fuller Queen who was considered one of America's best 19th-century lithographers. The initial technique involved the use of multiple lithographic stones, one for each color, which was an extremely expensive process at the time. (Library of Congress)

explained his view on army wages: "They could enlist in the Union army and get good wages, more food than they ever had, and have all the little gals wavin' at em when they passed." African American soldiers also supplemented their army income by selling, trading, and raising goods and by working for others. Some lent money and even charged interest on loans to white members of the military.

Regardless of the willingness of African Americans to serve, most Northern whites initially resisted the enlistment of African Americans, which can be attributed to racism and a lack of confidence that black soldiers would perform well in the heat of battle. Although most whites in nonsecessionist states were aligned with the Union, some were also slaveholders, and they were as concerned as their Southern counterparts about arming slaves (Berlin, Reidy, and Rowland 1998).

When blacks first tried to enlist, they were initially told that it was a "white man's war; no blacks need apply" (McPherson 1967). When the war dragged on longer than anyone had expected and when the army needed more men to suppress the Confederacy, African Americans were at first allowed to enlist, then were drafted, and finally were compelled to serve (Redkey 1992). When ex-slaves were permitted to enlist, they found the Northern military to be as prejudiced and repressive as the slavery system they had left (Berlin, Reidy, and Rowland 1998). As enlisted troops, they found their military roles often limited. Some concluded they were both second-class soldiers and second-class citizens (Grant 2000).

WHO WERE THEY?

At the beginning of the war, President Lincoln assured both North and South that it was a war about preserving the Union, not abolishing slavery. The president was more interested in trying to maintain the loyalty of slave states that joined the Union and believed that most Northerners, slaveholder or not, would not support ending slavery (Mays 1984). Early in the war when Indiana offered to provide two units of black soldiers, Lincoln balked at the offer, indicating that emancipation would turn border states against the Union and that their arms would be in the hands of Rebel forces within weeks (McPherson 1967). Many white Northerners, with the exception of the abolitionists, viewed African Americans as inferior. Northern whites, despite evidence to the contrary from the Revolutionary War and the War of 1812, believed that blacks lacked the technical skills, intelligence, and commitment to be effective military contributors. Besides, previous slave rebellions had demonstrated what African Americans could do when they had weapons. This gave rise to fear among Northern whites that arming blacks held an inherent risk. Others believed that whites would not fight next to African Americans and would abandon their duties. Finally, the initial assumption about the war was that it would not last very long and would be over in a few weeks, and because of this some questioned going to all of the trouble of enlisting African Americans for what was expected to be a minor skirmish.

In spite of these factors, as previously mentioned, approximately 9–10 percent of the enlisted Union troops were African American; most of these were ex-slaves, but several freemen also joined the Union Army (Smith 2002). In addition, Northern slave owners provided slave labor to the Union. Slave owners were expected, except in exempt regions, to provide slave labor for the Union cause. In exempt areas, owners had to be paid if their slaves served the military.

AFRICAN AMERICANS DISTINGUISH THEMSELVES IN THE WAR EFFORT

In 1862 Congress authorized President Lincoln to use African American soldiers at his discretion until the war was over. In spite of many barriers such as racist insults, poor treatment, and unequal pay, African Americans fought willingly and died bravely and in large numbers. One of the key reasons that it took until 1862 to allow blacks to serve in the military was the common belief that they were not up to the task of combat. Whites feared that blacks would not be trustworthy under fire and would turn and run in the heat of battle. However, African Americans who served shattered these racial stereotypes, and most served with distinction, bravery, and honor. Whether with individual acts of heroism or collectively as whole units, such as the famed Massachusetts 54th and 55th Volunteer Infantry Regiments and the Black Brigade of Cincinnati, black soldiers proved their courage, patriotism, and pluck to be every bit the equal of white soldiers.

One of the barometers of their bravery in combat is the notable number of African American Medal of Honor recipients. The Medal of Honor, created during the Civil War, was given to 1,522 Union combatants, of which 25 were awarded to African Americans (Hanna 2002; U.S. Army Center of Military History 2011). Of the 25 Medals of Honor awarded to African Americans in the Civil War, 14 of them were for valor in the battles at Chaffin's Farm and New Market Heights, fought during September 29–30, 1864, as part of the Siege of Petersburg. For all troops who participated in these conflicts there were 37 Medals of Honor awarded, of which the 14 went to black soldiers. Of these 14 recipients, 5 were awarded for taking command of their units when leaders had fallen in battle, 5 were awarded for rescuing the colors and rallying their troops when the standard-bearers had fallen, and 4 were awarded for other reasons.

One of the most notable of those was the case of Corporal Miles James, Company B, 36th U.S. Colored Troops, whose citation read "Having had his arm mutilated, making immediate amputation necessary, he loaded and discharged his piece with one hand and urged his men forward; this within 30 yards of the enemy's works" (U.S. Gen Web Project 2012). Though severely wounded, James did not want to be discharged from the service as long as the war raged on. He wrote a letter to General A. G. Draper requesting that he be allowed to remain in the army. Draper's response, which became part of James's service records in the National Archives, in part said:

If it be possible, I would most respectfully urge that his request be granted. He was made a Sergeant and awarded a silver medal by Major General Benjamin Butler for gallant conduct. He is one of the bravest men I ever saw; and is in every respect a model soldier. He is worth more with a single arm, than half a dozen ordinary men.

(Sunderland 2004, 227)

The first African American recipient of the Medal of Honor was Sergeant William Harvey Carney Jr., Company C, 54th Massachusetts Volunteer Infantry Regiment, for his leadership and bravery during the unit's assault on Fort Wagner in Charleston Harbor on July 18, 1863. Born into slavery in 1840 at Norfolk, Virginia, Carney made it to the North at about 15 years of age when his father, who had earlier escaped slavery through the Underground Railroad, later bought the rest of his family's freedom. The family settled in New Bedford, Massachusetts, and it was from there that Carney joined the army. He was quoted in an 1863 edition of the abolitionist newspaper the *Liberator*: "Previous to the formation of colored troops, I had a strong inclination to prepare myself for the ministry; but when the country called for all persons, I could best serve my God serving my country and my oppressed brothers. The sequel in short—I enlisted for the war" (Hammond 2007, n.p.).

Carney was among the 600 men of the 54th Massachusetts who were part of an overall 5,000-member Union assault force that attacked Fort Wagner. Of the 600 troops in the 54th Massachusetts, 272 African Americans were killed, wounded, or missing. The total Union casualties were 1,515 in the battle that was portrayed in the 1989 movie *Glory*. The 54th

Massachusetts spearheaded the Union assault from a strip of sand east of the fort. The soldiers were bunkered down during the day while artillery pounded the fort, and at nightfall the order was given for the 54th Massachusetts to attack. As the companies advanced, a barrage of fire immediately hit them. A bullet struck the color sergeant, and as he fell Carney dropped his own gun, seized the flag, and moved to the front of the 54th Massachusetts's ranks. He soon found himself alone while bullets and shell fragments flew around him. He wound the colors around the flagpole, crouched, and planned his move back to the Union lines. When he rose he was shot, but since the bullet did not fell him he continued on but was soon struck by another shot. Despite carrying two bullets, he persevered and shortly saw another Union soldier from the 100th New York coming toward him. Though the other soldier offered to take the colors, Carney refused, saying that he would not give the colors to anyone who was not a member of the 54th Massachusetts. As they talked, a third shot struck Carney's arm. The pair struggled on but did not get far before a fourth bullet shot Carney, grazing him in the head. When the two men finally managed to make it back to their own lines, Carney was taken to the rear to receive medical treatment. Throughout the ordeal, Carney held on to the colors. As he staggered into the ranks of the 54th Massachusetts, he said, "Boys, the old flag never touched the ground!"

A little more than a year after the battle, Carney was discharged from the army due to the lingering effects of his wounds. He settled back in New Bedford, where he worked as a mail carrier for the Postal Service until he retired. His valor at Fort Wagner was recognized on May 23, 1900, when he was awarded the Medal of Honor, to which he simply said, "I only did my duty" (Hammond 2007, n.p.).

Another of the Medal of Honor winners, Powhatan Beaty, showed great leadership at Chaffin's Farm and was awarded the Medal of Honor for taking command of his company after all officers had been killed or wounded. Beaty was born into slavery in Richmond in 1837 and moved to Cincinnati by 1849. He gained his freedom in 1861 and two years later joined the 127th Ohio Volunteer Infantry when Ohio governor David Todd was granted permission by the War Department to form an all–African American regiment. The 127th Ohio was later redesignated the 5th U.S. Colored Troops. In early September 1862 under rumor of a Confederate attack on Cincinnati, 700 African American males were rounded up involuntarily and pressed into service to become the Black Brigade to defend the city. They were later relieved by the volunteers, which included

Sergeant Beaty. After three weeks the threat of attack subsided, and the Black Brigade was disbanded. Many feel that the brigade was never given due credit for protecting the city at a time when there were no organized Union forces between Cincinnati and Richmond, 100 miles to the south. William M. Dickson, the commandant of the Black Brigade in 1864, wrote that "The Black Brigade was the first organization of the colored people of the North actually employed for military purposes" (Clark 1969, 3).

By the time of the Battle of Chaffin's Farm two years later, Beaty had risen to the rank of first sergeant in Company G of the 5th U.S. Colored Troops and was among a division of African American troops to attack the center of Confederate forces at New Market Heights (Hanna 2002). The attack was repulsed, and the regiment fell into retreat. The color-bearer was killed. Noticing the absence of the flag, Beaty went back the distance of 600 feet, recaptured the flag under fire, and, with the officers having been killed, took charge of the remnants of his company to mount a second charge. Of Company G's 8 officers and 83 enlisted men who mounted the first charge, only 16 enlisted men, including Beaty, survived the battle unwounded. Major General Benjamin Butler witnessed the incident, and when the Medal of Honor was presented, he also presented Beaty with a silver medal. After the war, Beaty settled in Cincinnati and became an actor, a playwright, and a public speaker. He died in 1916 at the age of 79.

Not all African American recipients of the Medal of Honor were from the infantry. John Lawson, born in Pennsylvania on June 16, 1837, served in the U.S. Navy during the war as a landsman (rank given to those with little or no experience at sea) aboard Admiral David Farragut's flagship, USS *Hartford*. Lawson most likely joined the *Hartford* when the ship was refitted in Philadelphia at the end of 1861. During the August 5, 1864, Battle of Mobile Bay, Lawson was serving on a six-man berth deck gun crew aboard the ship that was immortalized during the battle by Admiral Farragut's orders "Damn the torpedoes—full speed ahead" (Delaware Valley Rhythm & Blues Society 2011). Lawson's Medal of Honor citation in part reads "Wounded in the leg and thrown violently against the side of the ship when an enemy shell killed or wounded the 6-man crew as the shell whipped on the berth deck, Lawson, upon regaining his composure, promptly returned to his station and, although urged to go below for treatment, steadfastly continued his duties throughout the remainder of the action," continuing to supply the *Hartford*'s guns (Delaware Valley Rhythm & Blues Society 2011).

Another example of naval bravery was that of African American Robert Smalls, pilot of the Confederate gunboat *Planter*. The gunboat was stolen out of Charleston Harbor, South Carolina, on May 13, 1862, by Smalls and a crew of eight African American sailors when the entire white crew had gone to shore on unauthorized leave, entrusting the ship to the African American members of the crew (Adams and Cordial 2007). Although other crew members begged to change course, the daring Smalls steered the ship directly beneath the walls of Fort Sumter, blowing the steam whistle twice for passage and waving to the guards above while covering his face under the captain's hat. Once clear of the harbor, the *Planter* raised a white flag made of a bed sheet and surrendered to the nearest Union ship, USS *Onward*. The navy received both the *Planter* and the slaves on board as contraband property of the war. President Lincoln would later receive Smalls and his crew in Washington to recognize them for their bravery. The incident was a significant blow to Confederate morale.

Although not awarded the Medal of Honor, another African American soldier's narrative reminiscences from his participation in the Battle of Nashville certainly bring a human element to the accomplishments of African American troops. Moses Slaughter (IN) enrolled as a private in the 13th U.S. Colored Infantry, Company K, from Clarksville, Tennessee, on October 24, 1863. The regiment provided essential support for the construction of the 75-mile Nashville and Northwestern Railroad extension until being ordered back to Nashville in December 1864 to participate in the historic Battle of Nashville, the conclusion of which effectively ended the war in the western theater. Major General George H. Thomas was the commanding officer for the Union, while Private Slaughter's 13th U.S. Colored Infantry had been consolidated with the 12th and 100th U.S. Colored Infantry into the 2nd Colored Brigade under the command of Colonel Charles Thompson.

The following is Moses Slaughter's recollection of the battle as told to an interviewer in the 1930s during the WPA Federal Writer's Project. Slaughter, who would later be promoted to the rank of corporal in 1865, was living in Indiana when he supplied this:

I remember when our company was encamped at Johnsonville, Tennessee. We were in training and our camp was near a wilderness. We had heard that John Bell Hood, lieutenant-general of the Confederate army[,] was a natural born soldier. He had been given the command formerly held by J. E. Johnstone and had now been given command of the army of the Tennessee. General Thomas called an army to oppose Hood as he was planning a big battle at Nashville, Tennessee. So many Confederate soldiers were hiding in the wilderness our men could not march from Johnsonville to Nashville without surprising some party of Confederate skirmishers, so we were ordered to go by Clarksville[,] a much longer route than we would have had to travel only for our fear of the Confederate soldiers.

On that march we were afoot, carrying our packs. The roads were through the wilderness. We were in danger of becoming divided and in that case many would have been lost. Neither maps nor charts were given to us. We must just stay close together. Food was scarce and we were unpaid but one half of us guarded while the other half worked, cutting our way through that awful wilderness. We went by way of the Cumberland River and through the Gap. The Gap was always a point well guarded. General Grant was commander of all the armies of the United States and his plan was to crush Lee's army and all the Confederate forces.

General Thomas' command was made up of the army of the Cumberland and the army of the Ohio. Thomas was a thoughtful man, slow in all his ways of moving about. He was loved by all his men.

When we reached Nashville Hood's army was soon reduced to a handful. General Thomas commanded the Union corps although the regiment had been put under a general corps commanded by Charles H. Ottensteen, colonel of the Thirteenth Regiment.

Hood's army suffered severe losses in the battle of Nashville on December 15th and 16th, 1864. Although our men were tired, the Union soldiers were fighting for a cause that had both God and President Lincoln on its side, and the Thirteenth regiment fought for its own freedom.

Slaughter was wounded twice in the line of duty, the second time on December 16, 1864, on the last day of the Battle of Nashville as desperate Rebels attempted to steal food and supplies. The ruinous repulsion of the Confederate forces at Nashville precipitated General John Bell Hood's retreat into northern Alabama after losing nearly half of his 30,000 men, which further contributed to the dishonor that later befell him.

NORTHERN RESPONSE TO AFRICAN AMERICAN UNION SOLDIERS

Although they had served in earlier wars, at the beginning of the Civil War African Americans were barred from serving in state militias, and there were none in the U.S. Army (McPherson 1993). There was political resistance to their full participation on both sides of the Mason-Dixon Line. As previously noted, Northern resistance to the enlistment of blacks on the Union side was due mostly to the racially motivated concern that they would not make good soldiers and that they would be cowards in the face of battle (McPherson 1967).

It was a full year into the war when Congress authorized President Lincoln to use African American soldiers at his discretion (Redkey 1992). Earlier Lincoln had turned away African American volunteers, fearing a negative reaction from his proslavery constituents (Bailey 2006). Lincoln refused to use this new authority until war losses and few victories forced his hand. After a series of defeats and heavy Union casualties, the North increasingly became forced to involve blacks and even recruit them in the war effort. On November 7, 1862, Lincoln authorized the enlistment of African American regiments among the freed slaves on the South Carolina Sea Islands. The first such regiment was called the 1st South Carolina Volunteers (McPherson 1967). This had been preceded by Lincoln's July 22, 1862, executive order authorizing the employment of contrabands in the states of Virginia, South Carolina, Georgia, Florida, Alabama, Mississippi, Louisiana, Texas, and Arkansas (Woolley and Peters 1999). The order required military and naval commanders to employ as laborers "so many persons of African descent as can be advantageously used for military or naval purposes, giving them reasonable wages for their labor" (Lincoln 1862).

In 1850, the Fugitive Slave Act resulted in a number of free blacks being returned to the South. In 1857, the *Dred Scott* case denied African Americans rights that whites were legally bound to respect. The ruling reinforced the requirement that captured slaves were property and not persons with rights and that any captured slaves must be returned to the South and their owners. As the war progressed, Union officers started to ignore the Fugitive Slave Act and began employing runaway slaves as laborers in their camps and fortifications. These ex-slaves eventually became an important source of labor for the Union military, especially to the navy, which increasingly served as a sanctuary for runaways.

Northern abolitionists and African Americans had long argued for the enlistment of blacks in the Union Army (Bailey 2002). However, Northern conservatives and Southern planters doubted the slaves' willingness to fight (McPherson 1965; Smith 2003). While Northerners eventually accepted the assistance of African Americans in defeating the Confederacy, they remained skeptical of arming them due to the belief that African Americans lacked character. This, of course, was in marked contrast to the many black Americans who harbored no doubt in their ability and commitment to defeat the South (Berlin, Reidy, and Rowland 1998). Whether they were volunteers or forced in, African Americans yearned to dispel the misperception that they were inferior soldiers and wanted to be treated equitably.

African Americans seeking to join the Union forces or those conscripted in the Union effort found that soldiering was an ambiguous experience (Berlin, Reidy, and Rowland 1998). Those looking for equal treatment were disappointed. What they found was a white-dominated military system not unlike what some had experienced under slavery (Berlin, Reidy, and Rowland 1998). Often they were only allowed to perform menial jobs in support of white troops. For instance, Union generals Nathaniel P. Banks and Edward R. S. Canby only used black troops for fatigue and garrison duties (Wilson 2002). The belief was that they were better suited for hard labor in the warm, humid climate of the South. It was their lower pay that caused the most angst (Wilson 2002). In addition to lower pay and clothing allowances paid to black soldiers, white soldiers also received informal compensation for their families (Mays 1984). Widows and families of African American soldiers received no compensation.

Some African American units, specifically the 54th and 55th Massachusetts, protested unequal treatment and refused pay for a year on the principle that it was not equal to white compensation. To many African American families, the difference between $7 and $13 was important. The amount of the pay was important not only financially but also symbolically. Equal pay took on a special meaning because it represented equality, even though many federal officers were reluctant to grant equality to black soldiers (Shannon 1965). Finally, in June 1864 the War Department authorized equal wages for black soldiers, and for some, soldiering in the Union Army was a better financial opportunity than what they could manage on the outside.

The other reason for slave involvement in the Union military was that Northern slave owners sold their services. Owners were expected, except in exempt regions, to provide slave labor for the Union cause. In exempt areas, the government compensated owners if their slaves served in the military.

When the Union Army first activated black regiments in the autumn of 1862, Northern whites increasingly expected African Americans to pay the price of war with their lives, as had so many whites before them (Berlin, Reidy, and Rowland 1998). In a letter to Iowa governor Samuel J. Kirkwood dated August 5, 1862, General Henry W. Halleck makes the case that African American people should pay the same price for their freedom as whites had already. After pleading for more African American contrabands, General Halleck noted:

> I have but one remark to add and that in regard to the Negroes fighting—it is this—when the war is over and we have summed up the entire loss of life it has imposed on the country I should not have any regrets if it were found that a part of the dead are niggers and that they are not white men.
>
> (Berlin, Reidy, and Rowland 1998, 88)

The use of African American troops varied from state to state and from commander to commander. Key Union war figures, such as General Sherman, did not welcome African Americans into the army. Sherman refused to use them except in support roles, such as teamsters, cooks, and servants (Bailey 2002, 2006; Redkey 1992; Westwood 1992). Sherman's position on the use of armed African American soldiers never wavered throughout the war (Bailey 2006). In contrast, however, was Major General Benjamin Butler, commander of the Army Department in Virginia and North Carolina, who used them in combat roles. After initially turning down a regiment of African American soldiers, Butler changed his mind and recruited three regiments when threatened by a massive Confederate attack in New Orleans in August 1862 (Smith 2002; Westwood 1992).

The Union Navy did not implement the same discriminatory policies as the Union Army. The navy provided a different experience for African Americans (Hannon 2004). Unlike with the army, African American sailors received the same rates of pay, slept in the same quarters, were not segregated, and had similar ranks of boy, landsman, and petty officer. African Americans had similar rights as white sailors and made higher wages than their counterparts in the army. Free blacks had a long tradition of naval service to the country because they were never barred from enlisting (Mays 1984; Westwood 1992).

During the war, the navy actively recruited African American sailors early on and treated them favorably. While the navy took a position of general equality for its sailors regardless of race, white sailors at times practiced overt racism (Valuska 1993). In sharp contrast, the army was less egalitarian and more restrictive. In 1861, the navy actively recruited escaped slaves into its ranks. Secretary of the Navy Gideon Welles welcomed contraband sailors into the navy, as he needed more bodies to build the blockade ordered by President Lincoln (Ramold 2002). The navy also used contrabands as full-fledged sailors (Hannon 2004). However, contraband sailors were often limited to the role of "boys," a rank given to unskilled seamen. The navy expected black sailors to perform in full combat roles along with their white counterparts (Ramold 2002). The contributions of black sailors were critical to the success of the Union Navy. Skilled contrabands served valuable roles as coastal and river pilots on Union ships because they knew the river channels and currents better than most Northerners (Tomblin 2009).

UNION MILITARY ROLES FOR AFRICAN AMERICANS

African Americans serving in the Union Army were subjected to many indignities and hard physical labor (Mays 1984) and were not trained to the same degree as their white counterparts, giving them a slim chance of ever becoming officers. The military segregated them and made them serve under prejudiced white officers. Whites, both enlisted men and officers, often harassed and ridiculed black soldiers. Northern citizens in many of the cities also assaulted them. Despite these negatives, African American soldiers nevertheless served with honor and dignity. They proved themselves on the battlefield, much to the surprise of many Northerners. African American soldiers served in various roles in the military, including combat roles in the 54th and 55th Massachusetts and many other decorated units. They also worked in construction, served as rear guards and general laborers, built fortifications, protected occupied territories, guarded rail lines, and served as teamsters, body servants, and cooks and in other roles (Mays 1984; Redkey 1992). Thomas Cole (AL) reported helping General William Rosecrans set and load cannons at Chickamauga. Being body servants to union officers, similar to the South, was a common role. For example, Samuel Riddick (NC) said, "When the war broke out I left my marster and went to Portsmouth, Virginia. General Miles captured me and put me in uniform I waited on him as a body servant, a private in the U.S. Army." They also served in a number of different roles in the navy. Between the

army and the navy, African Americans made up about 15 percent of all
Northern forces.

While it is well documented that African Americans had combat roles,
most of their responsibilities were in support capacities. John Finnely, an
escaped slave from Alabama, described his work for the army: "Dere, us
put to work buildin' breastworks." He then added, "I's water toter dere for
de army and dere am no fightin' at first but 'fore long dey starts de battle."
African Americans also were charged with some of the labor-intensive and
menial jobs such as burying the dead, one of the most trying and difficult
tasks during the war. The collection and burial of putrefied bodies of the
fallen would have challenged even those of the strongest of heart and
stomach. The humidity and heat in the South, coupled with significant fa-
tal wounds and the fact that bodies often remained for days, weeks, and
even months after soldiers died, all made handling of the dead a nauseating
task. Louis Fowler (TX) described how he and other African Americans
worked the fields to clear out the bodies:

> De nex' day after de battle am over, mos' us cullud folks goes to de
> field. Some of 'em buries de dead, and I hears 'em tell how in de low
> places de blood stand like water and de bodies all shoot to pieces.

John Finnely (AL) provided this account:

> Dere am dead mens all over de ground and lots of wounded and
> some cussin' and some prayin'. Some moanin' and dis and dat one
> cry for de water and, God A' mighty I don't want any sich' agin.
> Dere am men carryin de dead uff de field, but dey can't keep up
> with de cannons. I helps bury de dead and den I gits sent to Mur-
> physboro and dere it am jus' de same.

As difficult as it was on the fields, some, such as James Lucas (MS),
admitted that the battlefield cleanup was an opportunity to harvest valuables from the bodies.

> Den I was put to buryin' Yankee sojers. When nobody was lookin' I
> stript de dead of dey money. Sometimes dey had it in a belt a-roun'
> dey bodies. Soon I got a big roll o' foldin' money. Den I come
> a-tramp-in' back home. My folks didn' have no money but dat
> wuthless kin'. It was all dey knowed 'bout. When I grabbed some if

it an' throwed it in de blazin' fiah, dey thought I was crazy, 'til I tol' 'em, "dat aint money; it's no 'count!" Den I give my daddy a green-back an' tol' him what it was.

SOUTHERN VIEWS OF AFRICAN AMERICANS SERVING IN THE NORTHERN MILITARY

As would be expected, Southern views of African American involvement on the side of the North were emphatically negative. African American Union soldiers faced immediate hostility from Southern whites (Winsboro 2007). The idea that blacks would fight for the Union outraged the Confederate sense of the old order. Consequently, Southern forces treated captured African American Union soldiers worse than white prisoners. Confederate president Jefferson Davis ordered that captured black troops be sent back to their home states and dealt with accordingly. Lincoln responded in kind by ordering that for every captured Union soldier enslaved, a captured Confederate soldier would be put into forced labor for the Union cause (Franklin and Moss 2000).

Rebel soldiers would shoot slaves rather than see them join with Union soldiers as the Northern armies advanced through the South in the later stages of the war. "Confederate soldiers regarded black troops as 'so many devils,' whose very presence in the South justified their deaths" (Faust 2008, 44). When African American soldiers were in the frontline fighting roles instead of in support roles, they faced the prospect of not only being killed or maimed in battle but also of being executed if they were captured by Confederates, who declared that all black men fighting for the Union were slaves regardless of whether they were actually former slaves or had been born free. African American prisoners were frequently executed or became victims of atrocities (Urwin 2004). Because of this and because they more frequently succumbed to disease, African American units on average suffered a casualty rate about 35 percent higher than white units (Varhola 2011).

Barney Stone (IN), who was born into slavery in Kentucky in 1847 and later witnessed his mother and younger brother sold away from him at a slave auction, recalled:

At the out-break of the Civil War and when the Northern army was marching into the Southland, hundreds of male slaves were shot down by the Rebels, rather than see them join with the Yankees.

One day when I learned that the Northern troops were very close to our plantation, I ran away and hid in a culvert, but was found and I would have been shot had the Yankee troops not scattered them and that saved me. I joined that Union army and served one year, eight months and twenty-two days, and fought with them in the battle of Fort Wagner, and also in the battle of Milikin's Bend. When I went into the army, I could not read or write. The white soldiers took an interest in me and taught me to write and read, and when the war was over I could write a very good letter. I taught what little I knew to colored children after the war.

After the war Stone became a preacher and a farmer and helped to build seven churches over a 69-year period.

It is well documented that the South committed atrocities against African American Union soldiers at Milliken's Bend (June 7, 1863), Port Hudson (May 22–July 9, 1863), and Mound Plantation (June 29, 1863). The battle at Milliken's Bend, Mississippi, although a relatively minor skirmish, was distinguished by the prominent participation of African American soldiers, who fought bravely and helped drive off the Confederates. After the battle Assistant Secretary of War Charles A. Dana wrote that "The bravery of the African Americans completely revolutionized the sentiment of the army with regard to the employment of negro troops. I heard prominent officers who formerly in private had sneered at the idea of negroes fighting express themselves after that as heartily in favor of it" (McPherson 1988, 634). But the feeling was very different among the Confederates, observed Dana. Infuriated by the arming of former slaves, Southern troops at Milliken's Bend shouted "no quarter!" and reportedly murdered several captured African Americans.

But there is scant documentation on how the South actually treated African American prisoners, since many never made it to prison camp. Not all Confederates even considered black Union troops as soldiers (Levin 2010). For Confederates to acknowledge them as such would have moved them closer to equal footing with whites. Because the Confederates refused to acknowledge African Americans as legitimate prisoners, few records were kept (McPherson 1988). In some parts of the South, captured African Americans were referred to as "negroes in arms" because to acknowledge them as soldiers would have given them rights (Barnickel 2010). "Negroes in arms" implied a slave insurrection and therefore no rights or protocols. Since they were not considered soldiers, they and their white officers were not included in prisoner exchanges and did not receive medical attention in the prison camps (Davis 2007). It has been suggested by some historians that black soldiers were inspired to fight with more passion because they knew that their capture would likely result in execution or excessive suffering in prison (Winsboro 2007).

On May 1, 1863, the Confederate Congress authorized President Davis to punish to the death captured white officers of black regiments for inciting slave insurrection. In addition, captured African American soldiers were to be turned over to the state from which they were taken and subjected to that state's laws, which was usually hanging (McPherson 1967). Furthermore, many Southern civilians, without official sanction, executed black soldiers they captured (Redkey 1992).

Confederate outrage toward the idea of African Americans in uniform reached a crescendo with the Fort Pillow affair. On April 12, 1864, the Union fort near Memphis fell to Confederate forces under the leadership of General Nathan Bedford Forrest. Since Confederates did not generally allow for the capture of African American soldiers to surrender, they were often shot or burned alive (Franklin and Moss 2000). The following is a description of the Fort Pillow aftermath as it appeared in an article titled "The Black Flag" on the front page of the April 16, 1864, edition of the *New York Times*:

The flag of truce was refused, and fighting resumed. Afterward a second flag came in, which was also refused. Both flags gave the rebels advantage of gaining new position. The battle was kept up until 3 P.M., when Major Booth was killed, and Major Bradford took command. The rebels now came in swarms over our troops, compelling them to surrender. Immediately upon the surrender ensued a scene, which utterly baffles description. Up to that time, comparatively few of our men had been killed; but, insatiate as fiends, bloodthirsty as devils incarnate, the Confederates commenced an indiscriminate butchery of the whites and blacks, including those of both colors who had been previously wounded. The black soldiers, becoming demoralized, rushed to the rear, the white officers having thrown down their arms. Both white and blacks were bayoneted, shot or sabered; even dead bodies were horribly mutilated, and children of seven and eight years and several Negro women killed in cold blood. Soldiers unable to speak from wounds were shot dead, and their bodies rolled down the banks into the river. The dead and wounded Negroes were piled in heaps and burned, and several citizens who had joined our forces for protection were killed or wounded.

(Anon. 1864, 1)

The Confederates' behavior at Fort Pillow ultimately led to the Union battle cry "Remember Fort Pillow." President Lincoln was so outraged that he declared that if the atrocities of Fort Pillow proved true he would retaliate, but he never did (Castel 2004).

Similar Confederate rage against blacks in Union attire was sworn to in an affidavit by Sergeant Samuel Johnson to his commanding officer, Major General Benjamin Butler, following the Rebels' recapture of Plymouth, North Carolina, in April 1864:

Upon the capture of Plymouth by the rebel forces all the negroes found in blue uniform, or with any outward marks of a Union soldier upon him, was killed. I saw some taken into the woods and hung. Others I saw stripped of all their clothing and then stood upon the bank of the river with their faces riverward, and there they were shot. Still others were killed by having their brains beaten out by the butt-end of the muskets in the hands of the rebels. All were not killed the day of the capture. Those that were not were placed in a room with their officers, they (the officers) having previously been dragged through the town with ropes around their necks, where they were kept confined until the following morning, when the remainder of the black soldiers were killed.

(Reed and Dickey 1910, 136–137)

At the Battle of Port Hudson both sides called a truce, allowing them to remove the bodies of fallen soldiers. However, the Confederates refused to let Union forces remove the bodies of the black Union soldiers. Following the Emancipation Proclamation, the Confederate Congress passed a resolution declaring that every commissioned white person who commanded, trained, armed, or prepared African American soldiers for war was guilty of inciting servile insurrection and, upon capture, would be put to death (Hollandsworth 2004). This threat was countered by a retaliatory warning from President Lincoln. In July 1863 he proclaimed that "To sell or enslave any captured person on account of his color and for no offense against the laws of war is a relapse into barbarism and a crime against the

The execution of Pvt. William Johnson, 23rd Regiment, United States Colored Troops (USCT), at Petersburg, Virginia, June 1864 as depicted in the left panel of a stereograph by Civil War–era photographers Taylor & Huntington. Johnson had confessed to desertion and rape and was executed within the outer breastworks at Petersburg near what is now the visitor center at the Petersburg Battlefield. (Library of Congress)

civilization of the age" (Barrett 1865, 482). The proclamation also declared that "For every soldier of the United States killed in violation of the laws of war a rebel soldier shall be executed, and for everyone enslaved by the enemy or sold into slavery a rebel soldier shall be placed at hard labor." Lincoln's proclamation had little effect on Confederate forces (Bailey 2006) because it was virtually unenforceable and was never carried out. Confederate troops continued to shoot on the spot, imprison, or impress into slavery captured African American troops. The Confederates reasoned that they could avoid federal retaliation by simply not taking prisoners (Hollandsworth 2004). Some captured black soldiers were sent to the horrible Confederate prisoner-of-war camps, such as Andersonville and the stockade at Florence, South Carolina (Westwood 1992). African

American Union soldiers were often put on special work details at prison camps such as Andersonville, where they were forced to work harder than other prisoners but also benefited from extra rations that helped them survive (Davis 2007).

There were some positive consequences for African Americans serving in the Union Army beyond their contributions to combat. One was that through their military participation, some African Americans used their free time to learn to read and write (McPherson 1967). The Union Army placed value on teaching black troops to read and write because it was thought that their education and literacy made them better soldiers (Wilson 2002). Many black soldiers continued to be members of the occupying forces following the war. This gave them the opportunity to provide leadership in some of the same communities in which they had fought for their freedom (Berlin, Reidy, and Rowland 1998).

OBSERVATIONS

African American participation in the Union Army and the Union Navy had a major impact on the war. Although slow to embrace the notion of African American soldiers, the Union would eventually fully equip and arm them for combat. This decision proved to be a wise decision, as African American troops approached their military roles with enthusiasm and commitment. While the eventual outcome of the war cannot be fully attributed to their participation, it is evident that they helped expedite a Union victory in many important ways. Eagerness to serve, bravery, and fighting to free all black men and women were themes echoed in many of the WPA narratives and documented by several historians (McPherson 1988, 1993; Quarles 1968; Smith 2002; Wilson 2002). Unfortunately, following the war African Americans' military contributions were not acknowledged, and many African American veterans struggled to get the benefits and recognition they so richly deserved (Shaffer 2004).

Besides their freedom provided by the Union victory, the status of African Americans did, however, change for the better in a number of ways. Union military service, though not on the same level of equity with whites, afforded them new opportunities that were not available under slavery. A case in point was that being in the Union military brought literacy to many black Americans that was for the most part forbidden under slavery (Tomblin 2009).

Many African Americans who served in the military went on to positions of leadership after the war, such as becoming legislators, businessmen, ministers, and leaders of groups devoted to furthering the rights of the newly freed blacks. Despite the frequent racial harassment that blacks were subjected to in the military, these newfound postwar roles would not have been available to them without the training they received as soldiers.

CHAPTER 6

Slave Involvement
with the Confederate Military

In the war time, when the Captain give the charge order, I would pick me out one of the enemy for my own personal fight and while I was making for him I would always say: "Bayonet to bayonet, skull to skull, if you ain't faster than I is, I get you in the rib!"— and then I would let him have it!

I use to be a fighting man and a strong Southern soldier, until the Yank's captured me and made me fight with them. I don't know what the year was, but there was some Southern Indians took in the same battle and they fought with the North too. There was whole regiments deserted from the South, but I was captured; never figured on running away from my own people. Some of the Cherokee Indians who fought with the North were Bob Crittenden, Zeke Proctor and Luke Six Killer. Luke's father was with the South and got killed; some of the folks said young Luke killed his own father in the war.

Some of the time I was fighting in Virginia against Lee's army, and there I saw many a man ripped with the bayonet and fall dead on the ground. I still got the bayonet I used in the war; the gun is gone. A white man borrowed it to take a picture of the old gun and he ain't never come back with it yet. He's a Muskogee man, but I forgot his name.

(Henry Henderson, OK)

Henry Henderson (OK) spoke of initially being a member of the Confederate Army in a combat role. He said that he was captured and then fought on the Union side. We cannot know for sure whether or not he served the Confederacy in a combat role other than by his claim that "I use to be a fighting man and a strong Southern soldier." When most people think about the Civil War and those who fought, we think of white soldiers on both sides and perhaps a few virtually all–African American units in the Union Army. What most do not think about is their participation in the Confederate Army. The role that African Americans played in supporting the Confederate cause is to this day controversial and much debated. African Americans in the Confederate military, especially when their involvement was voluntary, vexes historians and seems to represent a notable contradiction to modern perceptions about the Civil War. The notion of African American soldiers fighting for the Confederacy may have contributed to this being a relatively neglected area of study. Segars and Barrow (2007) observed that there is a shortage of books about common soldiers and that the story about all participants has not been fully told.

While the vast majority of historians agree that almost all African Americans were vehemently opposed to what the Confederacy stood for and to slavery, a few believe that many Southern blacks were loyal to the South and the way of life it represented. In this vein, the pro–Confederate Lost Cause mythology argues that the Confederacy was never defeated but was overwhelmed and betrayed by some key generals (Blight 2001). This view is part of the larger movement to reconcile to the white South the defeat. Part of this Lost Cause perspective emphasizes that the war was fought over states' rights rather than the issue of slavery. A war fought over states' rights made the conflict more justifiable than one fought over the morality of slavery. To support this idea, Lost Cause adherents typically look for historic examples of slaves and Southern freemen supporting the Confederate cause by their willingness to fight against the Union. This is coupled with the misguided notion that many slaves were content living under slavery and openly worked to counter the perceived attack by the North. Proponents point to Confederate veteran pension lists, war memorials to faithful slaves, photographs, eyewitness accounts, letters, and other documents that acknowledge African Americans who served on the battlefield or remained in the Southern factories or fields during the war. Much of the discussion surrounding African American Confederates is about who can claim a moral victory for their respective side.

In sharp contrast are the vast majority of Civil War scholars who find little support among African Americans of the period for the Confederate cause. They note that tens of thousands of African Americans fled to the North to gain their freedom, and tens of thousands willingly took up arms to defeat the South. Interestingly, this mass defection to the North early in the war was one of the reasons that began shifting its purpose from simply preserving the Union to freeing the slaves. Scholars also point to evidence indicating that African Americans hungered for a Confederate loss, which they believed would result in their freedom. From this perspective, it becomes incomprehensible that slaves would fight for the South, which by doing so would undermine their chance for freedom.

Answering the question of the nature of their participation is difficult. Evidence of African Americans fighting for the Confederacy is sparse. The National Archives and Records Administration has records that show that African Americans did not serve in combat roles for the Confederacy at any significant level, but there are several scattered records indicating that they served as cooks, musicians, laborers, and teamsters and in other supportive roles (Musick 2012). Complicating the issue is the fact that virtually all Confederate muster rolls do not contain any racial information. Mike Musick, a Civil War expert formerly with the National Archives, also cautions that precise definitions are needed, because African Americans serving with Confederate forces had separate status from enlisted white soldiers and therefore would not be labeled as "enlisted" in military service records of the Confederacy. They might be listed in some of the militias such as the Louisiana Native Guards, which was not part of the Confederate Army and never saw combat (Wesley 1919).

A few scholarly works have focused on the nature of African American involvement in the Confederate military and their support to the South (Barrow, Segars, and Rosenburg 2004; Brewer 1969; Segars and Barrow 2007). These studies focus on African American applications for Confederate military pensions, eyewitness accounts, newspaper references, photos, their participation at Civil War reunions, personal accounts, and war memorials to them located throughout the South. The Works Progress Administration (WPA) narratives seem to indicate that there was forced as well as voluntary slave participation in the Confederate military.

One of the earliest examples of African American support for the Confederacy occurred during John Brown's attack on Harpers Ferry on October 16, 1859, when an African American freeman named Heyward Shepherd, a civilian employee of the Baltimore and Ohio Railroad, was shot in the back by Brown's group as he tried to warn the town of the attack (Jordan 1995). In 1931 Shepherd's brief role in this historic event was memorialized by the United Daughters of the Confederacy and the Sons of Confederate Veterans. Although he was not part of the military, he was buried with full military honors.

There is no doubt that the Confederacy used slaves in support roles in the war to build fortifications, dig latrines, cook, prepare provisions, and haul supplies. Its army depended heavily on African American labor to support military efforts (Berlin, Reidy, and Rowland 1998). But owners were not always supportive of having their slaves impressed into service for the Confederacy (Reid 1950). The use of slaves in the military for menial jobs allowed the South to use more whites for combat and also reduced the number of African Americans remaining on the plantations, which then lacked white overseers and thus "proper" supervision (Bailey 2006).

While many owners forced their slaves to support the Confederate cause, other slaves willingly joined Confederate military forces. For example, 83 percent of male slaves working at Richmond's Jackson Hospital volunteered and then later went on to fight the Yankees in 1865 during the last month of the war. They proved themselves on the battlefield at Petersburg and were involved in combat roles in the first major battle of the war at the First Battle of Bull Run/Manassas (Jordan 1995). Eyewitness accounts credit them with some of the Union casualties during the battle. For example, John Parker and four other slaves were assigned to a battery and coerced to fight at Bull Run/Manassas. Parker's story has been selectively quoted by neo-Confederates to promote the idea that thousands of African American Confederates fought the Union. But Parker himself undercut this argument when he recalled that "We only fought because we had to. We wish[ed] to our hearts that the Yankees would whip and we would have run over to their side but our officers would have shot us if we had made the attempt" (Weinberg 2012). Other examples of Southern blacks in combat roles have been documented for both freemen and slaves.

Although seldom employed, the Confederate government could purchase slaves outright but found it cheaper to simply lease them from their owners, and this leasing process became a profitable enterprise for some owners (Jordan 1995). It should be acknowledged that the Confederate government required that owners send a quota of slaves to the army to directly support the war effort. Ex-slave Tines Kendricks (AR) detailed how the system worked and how cruelly slaves were treated by the Confederate Army:

It was this way, Boss, how come me to be in de War. You see, they 'quired all of de slaveowners to send so many niggers to de army to work diggin' de trenches an' throwin' up de breastworks an' repairin' de railroads what de Yankees done 'stroyed. Every mars was 'quired to send one nigger for every ten dat he had. Iffen you had er hundred niggers, you had to send ten of dem to de army. I was one of dem dat my mars 'quired to send. Dat was de worst times dat dis here nigger ever seen an' de way dem white men drive us niggers, it was something awful. De strap, it was goin' from 'fore day till 'way after night. De niggers, heaps of 'em just fall in dey tracks give out an' them white men layin' de strap on dey backs without ceastin'. Dat was zackly way it was wid dem niggers like me what was in de army work. I had to stand it, Boss, till de War was over.

Debate continues to focus on African Americans' role in the war, the magnitude and nature of their involvement, and whether their participation in the Confederate Army had any meaningful impact on combat (Segars and Barrow 2007). The notion that slaves and free African Americans would willingly support the Confederacy seems improbable and incomprehensible, but some records show that they did in significant numbers (Barrow, Segars, and Rosenburg 2004). Enslaved African Americans may have even supported the Confederate cause, believing that it offered the prospect for their freedom (Harper 2004). However, research also has established that the overwhelming majority of slaves believed that the North winning the war would secure their freedom. There is much evidence that voluntary participation in the Confederate military by slaves was very limited. When a handful of African Americans joined the Confederate Army in the spring of 1865, about 200,000 already had donned Union uniforms (Levine 2006). This numerical difference is testament to where the overwhelming majority of slaves' true sentiments lay.

Slave contributions to the Southern war effort were major, whether voluntary or not, and certainly slaves who became veterans believed that their contributions were significant. Pete Williams (AL) recalled doing much for the Confederate cause: "I done so much work fer de Confed'rates an' cum th'ough widout a scratch, dey orter take kere of me." It should be noted that Southern blacks were among the first to offer their services to the Confederate Army (Harper 2004). Estimates of the number of slaves participating in military efforts vary. In sheer numbers, conservative estimates range between 50,000 and 60,000 African Americans who served in the Confederate military (Barrow, Segars, and Rosenburg 2004). According to McConnell (1950), 104,487 African Americans were procured to serve the Confederate military. Hoar (2004, 71) estimated the number of blacks in the Confederate Army between 1861 and 1865 to be as high as 30,000 or more, and other estimates place the numbers much higher.

There are accounts of African Americans taking up arms to fight Union forces, but these are rare and never approach the magnitude of what occurred on the Union side (Brewer 1969; Jordan 1995; Levine 2006; Musick 2012; Wiley 1938). A Union private in the 5th New Jersey Infantry, Alfred Bellard, in his memoirs reported the shooting of two African American Confederate snipers by members of Berdan's Sharpshooters in April 1862. Bellard (1975, 56) wrote that "One of the Negro Confederates was only wounded, but the other was killed one afternoon after leaving the security of a hollow tree (probably to relieve himself). Two Confederates tried to get to his body but were driven away by the Union gunfire."

Other reports of African Americans in Confederate combat roles exist. Brewer (1969) reported that a small group of African American medical assistants was briefly armed and positioned in trenches at Richmond. Union major Charles S. Wainwright of the 1st New York Artillery wrote of a battle incident in which an African American Confederate sniper "had his own way for some days" (Yee 2007, 144). Yee provided other descriptions and accounts of African American sharpshooters, such as at Yorktown; Chickasaw Bayou; Suffolk, Virginia; and Morris Island in Charleston Harbor, South Carolina. There is some evidence that African Americans serving as armed Confederate soldiers does not hold up to the scrutiny of defining the term "free man of color" (Lowry and Ledoux 2009). There are at least eight instances where the Confederate Army counted persons of mixed European, African, and Native American descent as black Confederate soldiers. It is also known that lighter-skinned African Americans (mulattoes) served in the Confederate Army, with some becoming officers (Jordan 1995). They passed as whites and were undetected in the army.

One of the earliest examples of African Americans being armed and willing to fight for the Southern cause was the formation of Native Guard and militia units in the Deep South. In New Orleans, the 1st Louisiana Native Guard, consisting mostly of free persons of color, French-speaking Creoles, represented a military organization dedicated to fighting for the South. The Louisiana Native Guards had a white commander but also African American officers (Bailey 2006). On November 23, 1861, a parade of military forces, including Louisiana Native Guards, made its way through

New Orleans. Hollandsworth (1995) noted that what made this military parade notable was the inclusion of 33 African American officers and 731 enlisted men in the procession. These Native Guards were formed to protect the South from invasion by the North (Bailey 2006). Unlike white Confederate troops, the Native Guards had to purchase their own uniforms, a requirement that was irritating for some and caused some to abandon Native Guard units (Smith 2002). During the Union capture of New Orleans, Union major general Benjamin Butler attested to their commitment to defend their homeland:

> While I was waiting at Ship Island the Rebel authorities in New Orleans had organized two regiments from the free negroes, calling them National Guards, Colored. When General Lovell, Confederate commander, ran away from the city with his troops on the approach of union forces, these colored soldiers remained. Their organization was complete; the line officers were colored men, and the field officers white.
>
> (Segars and Barrow 2007, 49)

Even with their pro-Confederate motives, the Native Guards were concerning for white Southerners, who feared that arming African Americans posed a tremendous risk of slave insurrection. It was perhaps for this reason that the 1st Louisiana Native Guard was never used in battle, because in January 1862 the Louisiana legislature passed a law that reorganized the militia into only "free white males capable of bearing arms" (Louisiana State Legislature 1862). Fear among Southern whites of arming African Americans was partially due to their memories of the 1831 Nat Turner Rebellion and other slave insurrections (Wesley 1919).

By 1862, a large number of African Americans had been fully integrated into the Confederate Army according to an observation made by Captain Isaac W. Heysinger from Maryland, who wrote of a Confederate unit moving toward Sharpsburg:

> At four o'clock this morning the rebel army began to move from our town, Jackson's forces taking the advance. The most liberal calculation could not have given them more than 64,000 men. Over 3,000 Negroes must be included in that number. These were clad in all kinds of uniforms, not only cast off or captured United States uniforms, but in coats with Southern buttons, State buttons,

etc. They were shabby, but not shabbier or seedier looking than those worn by white men in the rebel ranks. Most of the Negroes had arms, rifles, muskets, sabers, bowie knives, dirks, etc. They were supplied, in many instances, with knapsacks, haversacks, canteens, etc., and were manifestly an integral portion of the Southern Confederacy Army. They were seen riding on horses, mules, driving wagons, raiding on caissons, in ambulances, with the staff of generals, and promiscuously mixed up with all the rebel horde.

(Harper 2004, 22)

A number of these slaves served their masters as body servants and cooks during the war and were pensioned by the state for that service later in life. The names of these slaves are given in the war records of Confederate soldiers. In addition, newspaper accounts provide a source of information about black participation in the Confederate military. The *Montgomery Advertiser* on May 1, 1861, reported the following:

We are informed that Mr. G. C. Hale, of Autauga County, yesterday tendered to Governor [A. B.] Moore the services of a company of negroes, to assist in driving back the horde of abolition sycophants who are now talking so flippantly of reducing to a conquered province the Confederate States of the South. He agrees to command them himself, and guarantees that they will do effective service. What will our Black Republican enemies think of such a movement as this? We have frequently heard the slaves who accompanied their masters to the "scene of action," assert that when fighting was to be done, they wanted to shoulder their muskets and do their share of it, and we do not have a shadow of a doubt but what they would be found perfectly reliable.

(Barrow, Segars, and Rosenburg 2004, 93)

Another account from the *Macon Daily Telegraph*, reprinted in the *Columbus Daily Sun*, on August 1, 1862, read:

We learn of a negro woman, wishing to go "in the war," dressed herself in the uniform of a soldier and went off with the Macon Light Artillery. She was arrested in Augusta and lodged in jail.

(Barrow, Segars, and Rosenburg 2004, 95)

STAYING ON THE PLANTATION OR WORKING
IN THE SOUTHERN FACTORIES

Most slaves stayed on their plantations or accompanied their owners as refugees who were transported deeper into the South, away from the conflict. Maintaining sufficient slave labor on plantations was critical to owners and to the Confederate cause. Slaves had to stay on to care for the crops and livestock and also maintain some degree of economic and social order. Numerous narratives provide descriptions of how slaves remained on plantations or farms serving their owners during the war. Alice Sewell (MO) recalled how slaves worked in the fields growing crops to feed the Confederate Army:

> Dey had to keep de money to care for de families de soldiers left behind, and send corn by de loads to de battlefield to feed de horses. Dey stopped raising cotton after de war started, and just raised food stuff cause dey had to send food to de battlefield for de soldiers.

Sometimes their support could be as simple as making clothing for the troops. Lizzie Gibbs (MS) recalled that "After Mrs. Henry told him goodbye she was so grieved, and to get her mind off the parting Lizzie suggested to her that they go to the school house an open up a sewing circle, where they made clothes all during the war for our soldiers."

The shortage of white labor left the Confederacy with little choice but to put slaves to work in Southern manufacturing. A case in point is the estimated 90 slaves who worked in the Columbus Naval Iron Works in Georgia building ships for the Confederate Navy and also turning out 12-pounders and other small cannons for the Confederate Army (Turner 1988). Pillai (2008) noted that slave contributions in industry and on the battlefield enabled the South to fight on longer than would have been possible otherwise.

Labor was at a high demand during the war, and some owners contracted out their slaves to work on other plantations or serve in the industrial factories, such as the Tredegar Iron Works in Richmond, in mines throughout the South, and in other industries (Franklin and Moss 2000; Jordan 1995). The demands of the war resolved the issue of whether or not slaves could be used effectively, safely, and efficiently in industry. The shortage of white manpower left the South with little choice other than to put slaves to work in its factories and mines. The Tredegar Iron Works, the primary production facility for Confederate artillery, employed thousands of slaves (Engs 2002). Other plants, such as the Confederate Powder Works plant in Augusta, Georgia, were primarily staffed by bondsmen. In 1862 the facility was the second-largest gunpowder factory in the world.

Owners were never enthusiastic about sending their most valuable possession, their slaves, off to war, and Engs (2002) suggests the reasons why. As valuable property, slaves could either be lost as war casualties or, as frequently happened, escape to the North. Owners viewed maimed or wounded slaves as less productive and as less valuable on the auction market. In addition, slaves serving in the war were usually overworked and mistreated in the military, which is documented in some of the narratives and corroborated independently by historians. Consequently, they frequently returned to their plantations exhausted and in very poor physical condition; again, this would also affect their value on the slave market. Many times slaves returned with injuries and illnesses. As a result, Engs (2002) observed that owners would often send their most unruly and rebellious slaves to the military and in doing so better managed their own local resources. This minimized owners' economic risk, although the less manageable slaves were also the most likely to escape to the North. As the Southern defeat became more evident, owners became more reluctant to send slaves to the military; instead, they increasingly clung to their most valuable and transportable slave property.

WHY WOULD AFRICAN AMERICANS WILLFULLY SERVE IN THE CONFEDERATE ARMY?

The reasons for African American participation in support of the Confederacy are complex and sometimes difficult to frame. It should be clear from the beginning that most African American involvement with the army was forced through the institution of slavery. However, loyalty to Southern culture and community, regardless of its oppressive nature, played a role for some slaves. Writing on slaves in Virginia, Jordan (1995, 216) observed that "Afro-Virginians volunteered and supported the Confederacy at the onset of the war even though they had been treated as inferiors and lived in a state of fear." Love of homeland and, yes, even slave devotion to some owners motivated some to continue to serve the South even in light of the obvious gains to be made by the abolishment of slavery. Jordan used the term "Afro-Confederates" to describe pro-Southern blacks who either privately or publicly supported and allied themselves with the Confederacy and called Southern blacks who supported the Union "Afro-Yankees" (xii).

These feelings and attitudes must be understood at the level of human interpersonal relationships. Although not politically popular or defensible in the

This 1862 *Harper's Weekly* cartoon entitled *Who are the nigger worshipers?* shows a Rebel Planter standing between an African American and a Confederate soldier, saying: "Yes, my son, you must go to the war. I can't spare Pomp; he cost me 1200 dollars, and he might get shot. Besides, you know, you coudn't stoop to work like a field-hand!" Plantation owners viewed slaves as property and were reluctant to send them off to war for fear of losing their "property" to escape, death, or dismemberment. This sarcastic cartoon pokes fun at the plantation owners and their preference for property over their sons. (Library of Congress)

modern context, they nevertheless were real to some slaves who lived through the destructive aspects of slavery. "Suffice it to say, black Confederates were not fighting for their own enslavement but sincerely believed that their ultimate freedom, prosperity, and destiny lay south of the Mason-Dixon Line" (Segars and Barrow 2007, 4). This was likely true for some of those not directly serving in the military but supporting the Southern cause. Other explanations have been offered such as that by Brewer (1969), who proposed that slaves continued their subjugation because they were psychologically disabled by oppression. It is equally true that some slaves' ties to the Confederacy and the Southern lifestyle were not strong and that the notion of freedom from oppression motivated them to move north of the Mason-Dixon Line.

McPherson (1993) wrote that local patriotism and the hope of better treatment during and following the war were motivating factors. He theorized that pressure from local officials and fear of impressment also played a part in African Americans being involved on the Confederate side. Some viewed participating as better than not participating and eventually being forced to participate. In addition, Jordan (1995) suggested that some African American Virginians were motivated by a desire to demonstrate their patriotism to the South to whites.

It was also the case for some slaves that they thought of themselves as Southerners or Confederates (Botkin 1945). Some believed that serving the Confederates would bring them nearer to equality with the whites and/or thought that their homeland was being invaded by a hostile Northern army (Segars and Barrow 2007; Wesley 1919). Similar to white Southerners, Southern blacks, slave and free, believed that the North would bring destruction to their homeland unless they resisted (Bailey 2006).

Yet others believed that they would gain their freedom regardless of which side won (Obatala and Maksel 1979). If the Union won they would be freed, and if the Confederacy won they would have earned their freedom by helping save the South. In fact some, such as Lieutenant General Nathan Bedford Forrest, independent of the Emancipation Proclamation, freed his slaves, who remained loyal to him, and he even armed them as bodyguards. However, it should also be remembered that this is the same individual who founded the Ku Klux Klan in Tennessee right after the war.

Some African Americans wanted to protect their homes from the perceived Northern invasion (Obatala and Maksel 1979). Some free blacks, such as those in New Orleans, had achieved relative success, including the ownership of property, and did not want to lose their gains to the North (Hollandsworth 1995). Charles W. Gibbons, a free African American from Louisiana, reported that following the war he joined the Native Guards in New Orleans because he feared losing his property and his life. He believed that having access to guns and ammunition via his participation in the Native Guards helped him defend his life and property (Hollandsworth 1995).

Another reason why some African Americans fought for and supported the South had to do with their ancestry. Hollandsworth (1995) suggested that New Orleans freemen had more in common with Europeans than with slaves living on the plantations. Specifically, he noted that 80 percent of New Orleans' freemen had some European ancestry, compared to 10 percent of Louisiana's plantation slaves. Hollandsworth wrote that these free African Americans had lighter skins and looked more like white Europeans than their slave counterparts living on the plantations.

As to the issue of whether slaves fought out of loyalty and love of the Confederacy, Jordan (1995) believed that African Americans fought because they were loyal to their masters and not because they were committed to the Confederate cause. In addition, body servants had opportunities to earn money while in the military. They could earn money on the side in a variety of ways, such as washing clothes, running errands, cooking, and gleaning items from the battlefield (Wiley 1938).

WHO WERE THEY?

Who were the slaves who went off to war? In addition to slaves who were problematic and as a result were simply shipped off to the Confederate Army, many slaves in the Confederate Army were house servants who had developed personal relationships with their masters. This latter group typically served as body servants to their masters in the field. They tended to be the more privileged or were those who posed fewer problems on the plantation:

> They were primarily able-bodied house servants of the more comfortable whites, rather than field hands; they were male blacks who had shown a willingness and adeptness for literacy and gentle manners, who had often won the hearts of their owner-employers and enjoyed positions of trust and privilege. Often they were treated as family, and this relationship had been true for generations.
>
> (Hoar 2004, 71)

A case in point was Isaac Pringle (MS), who worked as a house boy:

> Dey took me for a house boy, an' when de war started I went all through hit with him. We went to Atlanta an' went in de war in April 1862 an' come out in April 1865. Perryville, Kentucky, in August 1862, I was tied up all day in dat battle. Colonel W. F. Dowd was colonel of de 24th Miss. regiment, ridin' up an' down in front de lines, an', when de first shells come over, hit scared his horse so bad he run away straight through de Yankee army an' we never did see him no mo'.

THE EFFECTS OF THE WAR ON THE CONFEDERATES

The enthusiasm of Confederate soldiers and slave owners going off to war to whip the Union was expressed in many of the narratives. They depict troops marching off to war with great expectations of wreaking havoc on the enemy and expecting a quick and glorious victory. Just as there are accounts of optimism and enthusiasm for the war, there are as many that reflect beaten and downtrodden soldiers after the ravages of war. The return of beaten Confederates as the war turned sour provides a sense of the nightmarish reality of what was happening. Tom McAlpin (AL) provided this vivid description of energized and enthusiastic Confederate soldiers going off to war and their haggard and defeated return:

> But Boss, dere ain't never been nobody afightin' lak our 'Federates done, but dey ain't never had a chance. Dere was jes' too many of dem blue coats for us to lick. I seen our 'Federates go off laughin' an' gay; full of life an' health. Dey was big an' strong, asingin' Dixie an' dey jus knowed dey was agoin' to win. An' boss, I seen 'em come back skin an' bone, dere eyes all sad an' hollow, an' dere clothes all ragged, Boss, dey was all lookin' sick. De sperrit dey lef' wid jus' been done whupped outten dem, but it tuk dem Yankees a long time to do it. Our 'Federates was de bes' fightin' men dat over were. Dere warn't nobody lak our 'Federates.

At the beginning of the war, most citizens on both sides of the conflict assumed that the other side would cave in after a few minor engagements. On both sides, community and citizens rallied to the call of war. Some young men even expressed concern that the war would be over before they had a chance to participate in the glory. Significant numbers of young men enlisted and quickly joined regiments from their respective states, all to the sound of bands, much jubilation, and fanfare. There were exceptions to what would appear to be a cavalier attitude toward the war. General Winfield Scott and a few others did not assume that this would be a war fought in a few weeks but rather that it would be a long and bloody war with heavy casualties on both sides. The narratives reflect both the optimism for the war expressed on both sides and the hard reality of the hell that it actually proved to be.

MANY SLAVES DID NOT WANT TO SERVE IN THE CONFEDERATE ARMY

It is well established that most slaves did not want to serve the Confederate cause, and many took steps to avoid conscription into the military. Joe Nash (MO) spoke of his uncle fleeing to Kansas to avoid fighting for the

Confederates. Joe Clinton (AR) described what happened to a number of slaves who were sent by their masters to help the Confederate Army:

> My mars, he didn't go to de War but he sure sent er lot er corn en he sent erbout three hundred head er big, fat hogs one time dat I 'members. Den too, he sent somepin like twenty er thirty niggers to de Confedrites in Georgia. I 'members it well de time dat he sent dem niggers. They was all young uns, 'bout grown, en dey was skeered to death to be leavin' en goin' to de War. Dey didn't know en cose but what dey gwine make 'em fight. But mars tole 'em dat dey jus' gwine to work diggin' trenches en sich; but dey didn't want to go nohow en Jeff an' Randall, they runned off en come back home all de way from Georgia en mars let 'em stay.

Blacks were not alone in resisting service in the Confederate Army; a few Southern whites also did not want to serve. Mattie Curtis (NC) recalled that "De woods wus full of Rebs what had decerted, but de yankees killed some of dem." Poor whites who were not slave owners had little incentive to fight for the Confederacy. Alice Sewell (MO) provided an accurate account of this situation:

> De poor white folks what lived up in de hilly country, too poor to own slaves, while de war was going on, had to come down out of de hilly country. Dey lived on government land and dey had to have food for dem and der children. Der men folks was taken away from dem to war. Dey was called counterscript soldiers, and if dey refused to go to war dey got shot down like a dog. So de most of 'em rather go on and take chances of de war missing 'em dan get shot widout a doubt. Dey use to say dey had to go and fight a rich man's war but dey couldn't help demselves no better'n us slaves could.

THE SOUTHERN DILEMMA OF ARMING SLAVES

No slave could carry a gun, own property, travel without a pass, testify against whites in a court of law, or learn to read or write (Williams 2008). The Confederate Constitution formalized the prohibition of arming slaves and made it unlawful for a slave to carry a weapon (Bailey 2006). However, it should be noted that the narratives contain references to slaves using guns to hunt for wild game to augment their diets with meat to feed their families (Covey and Eisnach 2009). There can be little question that some slaves were adept at using firearms.

The arming of slaves was a major fear in the South, more so than in the North (Wesley 1919). One reason was that in much of the South, slaves outnumbered whites. To arm the slave majority represented a significant concern of empowerment and a first step toward slave rebellion, of which some Northerners and especially whites in the South had a deep-seated fear (Bailey 2006; Redkey 1992; Wesley 1919). This fear was certainly rational, as illustrated in a letter written by a "colored" soldier of the 25th U.S. Colored Infantry, Fort Pickens, Florida, dated between December 19, 1864, and February 5, 1865:

> The last scout we were on we met the rebs, who had six companies of colored soldiers with them, all armed with guns. As soon as the colored soldiers among the rebs saw our colored troops they threw down their arms and ran over to us, crying out "We are free, we are free!" This comes of putting arms in the hands of slaves to secure their own bondage. It will always be so, for they all know who are their friends.
>
> (Redkey 1992, 153)

The dilemma of arming slaves was not lost on the slaves. Louis Thomas (MO) was well aware of what arming the slaves might have meant:

> If de slaves could get as near as East St. Louis and Ohio without getting caught, dey would join de Yankees and help fight for free- dom. But the Rebs wouldn't think of giving slaves any guns, as mean as they had been to us. Dey knew too well, we would shoot dem first thing.

In a more elaborate description of arming slaves, William Irving (TX) ex- plained the issue the following way:

> De last year of de war de Confederate Government talked about let- tin' de slaves fight wid dem. De slaves dat had not run away wanted to do dis. Dey claim dat de Yankees had two hundred thousand nig- gers fightin for dem, an' de slaves dat stayed wid dey Masters said dey had rather fight for dey Masters dan for strangers. President Davis an' some of de Governors wanted Congress to free de slaves

for fightin, but some how dey never did do anything in Congress about hit. In some places dey did have dem to work on de breast-works when dey have dem whar dey could use dem. In most of de rebel army whar de young boys dat was slaves could be spared from home, dey went wid dey young master, an' cooked an' waited on dem, dey was dey body guards.

Did African Americans fight on the Confederate side during the war? Yes, but this was not openly sanctioned by the Confederate government until the war was essentially lost. Union soldiers frequently reported seeing black soldiers in Confederate units, but Redkey (1992, 7–8) argues that what they saw were "black servants of rebel officers; even though techni-cally civilians, such servants sometimes joined in the fighting to defend their masters." The circumstances may have been such that in the heat of battle, some African Americans would have joined in conflicts out of loy-alty to their masters or for their own self-defense.

There are several accounts of African Americans participating in major battles, such as the First Battle of Bull Run/Manassas in 1861 (Harper 2004). What this indicates is that Southern blacks, both free and slave, were occasionally engaged in armed conflicts with Union forces. William H. Harrison (AR) recalled being with his master during the battles at Get-tysburg, Bull Run/Manassas, and Bulls Gap. It cannot be determined whether he took up arms on the Confederate side but he did serve as a body servant. He did not consider himself a soldier until he was captured by the Union and "made a soldier." He said:

> The son was Gummal L. Harrison. I went with him to war. I was his servant in the battle-field till we fought at Gettysburg and Manassas Gap. Then I was captured at Bulls Gap and brought to Knoxville, Tennessee and made a soldier. I was in the War three and one half years.

Charlie Giles (SC) provided an account of armed slaves when he referred to covering his master and chasing Union soldiers:

> At Petersburg, April 1863, de Yankees act like dey was gwine to blow everything up. I crawl along de ground wid my Marster, and try to keep him kivered as best as I could. Us reached Chica-hominy River and go over to Petersburg. Den dey blow up Richmond. De

river turn to blood while I was looking at it. De cannons deafened me and I has been hard of hearing ever since. Some de blue tails clumb de trees when us got atter dem.

Isaac Stier (MS) mentioned in his narrative how he fought the Yankees. It is not too big of a leap to conclude that he likely fired a weapon in some instances:

When de big war broke out I sho' stuck by my marster. I fit de Yankees same as he did. I went in de battles 'long side o' him an' both fit under Marse Robert E. Lee. I reckon ever'body has heard 'bout him. I seen more folks dan anybody could count. Heaps of 'em was all tore to pieces an' cryin' to God to let 'em die. I toted water to dem in blue de same as dem in gray. Folks wouldn' b'lieve de truf if I was to tell all I knows 'bout dem ongodly times.

Sometimes it is unclear whether a narrative is referring to armed black Confederate soldiers or to white fathers of slaves. For example, Charlie Jeff Harvey (SC) described how his father was wounded at the Second Battle of Bull Run/Manassas but later how he was wounded again and shot at the Yankees. It is unclear whether he was referring to a white father or an African American father:

My own father was shot down for the first time at the Second Battle of Manassas. Here he got a lick over his left eye that was about the size of a bullet; but he said that he thought the lick came from a bit of shell. They carried him to a temporary make-shift hospital that had been improvised behind the breastworks. A soldier who was recovering from a wound nursed him as best he could.

The second time my father was wounded was in Kingston, N.C. He shot a Yankee from behind a tree and he saw the blood spurt from him as he fell. Just about that time he saw another Yankee behind a tree leveling a gun at him. Father threw up his gun but too late, the Yankee shot and tore his arm all to pieces. The bullet went through his arm and struck the corner of his mouth knocking out part of his jaw bone. Then it went under the neck vein and finally it came out on his back knocking a hole in one of his shoulder blades large enough to lay your two thumbs in. His gun stock was also cut into. He lay on the battlefield for a whole day and night; then he was carried to a house where some kind ladies acting as nurses cared for him for over four months. He was sent home and dismissed from the army just a mile below Maybinton, S.C. in Dewberry County. Father was unable to do any kind of work for over two years. The war closed a year after he got home.

SOUTHERN SUPPORT FOR ARMING SLAVES

Although there was reticence about arming slaves, Levine (2006) pointed out basic reasons why some Southerners supported arming them. First, many Southern partisans viewed the institution of slavery as benign and believed that it was beneficial to instill contentment in the lives of slaves. Some Southern partisans also believed that many slaves remained loyal to the South for these reasons, and so arming them would not be a risk. Those with this mind-set believed that blacks and whites understood the order of owner-slave relations, an order in which whites were superior and African Americans were subservient. Thus, there was no motive for African Americans to overturn this order. Another reason was that slavery was not the critical issue for the South in fighting the war; it began as a war for Southern states' control over their own self-government. Toward the end of the war, some leaders of the Confederacy increasingly called for the mobilization of armed black troops, but again it was too late to matter.

Slaves did serve in the U.S. Navy in the antebellum South (Ramold 2002) and became an important element of the Confederate Navy, and up to 5 percent of naval crews were African American (Jordan 1995). Robert E. Lee, Jefferson Davis, and General Patrick Cleburne, among others, urged the South to not only enlist but also to arm blacks. Among the other Confederate generals who favored enlistment of them were Richard Stoddert "Baldy" Ewell, William H. T. Walker, and Ambrose Powell Hill as well as others (Barrow, Segars, and Rosenburg 2004).

The North had demonstrated time and again that black troops were effective in combat. According to McPherson (1993, 245), "By 1864 the Northern example had convinced some Confederate leaders of the value of Negro soldiers. A few Southerners began to wonder out loud why the Confederacy did not take steps to utilize this powerful human resource."

Eventually for some, the survival of the Confederacy became more critical than maintaining the system of slavery (Barrow, Segars, and Rosenburg 2004). On January 2, 1864, Confederate major general Patrick Cleburne and several other Confederate officers proposed using slaves as soldiers since the Union was successfully using black troops. Cleburne drafted a proposal to enlist slaves in the Confederate Army in exchange for their freedom. President Jefferson Davis refused to consider Cleburne's proposal and forbade further discussion of the idea. The concept, however, persisted in spite of Cleburne's death at the disastrous Battle of Franklin (Levine 2006). By the autumn of 1864 the South was losing more and more ground, and some believed that only by arming slaves could defeat be averted. Union victories in the Deep South led to increasing calls for arming slaves (Durden 1972; Levine 2006). Southern awareness of African American adeptness in Union Army combat units had to have played a role in their thinking.

As the war continued and casualties grew, Southern resistance to arming African American soldiers began to fade. In June 1861 early in the war, Tennessee became the first state to legislate the use of free black soldiers for the Confederate cause (Jordan 1995). Acknowledging that they could fight effectively and bravely ran contrary to the Southern white assumption that they were incapable of fighting or of being trusted, similar to the view held by Northerners at the start of the war. It was only when war losses became significant that Confederate leadership changed its position (Barrow, Segars, and Rosenburg 2004). In a letter to Senator Andrew Hunter written in January 1865, General Robert E. Lee strongly recommended black enlistments in the Confederate Army:

> I think therefore we must decide whether slavery shall be extinguished by our enemies and the slaves be used against us, or use them ourselves at the risk of the effects which may be produced upon our social institutions. My own opinion is that we should employ them without delay. I believe that with proper regulations they may be made efficient soldiers. They possess the physical qualifications in a marked degree.
>
> (Segars and Barrow 2007, 6–7)

Expressing the counterpoint to Lee's argument, Confederate general Howell Cobb, owner of a large Georgia plantation, in a January 1865 letter to Confederate secretary of war James A. Seddon wrote that "The proposition to make soldiers of our slaves is the most pernicious idea that has been suggested since the war began. It is to me a source of deep mortification and regret to see the name of that good and great man and soldier, General R. E. Lee, given as authority for such a policy" (Jameson, Bourne, and Schuyler 1896, 97). As one of the strongest dissenting voices, Cobb declared that "If slaves will make good soldiers, our whole theory of slavery is wrong" (Brown and Morgan 2006, 279).

After debating the issue since the outset of the war, the Confederate Congress finally voted during the last days of the Confederacy on the issue of arming slaves. On March 13, 1865, the Confederate Congress authorized letting slaves serve in combat roles. The proposal was signed into law by President Davis on March 18, 1865 (Barrow, Segars, and Rosenburg 2004). An order was issued on March 23, 1865, but only a few African American companies were raised before Lee's surrender. Interestingly, one of these units accompanied Lee to the surrender at Appomattox (Fold3 2012).

The decision to enlist African Americans came in the waning days of the war and had little impact. Military historian Wayne R. Austerman (2004, 48) wrote that "Had Lee, Benjamin, and Davis had their way, slavery would have ended as an act of policy to secure Southern independence. Those who continue to insist that the south fought the war simply to defend slavery should ponder their words in the twilight hour of the Confederacy." By March 1865, all Southerners knew that the Confederacy was doomed, and the capital of Richmond fell less than 30 days later.

From the beginning, some Southern voices put a higher premium on secession and maintaining an independent Confederacy than on maintaining the institution of slavery. Even Jefferson Davis, toward the end of the war, proposed the emancipation of slaves in exchange for their service in the military. And though the legislation approving this did not require emancipation, Davis ensured that emancipation would be rewarded for faithful military service "by having the War Department regulations governing the enlistment of slaves require that masters consent to freedom before slaves could be enrolled" (Cooper 2000, 557). Davis was also politically motivated to abolish slavery in exchange for European diplomatic recognition, which was critical to the perpetuation of the Confederacy, even though he personally believed that slavery was the natural order for blacks since in his opinion they were inferior to whites (Cooper 2000, 553–554).

Some suggest that the Confederate failure to arm slaves in the war was a critical mistake and that had the South done otherwise it might have been victorious, although most historians believe that the reasons for the South's failure were much more numerous than this single issue. While arming slaves might have made some difference, it would not have changed the ultimate outcome of the war. The Union's more extensive and unified developed rail system as well as its telegraph system, factories, and larger

Marlboro Jones (ca. 1860s), slave manservant of Confederate Captain Randal F. Jones of the 7th Georgia Cavalry, sits for an ambrotype dressed in Confederate uniform. An ambrotype was a photograph that created a positive image on a sheet of glass using a wet plate process. In the United States, ambrotypes were first used in the early 1850s. They were very fragile and were usually carried in protective cases. During the Battle of Trevilian Station, Virginia, June 11–12, 1864, Captain Jones was mortally wounded and Jones brought his body back home to Savannah. It was common for slaves to accompany their masters into the Confederate Army and to work as body servants and also common for these servants to accompany their fallen masters' bodies back home. The back of the ambrotype has the words, "Marlboro the faithful slave who protected the women of the family while their husbands were in service—The Civil War." Trevilian Station was the largest all-cavalry battle of the Civil War and resulted in the loss of 735 Union and approximately 1,000 Confederate soldiers. The manservant was the basis for a character in the 1898 novel *Lyddy: A Tale of the Old South* written by Eugenia Jones Bacon (MacKethan 1998). (Courtesy The Museum of the Confederacy, Richmond, Virginia.)

population, in addition to other factors, undoubtedly were too much for the Confederacy to overcome even if slaves had been armed.

SLAVE LABOR WITH THE CONFEDERATE MILITARY

Most African Americans who assisted the Confederate Army were not volunteers but instead were coerced into service. Slaves were either hired out by their owners for monthly fees or were impressed into working for the Confederate Army. Free African American men were forced into service for manual labor. Pressing slave and free black men into service was a pattern that had been in practice in the antebellum South before the war. Local governments often forced the service of African American men to work on roads and public property.

White Southerners, though convinced of African Americans' inherent inferiority, were not reluctant in putting slaves to work in the military in support roles. Tens of thousands of slaves labored for the Confederacy, and for those providing labor on the front lines, the work often was not only more demanding than on the plantation but also more dangerous. The Confederate Army used slaves in a variety of ways, including building fortifications, cooking, serving as teamsters, being musicians, digging latrines, and hauling supplies (Durden 1972; Jordan 1995; Levine 2006; Reid 1950; Wesley 1919). George Kye (AR) served the Confederate Army as a teamster until liberated by Union troops. Jack Maddox (LA) was a laborer for the army. Bill Simms (KS) detailed his war effort: "When the war started, my master sent me to work for the Confederate army. I worked most of the time for three years off and on, hauling canons, driving mules, hauling ammunition, and provisions." In his narrative, Simms described how he was sent home when a Union army closed in on his Confederate unit, and when the army got close to his home he ran away and joined up. He drove a six-mule team hauling ammunition and provisions until the war ended, after which he returned to his old master.

The role of body servant was most common for slaves serving in the military. Slaves would accompany their owner or his sons when going off to war. Some free African Americans served as body servants for wages and because they also wanted to separate themselves from slaves. Freemen believed that publicly integrating and associating with white Confederate troops would enhance their status over slaves (Jordan 1995). A case in point was Samuel Page, who voluntarily worked for pay on the Manassas breastworks and later on an artillery battery until the end of the war. These wartime body servants were seldom armed and seldom fought but served their masters behind the front lines.

Elijah Green's (SC) account is typical of slaves who were used as servants during the war: "I was given to Mr. Wm. Jones's son, Wm. H. Jones as his 'daily give servant' who' duty was to clean his boots, shoes, sword, an' make his coffee." George Rogers (NC) mentioned that he went off with his young master: "His name was William Rogers, an' dey sent me to wait on 'im." Jim Threat (OK) remembered that "Bob Allen went to the war and as he was so used to having somebody to wait on him he took my mother's brother with him to be his special servant." Frank Childress (MS) accompanied his master to the war and served as a body servant and dispatch carrier. Women also served, including Josephine Hyles (TX) who remembered hearing the cannons in the background as she toted water for the soldiers. She also pitched tents, packed horses, prepared meals, maintained equipment, and laundered clothing. Millie Forward's (TX) description was typical: "When de sojers go to de war, every man take a slave to wait on him and take care he camp and cook." Wes Brady (TX) recalled that his

"Daddy went to war as a servant of Josh Calloway" and never came back. James Cornelius (MS) gave the following account of his servitude during the war:

> I heered dem talkin' 'bout de war but I didn' know whut dey meant an' one day Marse Murry said he had jined de Quitman Guards an' was goin'to de war an' I had to go wid him. Old Missus cried an' my mammy cried but I thought it would be fun. Is tuk me 'long an' I waited on him. I kept his boots shinin' to yer could see yer face in 'em. I brung him water an' fed an' cur'ied his hose an' put his saddle on de hose for him. Old Missus tol' me to be good to him an' I was.

A. M. Moore (TX) noted that some Confederates took more than one servant to wait on them: "Lots of the white soldiers from this county took one, two, three and four slaves with them to wait on them." The Confederate Army soon discovered that having slaves accompany their masters to war as servants was a burden on troop movements. An army unit of 2,000 soldiers might have as many as an additional 2,000 slaves in tow, which slowed down the entire unit. In addition, some of these servant slaves escaped to the Union at their first opportunity, and when they did they took with them useful information about troop movements and strengths. So, the idea of servants accompanying their masters to war was later abandoned by the South.

Some slaves who served as body servants also served as bodyguards. Charlie Giles (SC) recalled that "I was Capt. Jack's bodyguard during de whole entire war." Doc Quinn (AR) mentioned that being servants and bodyguards were common roles for slaves, "Because most uf us jined the Confederate Army in Colonel Ogburn's regiment as servants and bodyguards." Allen Price (TX) reported that his father served in a similar capacity: "When dey blockades Galveston, our old master done take my pappy for bodyguard and volunteers to help." Serving in the rear placed many slaves out of immediate danger, but risks were still present and very real. Shade Richards's (GA) interviewer wrote that "Bullets went through Shade's coat and hat many times but 'de Lord was takin' care' of him and he didn't get hurt." Benjamin Johnson (GA) provided a sense of just how close he was to the fighting and how he saw the carnage firsthand:

> When de war broke out ol' marster enlisted an' he took me 'long to wait on him an' to keep his clothes clean. I had plenty o' fun 'cause

dere wus'nt so very much work to do. I 'members seein' 'im fightin'
in Richmond an' Danville, Virginia. I had a good time jes' watchin'
de soldiers fightin'. I did'nt have to fight any at all. I used to stand
in de door of de tent an' watch 'em fight. It wus terrible—you could
hear de guns firin' an' see de soldiers fallin' right an' left. All you
could see wus men gittin' all shot up. One day I seed one soldier git
his head shot off fum his body. Others got arms an' legs shot off.
An' all de time all you could hear wus de guns goin'—bam, bam,
bam—it wus terrible to see an' hear. One mornin' as I wus standin'
in de door of de tent I had a dose of it. I wus leanin' against de side
of de tent wid my hand stretched out a load o' grape shot fum de
guns hit me in de hand an' de blood flew everywhere. I jes' hollered.
It come pretty near scaring me to death. After de doctor got it
patched up [and he held the hand up to exibit (*sic*) the scar] it wus
as good as it every wus.

Some ex-slaves expressed great loyalty to their masters when they went
with them to the army (Harper 2004; Levine 2006). When John Harris, the
son of Charlie Arrons's (AL) master, went to war, Charlie accompanied
him as a bodyguard and servant, looking after the horses and tents at the
Battle of Vicksburg. Charlie expressed his commitment to Harris when he
said, "I loved young Marster John, and he loved me, and I just had to watch
over that boy, and he came through all right." In his narrative, Gus Brown
(AL), who served as a battlefield servant to his master, recalled standing
by his side all the time.

A major role of African Americans on both sides during the war was to
serve as cooks. One of the most famous black Confederate cooks was Jeff
Shields, who cooked for General Thomas J. "Stonewall" Jackson. Shields
survived the war and was a well-recognized figure at many postwar reunions. Emma Chapman (AL) recalled cooking and transporting food for
Confederate soldiers. John Rogers (GA), who did not serve in combat,
said that he was Master Henry's body servant and "jest waited on him,
shined his boots, tended to his hoss, cooked his victuals like he wanted
them cooked, and did everything else I could 'round the camp."

Much effort during the war for both sides went to obtaining supplies.
Adequate food and supplies was rare, but the Union Army was better supplied and equipped than the Confederate Army. However, this fact did not
deter Northern armies from plundering whatever food and wealth they could
from the South. Some ways to offset meager and inadequate food supplies

was to forage, steal, plunder, or beg for food from locals. Many of the ex-slave accounts spoke of both Yankee and Confederate forces taking whatever they wanted from local food supplies. Confederate troops were no different in taking what they needed but were more often supported by Southern locals than were the Yankees, because many of the locals felt that in parting with their resources to Confederates they were supporting the war effort. Obatala and Maksel (1979) noted that the role that African Americans played as foragers in the Confederate Army was an important one.

A few slaves became very resourceful in obtaining food and water for Confederate troops. Tom Bones (MS) described in great detail how he supplied fish to troops near the "Chickihominey River." A relatively famous forager was Howard Divinity (MS), otherwise known as Uncle Divinity. He was born in the 1820s and served in the 12th Mississippi Regiment until the war's end. Uncle Divinity was so successful that he was thought of as the chicken provider for the Confederacy. He was not alone. Mattie Mooreman (AR) recalled how she and others supplied water to Confederate troops:

> Yes ma'am, the Confederates used to come through lots. I remember how we used to go to the spring for water for 'em. Then we'd stand with the buckets on our heads while they drank—drank out of a big gourd. When the buckets was empty we'd go back to the spring for more water.

Some slaves served as medical assistants and nurses, including Pet Franks (MS) who said that "When de war broke out I went right wid de Marster up to Corinth. I stayed up dere in de camp for de longes' time a-waitin' on de sojers an' nussing de sick ones. I never seen much o' de real fightin'. But I heard de cannons roar an' I waited on de sojers what got wounded." Martin Jackson (TX) said he served as an "official lugger-in of men that got wounded, and might have been called a Red Cross worker if we had had such a corps connected with our company." Rose Mercer's (OK) description of how she helped during amputations is vivid. She said:

> I also worked in the hospital at Greenville, Alabama. When they would bring the wounded soldiers into the hospital to have their arms or legs removed, I would hold the ceder "noggins" or pails which were used to catch the blood while the operation was being performed.

Amos Gadsden (SC) provided a similar account of his medical service to the Confederate Army:

> I went to Virginia with Dr. H. E. Bissell in the Army; he was a surgeon. A camp of Negroes went ahead to prepare the roads; pioneers, they called them. I remember Capt. Colcock [he mentioned several other officers], Honey Hill—terrible fighting—fight and fight! had to "platoon" it. I was behind the fighting with Dr. Bissell. I held arms and legs while he cut them off, till after a while I didn't mind it.

Some Southerners opened their homes up to take care of Confederate casualties. Ellen Claibourn (GA) spoke of her mistress caring for the war casualties in her home:

> During the war mistis had one room all fixed up to take care of sick soldiers. They would come stragglin' in, all sick or shot, an' sometimes we had a room full of 'em. Mistis had one young boy to do nothin' but look after 'em and many's the night I got up and helt the candle for 'em to see the way to the room.

Ella Belle Ramsey's (TX) memories of a Confederate hospital in Atlanta capture the misery that wounded soldiers and civilians experienced:

> After de War commence de Mistress make me help her prepare for de soldiers. Atlanta was crawling wit' soldiers den. Confederates was everywhere 'round dere. Dey open a soldiers' hospital dere an' de ladies take turns waiting on de sick soldiers. Mis' Goldsmith was one of de first ladies to help 'em. I use to go to de hospital wit' 'em an' carry her stuff. She always take 'em something to eat jes' like everybody do when dey go to a hospital. But I always hate to go dere. It was jes' a little wood building wit' cots in it for de soldiers to lay on, but de men was always screaming an' groaning an' taking on an' it stuck in my ears. I could hear 'em all night when I wen' dere in de day time. De ladies knit socks an' sweaters for de soldiers an' Mis' Goldsmith done her share dere too an' den some more.

Tom McAlpin (AL) recalled how he was sent to Richmond to bring home war casualties: "I was sont to Richmond to bring home some of our wounded 'Federates. They sont me caze dey knowed I warn't afeered of nothin'."

Slaves were also very involved in war-related construction. Franklin (1965, 1967) noted that blacks helped build fortifications and worked on many of the massive earthen breastworks throughout the South (Barrow, Segars, and Rosenburg 2004). The narratives mention slave contributions to the defensive installations at Vicksburg, Atlanta, and other locations. Ellen Campbell's (GA) narrative also referred to building breastworks, as interpreted by her interviewer:

> When asked about war times on the plantation Ellen recalled that when the Northern troops were around Waynesboro orders were sent to all the masters of the nearby plantations to send ten of their best men to build breastworks to hold back the northern advance.

Shade Richards's (GA) brother helped lay the railroad from Atlanta to Macon so Confederate soldiers and ammunition could move faster. John Rogers (GA) mentioned numerous roles that he played in supporting the Confederate Army: "Mostly, I dug ditches around de camp." In the first year of the war, blacks received into state or Confederate laboring units were substantially employed building fortifications and breastworks, raising crops, casting cannons, and working as teamsters, locomotive firemen, and hospital nurses (Harper 2004, 10). Cora Gillam (AR) said that slaves were used to build military sites for the South, such as a fort to protect Little Rock, Arkansas: "You see, so many white folks loaned their slaves to cessioners [Secessionists] to help build forts all over the state." Ella Belle Ramsey (TX) said that "De Confederates made 'em work helping 'em build bridges an' things dey need." Sam Kilgore (TX) remembered being sent to Birmingham, Alabama, to help build breastworks for General Lee that were never used. Kilgore was then sent to Lexington and Louisville, Kentucky, to do the same. Austin Pen Parnell (AR) said that his father went to war on the Confederate side as a laborer: "They cut down all the timber 'round the place where they were to keep the Yankee gunboats from shelling them and knocking the logs down on them."

The Confederacy impressed 900 enslaved laborers to build the notorious prison at Andersonville, Georgia (Davis 2007). Ex-slave Tines Kendricks (AR) spoke of building Camp Sumter, more commonly known as Andersonville Prison, and the conditions there:

> Did you ever hear 'bout de Andersonville prison in Georgia? I tell you, Boss, dat was about de worstest place dat ever I seen. . . . They would

just throw de grub to 'em. De mostest dat dey had for 'em to eat was
peas an' the filth, it was terrible. De sickness, it broke out 'mongst 'em
all de while, an dey just die like rats what been pizened [poisoned].

The unpleasant duty of burying the dead often fell to the slaves. A number
of WPA narratives contain references to this most unsanitary and foul-
smelling of jobs. Doc Quinn (AR) described it thusly: "And de onliest way
to bury dem was to cut a deep furrow wid a plow, lay de soldiers head to
head, an' plow de dirt back on dem." Charlie Sandles (TX) said that "Them
soldiers they fought all around us, and I'se helped pick up and bury lots of
them poor boys." A few sentences later he said:

> What I started to tell you, there was a white man there helping with
> the wounded and dead boys, and if he found one that he thought
> would not get well, he would hit that soldier on the back of his
> head and finish him up, then roll them all in a big hole together and
> pile the dirt over them. I did not help him much cause I'se got to
> where I would see spooks and he let me burn and bury the dead
> horses that was killed. I did not mind that like I did to bury them
> dead soldiers.

Louvenia Huff (AR) spoke of her grandfather and his responsibilities for
the dead:

> Father was a driver in the Civil War. He hauled soldiers and dumped
> them in the river. The Union soldiers wouldn't give them time to
> bury the other side. He took rations all but the times he hauled dead
> soldiers.

Ned Broadus (TX) told of the horror of recovering the wounded and dead
from battlefields:

> Dat war was shore a bad un. All us field niggers didn't hab no sense
> wid a gun. Dey sont us atter de battle out on de field to bring in de
> bodies of de dead an' wounded back to camp. It wa'n't no right wuk
> fo' me but I had to do it. Dem bodies handled like logs. Dere was
> my young Marses all cut up an' blood all ober dem an' dey beggin'
> ole Ned to gib 'em jus' a drink an' a easy place to lie an' moanin'
> an' it was dark an' I jus' don' lak to tell 'bout dat time, Miss.

This gruesome scene depicts the unpleasant job of burying the remains of fallen Union soldiers from the June 1864 battles of Gaines' Mill and Cold Harbor. This task has fallen to a group of black men doing the menial work while a white man standing at upper left acts as overseer. The man seated in the center, next to the stretcher laden with human parts, looks directly at the camera, revealing no emotion that can be reconciled with his grisly cargo. Already reduced to nothing more than a pile of bones, these bodies lay unburied for ten months until the war's end, while the blistering heat and humidity of the Virginia summer hastened their decomposition. It was common for bodies to remain where they had fallen for long periods following battles, such as was the case at Cold Harbor (Faust 2008). Local residents usually came forth to give a proper burial to the enemy troops that fell near their homes, but the scale of the casualties here—nearly sixty thousand Union soldiers were killed or wounded in this area—precluded this courtesy. Photo was taken in April 1865 by John Reekie, a Brady studio photographer, who shot many images of burying the Civil War dead, all graphically portraying the horrors of war. (Library of Congress)

Burying the dead left lasting impressions on many who carried out this duty. For at least one slave and perhaps others, burying the dead resulted in haunting memories that lasted long after the war. Charlie Cooper (TX) said:

> I'se seen several ghost 'specially after the war between the States.
> I'se had to help bury them dead soldiers. Boss, I'se never did sleep
> any much while that war was going on. One night while I was plum

sound asleep one of them soldiers they just walked right in the room and called Charlie, Charlie. Then the last time, he hollered Charlie real loud and wake me up and there he stood in the door. I set up in bed and ask him what he wanted, and you know he would not answer me no more. Just stood right there in that door. All of a sudden like he just completely disappeared and I could not see how he left like that.

On some occasions, slaves demonstrated their loyalty to their masters by staying with them even in death. Accounts of loyal slaves remaining with their fallen masters' bodies and accompanying the bodies home for burial have been documented (Harper 2004). O. W. Green (TX) told of his grandfather being a "wagon man," who on "De las' trip he made, he come home bringin' a load of dead soldiers to be buried."

OBSERVATIONS

African Americans, whether free or enslaved, were not passive bystanders to the Confederate cause. They supported, opposed, participated in, avoided, and undercut Confederate military efforts. Their involvement on the Union side is easily understood, but their support of the Confederacy is less easily comprehended. We do know that Southern blacks did not volunteer or enlist in the Confederate Army in any great numbers, partly for understandable reasons and partly because they were not allowed to as soldiers until very late in the war. They certainly did not enlist in the great numbers predicted by some supporters of the Confederacy. In Virginia, government officials estimated that between 4,000 and 5,000 free black Virginians would enlist in the Confederate Army when given the opportunity, but in reality that turned out to be between 40 to 50 enlistees (Levine 2006). Confederate propagandists clearly and consistently overstated slave loyalty to the South. Had Confederate leaders truly believed in slave loyalty and commitment to their cause, they would have more comfortably and rapidly armed slaves to fight rather than wait until the war was virtually over.

This is not to suggest that a few Southern blacks did not willfully support the South. Why some supported the very system that oppressed them was due more to personal relationships with their masters and their communities than to any other political cause, such as states' rights or the prospect of emancipation. Some were clearly motivated by self-survival, others by patriotism, and yet others by economic interest (Jordan 1995). To say that most slaves wanted freedom and to be viewed as equal are givens. To conclude that this desire was sometimes overpowered by personal relationships and loyalties, while not politically correct in a modern context, does characterize how some slaves must have felt. The narratives will not resolve this debate but instead will only fuel the controversy. As Isaac Potter (MS) would share:

> When de War come on I recon I jined hit. I wuked in de camp fer a long time. I was already trained ter look after horses an' be handy at eber ting in general. I injied watching de soldiers drill an' de sham battles. I was a takin' hit all in; soon I knowed how to march and draw de gun—hit was like dis [in his semi-blindness marched back and forth going through the motions]. I neber could understand why de soldiers could be so cheerful knowing dey might git kilt any time. Dey would sing an' dance an' joke all de time, right up to de time dey was called to battle. I've saw 'em come in after a hard battle, when de northern soldiers would be campin' near, dey would go to each other's camps an' swap coffee an' tobacco. Dey would laugh and wrestle an' hab de biggest time. When dey would part for de nite dey would say to each other, "We'll give you hell tomorrow." Long toward de end ob de War de southern soldiers got so hungry, de Calverymen had come through and destroyed eberthing ter eat. I have saw big army wagons wid dem big wheels run over big frogs, mashing dem flat as a rag, an' de soldiers come 'long an' shake de dust off an' eat 'em. Dey would eat horse flesh. I have eaten it and liked it a number of times.

Brasher (2012) recognized the presence of slaves in Confederate ranks but notes that those who might have shot at Yankees may have done so for reasons that had little to do with loyalty to the Confederate cause. Other historians, such as Harrison (2004), Lunsford (2004), and Barrow, Segars, and Rosenburg (2004), might reach a different conclusion. The best and most general summation is that most slaves did not willfully support the Confederate cause but did what they had to do to survive.

CHAPTER 7

The Day the Yankees Came

De Yankees got to de place and 'gin ransack it. Old Missy done lock dat stormhouse door and set down on it and she wouldn't git up when dey done tell her to. So dey takes her by de arms and lifts her off it. Dey didn't hurt her any. Den dey breaks de lock and comes down in dere. I didn't see why dey hadn't already found us kids, 'cause my heart beatin' like de hammer. Dey turned dat hogshead [large wooden cask] over and all us kids skinned out dere like de Devil after us. One de Yanks hollers, "Look what we done hatch out!" I tore out past de barn, thinkin' I'd go to mama, in de field, but it look like all de Yanks in de world jumpin' dere hosses over dat fence, so I whirls round and run in dat barn and dives in a stack of hay and buries myself so deep de folks like to never found me. Dey hunted all over de place befo' dey done found me. Us kids scart 'cause we done see dem Yanks' bayonets and thunk dey was dere horns.

(John Day, TX)

The day the Yankees came left lasting and deep impressions on many of the Works Progress Administration respondents. Some impressions were positive while others were negative, and such feelings remained so over the years. The memories of those experiences remained deeply embedded in the ex-slaves. Common elements of their recollections were the impressive blue uniforms or the shinny brass buttons of the Yankees, as Northern soldiers were disparagingly referenced by Southerners and slaves. It must have been quite a special occasion when the blue coats arrived compared to the Confederate troops, outfitted in their increasingly ragged uniforms. Harry Johnson (TX) recalled what he saw when Union forces arrived:

Dey was de cavalry. Dey had on very stylish jackets with tassels on dem, an' dere brass plates an' buttons shine like gol'. Dey shore was pretty. But dey was a tough-looking cavalry. Dey had sabres an' cutlass, an' dey'd holler, "Right! Left! Cut!" Dey shore had a pretty band. You'd think dey was harps from heaven dey play so pretty.

In a similar vein, Emma Blalock (NC) remembered Yankees dressed in blue uniforms with brass buttons: "I shore de 'member de Yankees wid dere blue uniforms wid brass buttons on 'em." Zeb Crowder (NC) also noted their appearance: "Yes sir, I seed de Yankees and I remember de clothes dey wore. Dey were blue and dere coats had capes on 'em and large brass buttons." Caroline Richardson (NC) said, "Yes mam, I 'members de blue uniforms an' de brass buttons, an' I 'members how dey said as dey come in de gate dat dey has as good as won de war, an' dat dey ort ter hang de southern men what won't go ter war." Georgiana Foster (NC) recalled their clothes: "I jes' can 'member de Yankees comin' through, but I 'members dere wus a lot of 'em wearin' blue clothes." Betty Brown (MO) said, "Dah was de' blue-coats'; some O' de folks call 'em 'Bluebelly Yank's, dey had fine blue coats an' the brass buttone all ovuh the front o' 'em shinin' like stahs." Rachel Cruze (OH) was taken in by the appearance of the Yankees. She saw their uniforms as "purty" compared to the drab uniforms of soldiers during the Great Depression of the 1930s. She added that "the blue of those Union uniforms was a beautiful bright shade, and all the men had those lovely capes lined in red, and bell pants coming well over the foot." Eva Martin (TX) had a similar description: "I 'member dey had pretty caps on wid pretty yaller t'ing on 'em, a bird like a eagle. . . . It was pretty shiny yaller like dat shiny t'ing on de en' of your pencil." Bud Jones (TX) recalled as vividly as if it had happened yesterday what he witnessed when the Yankees first appeared:

> I went into Lynchburg with old master in a buggy. We seen the blue bellies sojers. They was dressed up in the finest toggery I ever seen. They had big caps with tassels on them and pretty blue suits. They had big cannon guns on wheels. They went marching to a band and the drums were playin' to the way they steps up and down. They had the finest carriages; some of them drawn by a span of four horses. They was a extra fine carriage with six fine horses hitched up to it. I heared it was General Grant the biggest blue belly of all that rid in it. I never did see no call to call them blue bellies. I dont thing they had blue bellies. Leastways they looked alright to me.

These and other recollections of Yankees in uniform should not come as a surprise given the clothing of slaves and the uniforms of Confederate forces. The appearance of uniformed Yankees stood in stark contrast to the prevailing dress of most Southerners during the war. Most slaves were rationed minimal quantities of clothing. Shoes and boots were scarce if available at all, and what clothing was available lasted until threadbare.

In sharp contrast were some of the narrative observations of the Confederate forces. It is well established that the Confederate military was less equipped to fight the war than the Union, and this was reflected in part by the tattered clothing worn by troops as the war progressed. Samuel Sutton (OH) used the adjective "fine" when he described Union troops, but he was less flattering in describing Rebel troops: "But de Rebels now, I recollect day had no uniforms fo dey was hard up, an dey cum in jes common clothes." Martin Jackson (TX) characterized Rebel troops as a "sorry-lookin' bunch of lost sheep. They didn't know where to go, but most of 'em ended up pretty close to the towns they started from." He also said that "They was like homing pigeons, with only the instinct to go home and, yet, most of them had no homes to go to." William Irving's (TX) account of Sherman's March to the Sea contains a reference to Confederate general John Bell Hood's troops in Tennessee and the condition of their shoeless feet and tattered clothing:

> His soljers was ragged an' bloody dey say, an' widout food, w'en de Yankees was following dem, dey had to put de infantry men in de wagon for dey feet was barefooted an' dey had to stop long enough fer dem to skin a mule or cow dat had been killed to get de hide to make dey sandals. Dey even took dey felt hats, if dey had any, to make moccasons for dey feet.

YANKEES AS LIBERATORS AND HEROES

Many slaves welcomed the arrival of Union troops. For some slaves, this meant not only liberation (see Chapter 9) but also that they would benefit in more immediate ways. Callie Elder (GA) recalled that the Yankees took everything they wanted and gave the rest to the slaves. When the Yankees left, William Neal's slaves returned everything back to their master because he had been good to them. It was a common occurrence for Yankee troops to open food stores and clothing supplies to resident slaves. For example, John Smith (NC) said, "I had no clothes and shoes till de Yankees come. Dey gimme clothes and shoes, but I slipped away from 'em because dey wanted me to do things I didn' want to do."

A Thomas Nast illustration of a southern plantation that appeared in *Harper's Weekly* newspaper on April 4, 1863. The Nast print, entitled *Arrival of a Federal Column at a Planter's House in Dixie*, shows a group of Union soldiers arriving at a plantation. Three women, who appear confused, stand on the porch steps as men, women, and children gather around the Federal Column. A Union officer tips his hat to the women while a soldier is shown gallantly posing in the center right of the image with his eyes looking toward the heavens. Southern men are not obvious as they were likely off fighting the war. The recently liberated slaves are celebrating because of their newly found freedom. In the foreground, one slave is shown bowing in gratitude to one of the Union soldiers as an older slave respectfully bows and tips his hat to the same soldier. (Courtesy Wisconsin Historical Society, Image ID: 82138.)

Ryer Emmanuel (SC) viewed Yankees as heroes because of the food they left behind for slaves. The Yankees did not bother slave children but would take the master's food and prepare it during visits to the plantation. Emmanuel reported that Union soldiers would kill livestock and cook it on the spot. When they had eaten their fill, they would let slave children eat what remained. Emmanuel said hunger was felt by many slaves on his plantation, and they were grateful to have these windfalls of food. He also noted that his widowed mother did not receive anything from her master:

Oh, Lord, us was glad to get dem vitals, too. Yes, mam, all dey had left, dey would give it to de poor colored people. Us been so glad, us say dat us wish dey would come back again. Den after dey had left us plantation, dey would go some other place where dere was another crowd of little niggers en would left dem a pile of stuff, too. Old Massa, he been stay in de swamp till he hear dem Yankees been leave dere en den he come home en would keep sendin to de colored people houses to get a little bit of his rations to a time. Uncle Solomon en Sipp en Leve, dey been eat much of boss' rations dey wanted cause dey been know de Yankees was comin back through to free dem. But my mammy, she was a widow woman en old man Anthony Ross never left nothin to her house.

THE APPEARANCE OF YANKEES WAS MET
WITH MIXED REACTIONS

When Union troops began overrunning the South, it was not always a welcome sight to slaves. John Beckwith (NC) thought he had a pretty good life and did not challenge the fact that he was born into bondage. For Beckwith, having his basic needs met and having an enduring personal relationship with his owner were more important than the prospect of his freedom. Beckwith did not question the fact that his mother was working in the fields and could not be with him as a small child. Instead, he was raised by "de missus." He may have bonded as much to his white caretaker as he did his own family members. Beckwith spoke of his happiness and the disruption caused when the Yankees raided his owners' property:

> When dey told us dat de Yankees was comin' we was also told dat iffen we didn't behave dat we'd be shot; an' we believed it. We would'uv behaved anyhow, case we had good plank houses, good food, an' shoes. We had Saturday an' Sunday off an' we was happy.
>
> De missus, she raised de nigger babies so's de mammies could wuck. I 'members de times when she rock me ter sleep an' put me ter bed in her own bed. I was happy den as I thinks back of it, until dem Yankees come.
>
> Dey come on a Chuesday; an' dey started by burnin' de cotton house an' killin' most of de chickens an' pigs. Way atter awhile dey fin's de cellar an' dey drinks brandy till dey gits wobbly in de legs. Atter dat dey comes up on de front porch an' calls my missus. When she comes ter de do' dey tells her dat dey am goin' in de house ter look things over. My missus dejicts, case ole marster am away at de war, but dat doan do no good. Dey cusses her scan'lous an' dey

dares her ter speak. Dey robs de house, takin' dere knives an' split-
tin' mattresses, pillows an' ever' thing open lookin' fer valerables,
an' ole missus dasen't open her mouth.

    Dey camped dar in de grove fer two days, de officers takin' de
house an' missus leavin' home an' goin' ter de neighbor's house.
Dey make me stay dar in de house wid 'em ter tote dere brandy
frum de cellar, an' ter make 'em some mint jelup. Well, on de secon'
night dar come de wust storm I'se eber seed. De lightnin' flash, de
thrunder roll, an' de house shook an' rattle lak a earthquake had
struck it.

But not all interaction between Union soldiers and slaves ended negatively.
Another basic scenario in the narratives was that during their plundering,
some Yankee troops would share their spoils with the slaves. For example,
Sarah Harris (NC) remembered that "I can see how de chickens and guin-
eas flew and run from 'em. . . . De Yankees killed 'em and give part of 'em
to the colored folks." Jim Threat (OK) recalled Yankees distributing food
to slaves but also destroying much of it:

    The next morning after the Yankees camped at our house the captain
    put me and my brother on a horse and told us to go show him where
    old man Kelso lived. When we got there the old man was setting in
    the yard in the shade and the cap'n ordered his men to go to the
    smokehouse and bust it open. You never saw the like of fine meat.
    He divided it out among the slaves. There must have been at least a
    thousand pounds of flour they busted the ends out of the barrels and
    just scattered it all over the place. Next they emptied three hogs-
    heads of lard. There was about twenty barrels of New Orleans mo-
    lasses, they split the barrels and let the syrup all spill. You never saw
    such a mess of flour, lard and syrup. They got on their horses and
    went on their way and old man Kelso didn't say a word.

Other accounts portray Yankees in a more positive light. Malinda Murphy
(MO) remembered how she and others were invited to eat with them:

    When de soldiers came we had a good meal. De soldiers had on
    blue coats, and when dey came we would be switching off de flies
    with a long pole with paper on the end. De soldiers would then say
    "We don' need that, come on and eat with us."

When the Yankees came, some slaves, emboldened by the appearance of soldiers in blue coats, took advantage of the opportunity to settle old scores with cruel owners. In his narrative, Jim Threat (OK) shared a story of how the Yankees imparted justice on both his owner and a particularly mean neighboring owner. Threat told of how the Yankees came to his master's property, took the guns from the owner's house, and broke them and then took all the corn and fed it to their 300 horses. Next, the Yankees turned their attention to the neighbor:

> We had a neighbor named Kelso who was terrible mean to his nig-gers. He had about seventy-five and all he fed them was cottonseed boiled and thickened with corn meal. This was poured into long troughs and the people ate it with wooden spoons. Most any night you could see a light in his gin house till nine o'clock and you could hear them beating some one and hear them crying, "Oh, pray Mas-ter." Every body knowed how mean he was and several times the white men in the country went to him and tried to git him to treat them better but he kept it up.

Not all slaves took advantage of what the Yankees offered. The slaves on Melissa Munson's (MS) plantation returned sugar back to their owner after the Yankees left. Whether their motive was loyalty, fear of reprisal, or something else was not disclosed.

> Ole Marster had barrels of brown sugar dat he brought from de market once a year, an' dey 'vided de sugar an' all de s'plies amongst us niggers an' tol' us to have a feast. But we didn't have no feast. No, mam. When dem Yankees got gone we went an' carried ever speck of dem eats back an' give 'em to Old Marster.

FEAR OF YANKEES AS AN INSTRUMENT OF CONTROL

A good number of slaves feared the day when the Yankees would arrive because they had lived in an environment where virtually everything they had heard about the Yankees was negative. To limit slaves from communi-cating and consorting with the Yankees, Southerners often demonized them and characterized them as being banshees, which were evil spirits that haunted the swamps of the South and would harm and perhaps kill Southerners (Ward 2008). Susie King Taylor wrote a firsthand account of being a black Civil War nurse. In her memories of the war, published in 1902, she shared her grandmother's insight into why slaves were taught to fear the Yankees:

> I had been reading so much about the "Yankees" I was very anxious to see them. The whites would tell their colored people not to go to the Yankees, for they would harness them to carts and make them pull carts around in place of horses. I asked grandmother, one day, if this was true. She replied, "Certainly not!" that the white people did not want slaves to go over to the Yankees, and told them these things to frighten them.
>
> (Taylor 1902, 7–8)

Owners seldom missed opportunities to create or reinforce the fear that slaves had of Yankees. Steve Jones (TX) recalled that as cannons roared in the background, his master told him "that is them blue bellies coming after you, that's what they called them Yankees." Charlie Crump (NC) believed that the Yankees would skin him alive. William Mathews (TX) believed that the Yankees would kill him, and he recalled that "Some say de Yankees fight for freedom and some say dey'll kill all de slaves." Reverend Squire Dowd (NC) said that he "did not like the Yankees" because "We were afraid of them. We had to be educated to love de Yankees, and to know that they freed us and were our friends." Melissa Williamson (NC) said, "We was told dat de Yankees would kill us an' we was skeered of dem too, an' I was always runnin' fer fear de Yankees would git me." Letha Taylor Meeks's (MO) reaction to their approach was typical; she ran to warn the others. When she looked down the grove and spotted the Yankees, she ran "back to de house ahollerin' 'De Yankees is comin.'"

Richard Franklin (OK) worried that the Yankees would kill him: "I went back home for I thought the Yankees would kill me, because my master told me that the Yankees were bad people." Jennie Small (OH) acknowledged that "We were always taught to fear the Yankees." Some slaves, such as Chane Littlejohn (NC), thought that Yankees actually had blue bellies. James Gill (AR) had been told that Yankees had horns and was surprised to discover they did not:

> But de Yankees, dey didn' know dat we was Confedrits, dey jus' reckon we like most all de res' of de niggers. Us was skeered of dem Yankees though 'cause us chillun cose didn' know what dey

was and de oberseer, Jim Lynch, dey done tole us little uns dat a Yankee was somepin what had one great big horn on he haid and just one eye and dat right in de middle of he breast and, boss, I sure was s'prized when I seen a sure 'nough Yankee and see he was a man just like any er de res' of de folks.

J. H. Day (TX) reported a similar perception of Yankees that was held by slave children. Day recalled that slave children believed that Yankees were so evil they had horns. Day said, "We kids was all scared of de Yankees as we could be because de grown folks told us that de Yankees had horns." Henry Barnes (AL) recalled:

Den, I 'members atter I growed up dey tell 'bout how de Yankees comin' here an' how dey pester de white folks an' de niggers, too. Broke in dey smoke-houses, burn 'em up an' t'row t'ings away an' lef' nobody nuttin' to eat. I don't 'member dat 'cuz I was too li'l.

Steve Jones (TX) described how he feared Yankees as they approached his plantation:

I'se member one day when I was with Maser feeding the mules we was going to a place out close to Chattanooga and we heard the canons roaring. Maser says: did I'se knows what that racket was—and I'se says no. He say that is them blue bellies coming after you, that's what they called them Yankees. I'se so scared he couldn't get me way from his coat-tail. When the Civil War ended I'se in Richmond, Virgina, when Vicksburg surrendered. The day we is sot free it was bout 8 o'clock in the morning. Maser told my papa we could go anywhere where now we wants to go cause we is freed.

Andrew Boone's (NC) comments reveal his trepidation borne of Southern propaganda versus what actually happened:

I wus afraid of de Yankees 'cause de Rebels had told us dat de Yankees would kill us. Dey tole us dat de Yankees would bore holes in our shoulders an' wurk us to carts. Dey tole us we would be treated a lot worser den dey wus treating us well, de Yankees got here but they treated us fine.

Fear can be an effective tool in controlling any group, including slaves. Portraying Yankees as evil demons helped instill a fear among slave populations. Children were particularly susceptible to folklore and misinformation. Beckwith's response to the Yankees was typical for some slaves. In addition, some slaves identified with their masters and believed that what their masters owned was also theirs. They were taught and believed that the Yankees were trying to take everything away (Ward 2008). Jennylin Dunn (NC) remembered as a small child that she and others were told that Yankees would harm black children. She said, "When dey hyard dat de Yankees was on dere way ter hyar dey says ter us dat d em Yankees eats little nigger youngins, an' we shore stays hid."

Slaves had encounters throughout the war with both Confederate and Union troops that ran the gamut from positive to very negative. Sarah Debro (NC) recalled experiences with troops from both sides that showed the callous and dreadful nature of the war in her eyes. First, the encounter with Confederates:

I 'members when Wheeler's Cavalry come through. Dey was 'Federates but dey was mean as de Yankees. Dey stold everything dey could find an' killed a pile of niggers. Dey come 'roun' checkin'. Dey ax de niggahs if dey wanted to be free. If dey say yes, den dey shot dem down, but if dey say no, dey let dem alone. Dey took three of my uncles out in de woods an' shot dey faces off.

And then the Yankees:

I 'members de first time de Yankees come. Dey come gallupin' down de road, jumpin' over de palin's, tromplin' down de rose bushes an' messin' up de flower beds. Dey stomped all over de house, in de kitchen, pantries, smoke house, an' everywhere, but dey didn' find much, kaze near 'bout everytiing done been hid. I was settin' on de steps when a biig Yankee come up. He had on a cap an' his eyes was mean.

"Whare did dey hide do gol' an silver, Nigger?" he yelled at me. I was skeered an my hands was ashy, but I tole him I didn' [know] nothin' 'bout nothing; dat if anybody done his things dey hid it while I was sleep.

When the war was over, things got no better in Debro's opinion, and interaction with Yankees was just as dismal. Her parents moved off the plantation to housing built by Yankee soldiers, and she found herself hungry and struggling against soldiers who would force themselves on her:

> When de war was over de Yankees was all 'roun' de place tellin' de niggers what to do. . . . Dem was bad days. I'd rather been a slave den to been hired out like I was, kaze I wuzn' no fiel' hand, I was a hand maid, trained to wait on de ladies. Den too, I was hungry most of de time an' had to keep fightin' off dem Yankee mens. Dem Yankees was mean folks.

Some Yankees blamed the slaves for causing the war and as a result openly confronted them. The narrative of Blount Baker (NC) contains such a reference. In recalling how his master discussed the war and the "yaller bellied Yankees," Baker told his interviewer that "We ain't seed no Yankees 'cept a few huntin' Rebs. Dey talk mean ter us an' one of dem says dat we niggers am de cause of de war." Baker responded, "'Sir,' I sez, 'folks what am a wantin' a war can always find a cause.'"

However, some slaves were not scared, as Sarah Ann Green (NC) shared: "I wuzn' skeered of de Yankees." They welcomed the day when the Yankees would arrive. Louisa Adams (NC) offered a similar response to the arrival of the Yankees: "It didn't sturb me at tall. I was not afraid of de Yankees." Margaret Hughes (SC) told of how she was scared, but her aunt was not:

> When I used to hear de older niggers talking 'bout de Yankees coming, I was scared, 'cause I thought it was some kind of animal they was talking 'bout. My old aunty was glad to hear 'bout de Yankees coming. She just set and talk 'bout what a good time we was going to have after de Yankees come. She'd say, "Child we going to have such a good time a settin' at de white folks table, a eating off de white folks table, and a rocking in de big rocking chair."

HIDING FROM THE YANKEES

When it became apparent that the Yankees were near, many owners and slaves prepared for their arrival by hiding valuables, supplies, food, and even themselves. Examples include Fannie Dunn (NC), who did not know her age but remembered the day the Yankees came. Like many slaves, she hid from them. In her case, being a little girl, she hid under the bed.

Andrews Moss (TN) said, "I hit it out from dar and hide behind two little hills down by de big spring." Annie Groves Scott (OK) spoke of how her owner warned of the Yankees coming and how anything of worth needed to be hidden from them:

> The master was always afraid of the Yankees coming and one day during the war he called Maw and some of the other slaves in one of the big rooms and say to them, "The damn Yanks ain't here, but they is coming soon enough! They'll take everything on the place unless we hide it. That's what I want you all to do, hide the lard, put the meats in a hard place and all the trinkets of things that you don't want to lose."

Robert Laird's (MS) owners hid him from the approaching Yankees. He willfully cooperated because he feared what they might do to him:

> We was scared ob de yankees an' while de war was gwine on dey was having a battle over at Vicksburg, Mississippi. We could hear de cannons an' see de lights. I can tell yo' us was all a scart a plenty. One day Ole Missus heard de yankees a commin', right in de middle dat awful battle dey hid de slaves. I can recollect dey hid me in de barn. I was under some hay an' to scart to breath. I was dier, still an' quiet till I thought I was a gwine to die. After ages Marse say fer us to come out. I slipped out fearin' dey would kotch me no how.

In a similar vein, Peter Ryas (TX) described how owners in his area hid their slaves on an island for two basic reasons. One was to keep the Yankees from finding them, and the other was to keep slaves from joining the Yankees. This strategy failed on both accounts.

> De war goin' on. Us see sojers all de time. Us hide in bresh and play snipe at dem. All de white folks in town gang up. Dey send dere slaves out on Cypress Island. Dey do dat try keep Yankee sojers from find dem. It ain't no use. Dem Yankee find dat bridge what lead from mainland to island. Dey come 'cross dat bridge. Dey find us all. Dem white folks call deyselves hidin' us but dey ain't do so good. Dey guard dat bridge. But some de niggers dey slip off de Island. Dey jine de Yankees.

Elias Thomas (NC) mentioned that his owners told him that the Yankees would kill him or carry him off, so he "hid in the woods while they were there." Wylie Miller (MO) recalled that all of the children, both black and white, hid from the Yankees:

> De fust time we ever seed sojers, dey was a big crowd o' 'em cum up to our place, when us chillern seed 'em we crawl unner de house—white and black, all o' us. De Blue Coats look unner dere an' dey say, "Come out o' der, you, or we kill all o' you." We's sure scared but we crawls out. Dey didden hurt us none, but dey 'reets Ole Boss.

Another common response was to run at first sight of Yankee forces. Harry Johnson (TX) said, "Some of de niggers run 'way soon as dey seen de Yankees." According to Johnson, they ran because whites had told them Yankees would "kill 'em." Zeb Crowder (NC) reported a similar reaction: "All de niggers 'cept me an' de white folks ran to de woods." Crowder attributed his staying to the fearlessness of youth. Charlie Crump (NC) ran at first sight: "I had started fer de cane fil' wid a bucket o' water on my haid, but when I sees dem Yankees comin' I draps de bucke an' runs."

Dilly Yellady (NC) also described how owners fearfully moved slaves about when the Yankees came to prevent them from being set free, and some slaves ran to warn their owners:

> Dey shifted niggers from place to place to keep de Yankees frum takin' 'em. When dere got to be too many Yankees in a place de slaves wus sent out to keep 'em from bein' set free. Mother said onct when she wus carrying the cows to de pasture dey looked down de railroad an' everything wus blue. A nigger girl by the name of Susan wus with her. My mother wus named Rilla Pool. Dey said dey jus fell down an' de Yankees commenced sayin' "Hello Dinah," "Hello Susie." Mother an' Susan run. Dey just went flyin'. When dey crossed a creek my mother lost her shoe in de mud, but she just kept runnin'. When she got home she tole her missus de Yankees were ridin' up de railroad just as thick as flies. Den my great-grandmother said, "Well I has been prayin' long enough for 'em now dey is here." My great-grandmother wus named Nancy Pool an' she wus not afraid of nothin'.

Slaves were not the only ones to hide or be hidden from the Yankees. Whites also had reason to avoid them. Jake Wilson (TX) detailed in his narrative how his sick young master returned from the war and needed to be hidden for fear of being imprisoned:

> One time, one ob de young Marsters come home on er furlough kase he was kinder porely f'om de swamp feber. Well, us heard dat some Yankee soljers was er comin', so, ole Mistis, she git all worrited up, kase she 'feared dat effen de Yankee officers kotch young Marster, dey gwine put him in one ob dem Northern prison places. So, she ax some ob de oldest slaves w'at us gwine do, an' dey take de young Marster an' some beddin' an' things an' slip erway down through de woods an' take him ter de "prayin' cave" ez us all call hit. Er meny an' er meny er time, I'ze snuk down dar an' tuk him somefin' ter eat an' things. Us had put brushes in front an' fix hit so dat onles' you know 'bout hit, you ain't gwine git inter dat cave. Marse stayed dar 'twil he git ready ter go back ter his company. All endurin' de war, 'twarn't no onusual thing, way 'long in de dark ob de mawnin' fer ole Mistis ter wake up some ob de oldest slave men an' rush dem off ter dis cave an' thicket wid things dat she didn't want no Yankee ter git er holt ob, kase she done git de word dat "de Yanks am comin'."

Food supplies were critically important for the South, especially salt, which was essential for food storage. Survival for some Southerners depended on maintaining adequate food supplies. If the Yankees destroyed or plundered these supplies, it meant disaster. Bell McChristian (MS) remembered that her master had the slaves hide all the meat by burying "it in holes in de ground to keep dem Yankees from stealin it." In virtually all cases, slaves had a big stake in hiding food from Union troops. For example, Robert Wilson (TX) said:

> Ise only sees big bunch Yankee sojers gwine North. 'Twas de day befo' dey comes dat Marster digs big hole in de field 'bout 15 feet f'om big tree. Den he takes big hogshead barrel dat Ise could stand in also lay down in an' puts it in de hole. Den he takes neahly all de meat f'om de smokehouse an' fills it wid de meat an' waht else would keep. W'en de barrel am full he puts de lid on an' finishes fillin' de hole wid dirt. He fells de tree so 'twould be de branches

coverin' de top of de hole. Den he spreads dis leftover dirt 'round on de field an' tells weuns not to tell nobody 'bout it. De next day w'en de sojers comes some goes into de smokehouse an' takes all de meat dey could find. Dey even comes into de house an' takes what de finds 'cept 'nough fo' 'bout two days. 'Twas luck fo' sho de Marster beats dem to de punch. De sojers even cusses him 'cause he have so little rations.

A similar approach to hiding food was mentioned by Sarah Ann Green (NC). In her case, burying food and valuables under a woodpile proved ideal:

De day Ole Marse heard dat de Yankees was comin' he took all de meat 'cept two or three pieces out of de smoke house, den he got de silver an' things an' toted dem to de wood pile. He dug er hole an' buried dem, den he covered de place wid chips, but wid dat he wuzn' satisfied, so he made pappy bring er load of wood an' throw it on top of it, so when de Yankees come dey didn' fin' it.

Gus Brown (AL) reported hiding valuables that were never discovered and how none of the slaves revealed their location. In Brown's interview, Alexander B. Johnson wrote of Gus's account:

Beforehand the master called all the servants he could trust and told them to get together all of the silver and other things of value. They did that, he explained and afterward they took the big box of treasures and carried it out in the forest and hid it under the trunk of a tree which was marked. None of the Negroes ever told the Yankees where it was so when the war ended the master had his silver back.

Since concealing food from the Yankees was critical to many, both slaves and their owners did what they could to keep troops from finding their stockpiles of food. Callie Gray (MS) described how she and others were able to hide their turkeys:

The Yankees stole the corn and wheat and drove off the horses and mules and killed the hogs and sheep, and took all the chickens, but we sho saved the turkeys. We could hear the Yankees coming, and we dropped corn under a old house and when the turkeys all wus under the house, we nailed planks 'round the bottom. Then we swept away all the tracks. Yes, we sho saved the turkeys. I remember seeing 'em kill a hog, cut off his head and split him open down the middle, then they took out his intrels and dropped him in a tole sack and carried it off.

Henrietta Murray (MS) recalled her owners hiding animals and possessions in the woods, which was a common practice:

When de Yankees come through old Marsa had had us take Missus saddle horse an' his two carriage horses to de woods. They went an' got a barrel o' sugar an' flour, killed a cow, got heep o' chickens an' hams. They eat what they wanted an' left de other in de woods. Us chillun went to where camp was after they was gone an' saw all de stuff they had left. We told our white folks an' they gathered it up an' saved most o' it.

Sam McAllum (MS) remembered hiding the owner's valuables: "Us hid all de bes' things lak silver, an' driv' de stock to de swamp." Mary Anngady (NC) commented that "We had all the silver and valuables hid and the Yankees did not find them, but they went into marster's store and took what they wanted."

Ben Brown (OH) spoke of hiding his owner's gold and silver:

When dere was talk of Yankies cumin' de missie told me to git a box an she filled it with gold an' silver, lots of it, she was rich, an I dug a hole near de hen house an put in de box an' covered it with dirt an' smoothed it down an scattered some leaves an twigs ovah it. She told me nevah, nevah to tell about it and I nevah did until now. She showed me a big white card with writin' on it an' said it say "This is a Union Plantation" an' put it on a tree so the Yankies wouldn't try to find do gold and silvers.

Mary Wallace Bowe (NC) told a similar story about her two sister mistresses, Fanny and Virginia:

When she [Virginia] seed dem Yankees comin' 'cross de hill, she run 'roun' an' got all de jewelry. She took off de rings an' pins she an' Mis' Fanny had on an' she got all de things out of de jewelry box an' give dem to pappy. "Hide dem, Lillman," she tole pappy, "hide dem some place whare dem thieves won' fin' dem."

Pappy had on high top boots. He didn' do nothin but stuff all dat jewelry right down in dem boots, den he strutted all 'roun' dem Yankees laughin' to heself. Dey cussed when dey couldn' fin' no jewelry a tall. Dey didn' fin' no silver neither kaze us niggers done he'p Mis' Fanny an' Mis' Virginia hide dat. We done toted it all down to de cottin gin house an' hid it in de loose cotton piled on de floor. When dey couldn' fin' nothin' a big sojer went up to Mis' Virginia who was standin' in de hall. We look at her an' say: "Yo's skeered of me, ain' yo'?"

Mis' Virginia ain' batted no eye yet. She tole him, "If I was gwine to be skeered, I'd be skeered of somethin'. I sho ain' of no ugly, braggin' Yankee."

De man tu'ned red an he say: "If you don' tell me where you done hide dat silver I'se gwine to made you skeered."

Mis' Virginia's chin went up higher. She set her mouf an' look at dat sojer twell he drap his eyes. Den she tole him dat some folks done come an' got de silver, dat dey done toted it off. She didn' tell him dat it was us niggers dat done toted it down to de cotton gin house.

Sometimes hiding valuables went for naught, as slaves would readily disclose where items were hidden. A case in point is the narrative of Samuel Boulware (SC):

I 'members lak yesterday, de Yankees comin' 'long. Marster tried to hide the best stuff on de plantation but some of de slaves dat helped him hide it, showed de Yankee soldiers just where it was, when they come dere. They say: "Here is de stuff, hid here, 'cause us put it dere." Then de soldiers went straight to de place where de valuables was hid and dug them out and took them, it sho' set old marster down. Us slaves was sorry dat day for marster and mistress. They was gittin' old, and now they had lost all they had, and more that dat, they knowed their slaves was set free. De soldiers took all de good hosses, fat cattle, chickens, de meat in de smoke house, and then burnt all empty houses. They left de ones dat folks lived in. De Yankees 'pear to me, to be lookin' for things to eat, more than anything else.

Henry D. Jenkins (SC) described a similar scenario:

When de Yankees come, what they do? They did them things they ought not to have done and they left undone de things they ought

to have done. Yes, dat just 'bout tells it. One thing you might like
to hear. Mistress got all de money, de silver, de gold and de jew-
els, and got de well digger to hide them in de bottom of de well.
Them Yankees smart. When they got dere, they asked for de ve'y
things at de bottom of de well. Mistress wouldn't tell. They held a
court of 'quiry in de yard; called slaves up, one by one, good
many. Must have been a Judas 'mongst us. Soon a Yankee was let
down in de well, and all dat money, silver, gold, jewelry, watches,
rings, brooches, knives and forks, butter-dishes, waters, goblets,
and cups was took and carried 'way by a army dat seemed more
concerned 'bout stealin', than they was 'bout de Holy War for
de liberation of de poor African slave people. They took off all de
hosses, sheeps, cows, chickens, and geese, took de seine and de
fishes they caught, corn in crib, meat in smoke-house, and everything. Marse General Sherman said war was hell. It sho' was.
Mebbe it was hell for some of them Yankees when they come to
die and give account of de deeds they done in Sumter and Rich-
land Counties.

YANKEES PILLAGE THEIR WAY THROUGH THE SOUTH

There was good reason to hide food supplies and valuables from the
Yankees. Numerous narratives spoke of looting by the Yankees. Amy Perry
(SC) remembered the forays of both Yankee and Confederate soldiers alike
as being dreadful. "I 'members w'en de Yankee come tru, and Wheeler
a'amy come after um. Doze bin dreadful times. De Yankees massicued de
people, and burn dere houses, and stole de meat and eberyting dey could
find," she said.

Rachel Santee Reed's (MS) mother tried to accommodate the Yankees
when they were around and noted that when they rode away "dey flung
out fish hooks and strings and cotch Ole Missus' chickens and take dem,
and Ole Miss she was sho mad—but didn't do no good." Jessie Davis
(SC) said that when an advance column of Yankee soldiers came through,
"They gallop right up, jump down and say: 'Hold dese hosses! Open dat
smoke-house door!' They took what they could carry 'way." When the
master arrived, "They surround him, take his watch, money, and hoss, and
ride 'way."

Louisa Adams (NC) recalled how they came and ransacked the prem-
ises for food. What they did not take they destroyed:

The Day the Yankees Came 175

I 'member dey went to Miss Emma's house, and went in de smoke house and emptied every barrel of lasses right in de floor and scattered de cracklings on de floor. I went dere and got some of 'em. Miss Emma was my missus. Dey just killed de chickens, hogs too, and old Jeff the dog; they shot him through the thoat. I 'member how his mouth flew open when dey shot him. One of 'em went into de tater bank, and we chillun wanted to go out dere. Mother wouldn't let us.

In his interview, Fountain Hughes (MD) spoke of the Yankees destroying food supplies:

I remember when the Yankees come along an' took all the good horses an' throwed all the meat an' flour an' sugar an' stuff out in the river an' let it go down the river. An' they knowed the people wouldn't have nothing to live on, but they done that.

Reverend James W. Washington (MS) provided a similar account:

I remember de Yankees when dem cum. Sum of dem wus on horses en sum uf dem wus walking. Dey all wore blue close, two uf de men hed big brass buttons on deir close. Dey talk wid de Dr. en dey took his fine horses en mules en left us deir old scrubs. Dey killed one cow en took her down de road en roasted her. Dey tuk our meal en flour. When dey left we went down de road to git whut dey left. Sum of de folks sed de meat wus not fittern to eat, but I et it en thought it wus good. Dr. had his Carriage hid in de woods en all de silver. Dey did not git dat.

Sally Nealy (AR) shared a similar experience: "When the Yankee soldiers come through old mistress run and hide in the cellar but the Yankees went down in the cellar too and took all the hams and honey and brandied peaches she had." Ann May (MS) also gave a flavor of the times:

When the Yankees came to the white folks houses they killed all the hogs, chickens, cows and carried away all the flour, sugar and left us mighty little to eat. They carried off the fine horses too. Mistress would not talk sassy to them because she was afraid they would burn her house. They did burn some white folks houses.

The Yankees were not always respectful or concerned with the well-being of the slaves they were liberating. In fact, some Union troops engaged in shameful behavior, using food to demean slaves. Tiney Shaw (NC) was only a child when Yankee soldiers came through the plantation where he lived, and when interviewed he recalled the humiliation that both he and his mother suffered at the hands of the Federals as they tried to help feed the soldiers:

> Me an' my mammy was sittin' by de fireplace when de Yankees come. I crawled under de wash bench but de Yankee officer drug me out an' he sez, "Go fetch me a dozen aigs, an' I wants a dozen now, mind yo'."
>
> I looked till I found twelve aigs an' I started ter de house wid 'em, but bein' so excited I drapped one uv dem an' cracked it. I was sceered stiff now sho' nuff, an' I runned inter de back do' an' crawled under de bed. De officer seed me do' an' he cracks his whup an' makes me come out den he sez, "Nigger what's dat out dar in dat barrel in de hallway?"
>
> I sez, "Lasses sir," an' he sez "draw me some in dis cup." I draws 'bout a half a cupful an' he sez, "Nigger dat ain't no 'lasses," an' he cracks his whup ag'in.
>
> I den draws de cup full as it could be an' he tells me ter drunk it. I drinks dat whole cupful uf 'lasses 'fore he'll lemmie 'lone. Den I runs back ter my mammy.
>
> Atter awhile de Yankee comes back an' sticks his haid in de do' an' he 'lows, "ole woman, yo' 'lasses am leakin'."
>
> Sho' nuff it was leakin' an' had run all down de hall an' out in de yard, but he done pull de stopper out fer meanness so he could laff at mammy when she waded through dat 'lasses. Dey laffs an' laffs while she go steppin' down through de 'lasses lak a turkey walkin' on cockleburs.

Dilly Yellady (NC) said, "Yes, de Yankees freed us but dey lef' nuthin' for us to live on." Mrs. Mary Wood (VA) recalled how the Yankees also treated slave children in this account: "Yankees search cellars; rolled all 'lasses barrels out and poured hit all out on de ground and called all de little slave nigger chillum to lick 'lasses off de dirty ground." Josie Martin (AR) described how an elderly couple lost their hog to the Yankee troops:

> I used to run from the Yankees. I've seen them go in droves along the road. They found old colored couple, went out, took their hog and

made them barbecue it. They drove up a stob, nailed a piece to a tree and stacked their guns. They rested around till everything was ready.

Adeline Green (SC) depicted what happened when the Yankees came to her plantation:

> Dey burn de ginhouse, de shop, de buggyhouse, de turkeyhouse an' de fowlhouse. Start to set de cornhouse afire, but my Ma say: "Please sir, don't burn de cornhouse. Gie it to me an' my chillun." So dey put de fire out. I member when dey started to break down de smokehouse door, an' ole Missus come out an' say: "Please don't break de door open, I got de key." So dey quit. I remember when dey shoot down de hog. I remember when dey shoot de two geese in de yard. Dey choked my Ma. Dey went to her an' dey say: "Where is all de white people gold an' silver?" My Ma say she don't know. "You does know!" dey say, an' choke her till she couldn't talk. Dey went into de company room where de ole Miss was stayin' an' start tearin' up de bed. Den de captain come an' de ole Miss say to him: "Please don't let 'em tear up my bed," an' de captain went in dere an' tell 'em "Come out!"

John A. Holt (MO) recalled how the Yankees were starving when they raided the food supplies: "They dumped every apple in our celler out on the ground and dem soldiers eat like hogs." In addition, he added, "Bee hives was turned over and men and dogs eat all our honey." Gabe Emanuel (MS) remembered stealing food back from the Yankees:

> I 'member one time de Yankees camp right in de front yard. Dey took all de meat we done had in de curin' house, out to de camp. Well suh! I done decide by myse'f dat no Yankee gwine eat us meat. So dat night I slips in dey camp an' stole back dat meat from dem thievin' sojers an' hid it, good. Dem men was sho' plenty mad de nex' mornin'—Ho! Ho! Ho! Dey never did fin' dat meat.

CONFEDERATES RAVAGE THE COUNTRYSIDE OF THE SOUTH

It is important to note that some slaves feared Confederate troops as much as or more than they did the Yankees. Confederate troops also looted and harmed slaves during the war. Many Confederates blamed slaves for the conflict and did not hesitate to assault, molest, and otherwise punish them. Troops also looted owners, stealing food and valuables.

John C. Bectom (NC) told of Yankees and Confederates fighting near Fayetteville, Arkansas. Bectom said that General Joseph Wheeler's Confederate cavalry "came first and ransacked the place." Betty Brown (MO) said, "Dem 'Blue-coat's' was devils, but de 'gray-coats' was wusser. Dey turn over our bee-gums an' dey kill our steers, an' carry off our provisions, an' whut dey couldn't carry off dey ruint. Den dey go roun' killin' all de cullud men an' bayanettin' de chillern."

Andrews Moss (TN) said that when the Rebels came, they burned food supplies to keep the Yankees from confiscating them. Moss added that some of the Rebels "was mean as the Yanks—And dat was bein' mean." Other narratives also report how food was destroyed or taken so it would not fall into the hands of the Yankees. For example, Patsy Mitchner (NC) noted how Wheeler's cavalry "grabbed everything and went on. Dey had a reason for leavin'; de Yankees wus at dere heels." Charley Roberts (FL) commented on feeding the looting Confederate troops:

We have to milk the cows and carry the milk to the Confederate soldiers quartered near us. At that time, I can 'member of the soldiers comin' 'cross the Savannah River. They would go to the plantations and take all the cows, hogs, sheep, or horses they wanted and "stack" their guns and stay around some places and kill some of the stock, or use the milk and eat corn and all the food they wanted as they needed it. They'd take quilts and just anything they needed.

Willie McCullough (NC) contrasted the behavior of Yankee troops to Confederates, pointing out that "The Yankees took chickens and things, and they gave us some things, but Wheeler's Cavalry gave us nothin'." Willie added, "They took what they wanted and went on." Lindsey Faucette (NC) complained that Confederate troops were more harmful than the Yankees, even when it came to lice:

Our own sojers did more harm on our plantation den de Yankees. Dey camped in de woods an' never did have nuff to eat an' took what dey wanted. An' lice! I ain't never seed de like. It took fifteen years for us to get shed of de lice dat de sojers lef' behind. You jus' couldn' get dem out of your clothes les' you burned dem up. Dey wuz hard to get shed of.

Hannah Jones (MO) shared what Rebel troops did:

> Dey killed three of us niggers in our camp det morning. All de nig-
> ger men been taken away just leaving us nigger women and chillun.
> Dey burned down frame and log huts just de same.

OBSERVATIONS

The day the Yankees came left lasting impressions on slaves and was a mixed blessing for many of them. It was a time that many awaited with great anticipation, yet some slaves dreaded the day. Others prayed for the appearance of blue coats and could hardly wait to be liberated. Clearly, all prepared one way or another by hiding things that they or their owners valued. Given what many experienced with the foraging and pillaging for food by troops from both sides, preparing for the coming of the Yankees was important and necessary.

What conclusions can we draw from these events? Most slaves were touched in some very profound ways by the arrival of the Yankees. Undoubtedly, some learned that Yankees were indeed the evil beings that slaves had been led to believe they were. Other slaves found Yankees to be compassionate compared to the whites they had lived with and worked for in the antebellum South. The narratives are liberally laced with stories of barbaric and rapacious behavior by troops of both sides and in some cases by gallantry displayed by both, particularly Union soldiers.

Although the Civil War was replete with stories of heartache and moments of pathos, there were also moments of outright humor. Hecter Hamilton (NC) told the story of the two General Lees in his narrative. Working for Virginia planters Peter and Laura Hamilton, Hecter was assigned the duty of watchman over the plantation's commissary to prevent the pilfering of food. He taught a gander to drive cattle and sheep and sic vicious dogs, and he named the goose "General Lee" after the patriarch of the Army of Northern Virginia. Everywhere Hecter went "dat gander wuz right at my heels." One day when the Yankees advanced to the Hamilton plantation, a soldier spied Mrs. Hamilton on the porch wearing diamond earrings. Hecter picked up the story from there:

> When de sojer seed dem diamon's his eyes 'gun to shine. He went
> out on de po'ch an' went up to Mis' Laura. "Gim me dem ear rings,"
> he say jus' like dat. Mis' Laura flung her han's up to her ears an' run

out in de yard. De sojer followed her, an' all de other sojers come too. Dat big Yankee tole Mis' Laura again to give him de ear rings, but she shook her head. I wuz standin' 'side de house near 'bout bustin' wid madness when dat Yankee reach up an' snatch Mis' Laura's hands down an' hold dem in his, den he laugh, an' all de other sojers 'gun to laugh too jus' like dey thought 'twuz funny. 'Bout dat time Ole General Lee done smell a fight. He come waddlin' 'roun' de house, his tail feathers bristled out an' tawkin' to he' sef. I point to dem sojers an say, "Sic him, General Lee, sic him."

Dat gander ain't waste no time. He let out his wings an' cha'ged dem Yankees an' dey scatter like flies. Den he lit on dat big sojer's back an' 'gun to beat him wid his wings. Dat man let out a yell an' drap Mis' Laura's hands; he try to shake dat goose, but General bit into his neck an' held on like a leech. When de other sojers come up an' try to pull him off, dat gander let out a wing an' near 'bout slap dem down. I ain't never seed such fightin! Every time I holler, Sic him, General Lee start 'nother 'tack.

Bout dat time dem Yankees took a runnin' nothin. Dey forgot de ear rings an' lit out down de road, but dat gander beat dat bigoty yellin' sojer clear down to de branch befo' he turned him loose, den he jump in de water an' wash hese'f off. Yes, suh, dat wuz sho some fightin' goose; he near 'bout out fit de sho nuff Marse General Lee.

CHAPTER 8

How the Slaves Saw the Major Figures of the War

It was rumored that Abraham Lincoln said to Jefferson Davis, "Work the slaves until they are about twenty-five or thirty years of age, then liberate them." Davis replied: "I'll never do it, before I will, I'll wade knee deep in blood." The result was that in 1861, the Civil War, that struggle which was to mark the final emancipation of the slaves, began. Jefferson Davis' brothers, Sam and Tom, joined the Confederate forces, together with their sons who were old enough to go, except James, Tom's son, who could not go on account of ill health and was left behind as overseer on Jack Davis' plantation. Jack Davis joined the artillery regiment of Captain Razors Company. The war progressed; Sherman was on his famous march. The "Yankees" had made such sweeping advances until they were in Robertsville, South Carolina, about five miles from Black Swamp. The report of gun fire and cannon could be heard from the plantation. "Truly the Yanks are here" everybody thought. The only happy folk were the slaves, the whites were in distress. Jack Davis returned from the field of battle to his plantation. He was on a short furlough. His wife, "Missus" Davis asked him excitedly, if he thought the "Yankees" were going to win. He replied: "No if I did I'd kill every damned nigger on the place." Will who was then a lad of nineteen was standing nearby and on hearing his master's remarks, said: "The Yankees aint gonna kill me cause um goin to Laurel Bay" [a swamp located on the plantation]. Will says that what he really meant was that his master was not going to kill him because he intended to run off and go to the "Yankees." That afternoon Jack Davis returned to the "front" and that night Will told his mother, Anna Georgia, that he was going to Robertsville and join the "Yankees." He and his cousin who lived on the Davis' plantation slipped off and wandered their way to all of the

surrounding plantations spreading the news that the "Yankees" were
in Robertsville and exhorting them to follow and join them. Soon the
two had a following of about five hundred slaves who abandoned
their masters' plantations "to meet the Yankees." En masse they
marched breaking down fences that obstructed their passage, care-
fully avoiding "Confederate pickets" who were stationed throughout
the countryside. After marching about five miles they reached a
bridge that spanned the Savannah River, a point that the "Yankees"
held. There was a Union soldier standing guard and before he realized it, this group of five hundred slaves were upon him. Becoming
cognizant that someone was upon him, he wheeled around in the
darkness, with gun leveled at the approaching slaves and cried
"Halt!" Will's cousin then spoke up, "Doan shoot boss we's jes
friends." After recognizing who they were, they were admitted into
the camp that was established around the bridge. There were about
seven thousand of General Sherman's soldiers camped there, having
crossed the Savannah River on a pontoon bridge that they had con-
structed while enroute from Green Springs, Georgia, which they had
taken. The guard who had let these people approach so near to him
without realizing their approach was court martialed that night for
being dilatory in his duties. The Federal officers told the slaves that
they could go along with them or go to Savannah, a place that they
had already captured. Will decided that it was best for him to go to
Savannah. He left, but the majority of the slaves remained with the
troops. They were enroute to Barnwell, South Carolina, to seize Blis
Creek Fort that was held by the Confederates. As the Federal troops
marched ahead, they were followed by the volunteer slaves. Most of
these unfortunate slaves wore slain by "bush whackers" [Confeder-
ate snipers who fired upon them from ambush]. After being killed
they were decapitated and their heads placed upon posts that lined
the fields so that they could be seen by other slaves to warn them of
what would befall them if they attempted to escape. The battle at
Blis Creek Fort was one in which both armies displayed great heroism; most of the Federal troops that made the first attack were killed
as the Confederates seemed to be irresistible. After rushing up rein-
forcements, the Federals were successful in capturing it and a large
number of "Rebels."

General Sherman's custom was to march ahead of his army and
cut rights of way for them to pass. At this point of the war, many of

the slaves were escaping from their plantations and joining the "Yankees." All of those slaves at Black Swamp who did not voluntarily run away and go to the "Yankees" were now free by right of conquest of the Federals.

Will now found himself in Savannah, Georgia, after refusing to go to Bareswell, South Carolina, with the Federals. This refusal saved him from the fate of his unfortunate brothers who went. Savannah was filled with smoke, the aftermath of a great battle. Lying in the "Broad Biver" between Beauport, South Carolina, and Savannah, Georgia, were two Union gun boats, the "DeManh" and "Man O War" which had taken part in the battle that resulted in the capture of Savannah. Everything was now peaceful again; Savannah was now a Union city. Many of the slaves were joining the Union army. Those slaves who joined were trained about two days and then sent to the front; due to lack of training they were soon killed. The weather was cold, it was February, 1868, frost was on the ground. Will soon left Savannah for Beaufort, South Carolina, which had fallen before the "Yankee" attack. Soldiers and slaves filled the streets. The slaves were given all of the food and clothes that they could carry—confiscated goods from the "Rebels." After a bloody struggle in which both sides lost heavily and which lasted for about five years, the war finally ended May 15, 1865. Will was then a young man twenty-three years of age and was still in Beaufort. He says that day was a gala day. Everybody celebrated (except the Southerners); the slaves were free.

Thousands of Federal soldiers were in evidence. The Union army was victorious and "Sherman's March" was a success. Sherman states that when Jefferson Davis was captured he was disguised in women's clothes.

Sherman states that Florida had a reputation of having very cruel masters. He says that when slaves got very unruly, they were told that they were going to be sent to Florida so they could be handled. During the war thousands of slaves fled from Virginia into Connecticut and Hew Hampshire. In 1867 William Sherman left Beaufort and went to Mayport, Florida, to live.

The previous detailed account by William Sherman (FL) is a combination of fact and hearsay. Sherman, similar to some of his ex-slave counterparts, had formed ideas about the unfolding of events and major figures of the war. The slave narratives contain many references to the main figures of the war, including U.S. president Abraham Lincoln; Confederate president Jefferson Davis; Union generals Ulysses S. Grant, Benjamin Butler, and William Tecumseh Sherman; and Confederate generals Robert E. Lee and Joseph Wheeler. Some of these references are based on hearsay and secondhand accounts, while others are rooted in firsthand observations. Since the war was fought on several fronts and there were movements of military forces throughout the South and occasionally in the North, chances were good that some or maybe many of the observations, especially of military leaders, occurred. These observations and in some cases personal contact as well as information gleaned from other sources, such as owners, provide insight into the wide range of perspectives that slaves had and why they felt the way they did about the major figures of the war.

ACCOUNTS INVOLVING PRESIDENT LINCOLN

More than any other figure, ex-slaves referenced President Lincoln in their narratives. It is evident from these accounts that they had strong opinions about Lincoln well after the war. Blacks, free and in bondage, perceived Lincoln as a larger-than-life individual. Some viewed him in a positive light, while others saw him in the most negative terms. How is it that views on the single biggest symbol of freedom and emancipation could be viewed with such a wide range of perspectives? The answer to this question is complex, and some of the narratives suggest clues that may help provide answers.

THE OMNIPRESENT AND MYTHICAL LINCOLN

Many of the former slaves claim in their narratives to have personally seen Lincoln. From this one might have the impression that before and during the war, Lincoln was omnipresent in the South. While a few may have actually seen Lincoln, it is highly improbable that every former slave who claimed to have seen him actually did. As a presidential candidate and later the president, Lincoln, although known for his courage, was never popular in the South and would not have taken the risk of venturing into the antebellum South, as is often suggested by the "eyewitness" accounts found in the narratives. For him to do so would have been extremely dangerous and foolhardy. It is true that Lincoln was no stranger to the battlefield and did visit his commanders in the field at some risk. Andrew Ward (2008, 9–10) suggests that in some of the Lincoln "sightings" he may have been confused with someone else:

> In their recollections, a number of former slaves would claim to have laid eyes on Lincoln before the war. Some may well have encountered not the Abraham Lincoln but his cousin and contemporary of the same name, or perhaps an English immigrant named William Ellaby Lincoln, a somewhat unbalanced Oberlin College student who roamed the South before the Civil War, preaching against the sins of slavery.

The narratives contain mythical or legendary sightings and encounters of slaves with Lincoln, and most historians lay these accounts to folk legend. For example, Julius Jones (TN) reported meeting Lincoln when Yankee troops marched through. He described how Lincoln offered them freedom if they would fight for the Union:

> That was in the year 1863, at that time the southern folks had the Yankees whipped, and they could have won the war if it hadn't been for a great man by the name of Abraham Lincoln. That man held a council right then. He 'greed to take all the colored people. Said if they fought on his side he would set them all free. When them niggers heard that free part, they all joined the army.

Another example of "seeing" Lincoln includes the narrative of Georgianna Foster (NC), who mentioned that her mother and father claimed to have seen Lincoln on his way to meet with President Davis. Foster noted that Lincoln came south three times to meet with Davis. According to Foster, Lincoln said on his third visit, "'Is you gwine to set dem slaves free Jeff Davis?'" Then Davis replied, "'Abraham Lincoln, you knows I is not goin' to give up my property,' an' den Lincoln said, 'I jest as well go back an' git up my crowd den.'" Foster then went on to say that Lincoln came back with 140,000 men and "whupped" the South and set us free.

Louis Meadows (AL) claimed to have seen Lincoln before his election:

> I stood on de side of de road an' seed Mr. Lincoln ridin' by wid Mr. Buchanan. [His version is doubtful.] Mr. Buchanan was de President den and Mr. Lincoln was runnin' fer 'lection. Dey was ridin' in

one of dem carriages wid de seat high up. It was a rockaway carriage. A nigger coachman, all dressed up, was sittin' up in front an'
a little black boy was sittin' on de seat behind. His foots was restin'
on de low steps.

The only historically known time that Lincoln and James Buchanan rode
together in a carriage was on the way to Lincoln's first inauguration on
March 4, 1861, and since this was in Washington, D.C., it is doubtful that
a slave from the South witnessed the event.

VIEWING LINCOLN AS A MAN OF THE PEOPLE

Some ex-slave accounts seem to normalize Lincoln as an ordinary person,
one who shared meals, asked questions, and observed the oppression in the
South. While his stature was intimidating and scared some slave children,
he was viewed as a common man with an interest in the welfare of the
slaves. Mary Jane Wilson (VA) claimed in her narrative interview to have
had Lincoln visit her cabin. Her interviewer wrote:

At one time Abraham Lincoln visited her home county and while
investigating conditions of the slaves stopped at her family cabin.
His height and dignity frightened the children and they fled in
hiding. It was not until her father assured them that "Massa
Lincoln" wouldn't harm them that they left their places of refuge.

Sam Mitchell (SC) asserted that Lincoln came to Beaufort before the war
and had dinner with his owner:

I got his history right here in my house. He was de president of de
United States that freed four million slave. He come to Beaufort
befo' de war and et dinner to Col. Paul Hamilton house at de Oaks.
He left his gold-headed walking cane dere and ain't nobody know
de president of de United States been to Beaufort 'till he write back
and tell um to look behind de door and send um his gold-headed
walking cane.

Margret Hulm (AR) made a similar reference to a supposed visit by
Lincoln to her Tennessee plantation before the war:

I waited on my mistress and her chillun, answered the door, waited on de table and done things like that. I remember Mr. Lincoln. He came one day to our house (I mean my white folks' house). They told me to answer the door and when I opened it there stood a big man with a gray blanket around him for a cape. He had a string tied around his neck to hold it on. A part of it was turned down over the string like a ghost cape. How was he dressed beneath the blanket? Well, he had on jeans pants and big mud boots and a big black hat kinda like men wear now. He stayed all night.

Lou Griffin (MO) also shared a story of Lincoln visiting to look at the plight of slaves. Griffin's narrative seems to romanticize the view of Lincoln as a compassionate and concerned president who visited slaves to better understand their situations and living conditions:

Dis heah old Abe Lincoln come through our town. I guess you done heard 'bout him, is you, honey? If you ain't, I'll tell you. He just come 'round to see how de Rebs do de slaves. I gets so full thinkin' how de good Lawd fix it for us. He come 'round when nobody's lookin' for him. Bye and bye he says, fight for your freedom in de Yankee army instead of standing 'round here being sold and treated like beasts.

Charlie Davenport (MS), who claimed that he was about 15 years old when Lincoln came to talk with the slaves, in his narrative described Lincoln's behavior that stirred the slaves:

He went all through de country jest a rantin and preachin 'bout us bein his black brudders. Ole Marse didn't know nothin 'bout hit 'cause hit was sorta secret like. Hit shore riled de niggers up en lots ob 'em run away. Yas ma'am, I shore heard him but didn't pay him no mind.

J. T. Tims (AR) portrayed Lincoln as a fairly ordinary man looking for work but also a man with, interestingly enough, bodyguards:

They say Abe Lincoln come down in this part of the country and asked for work. He had his little grip just like you got. The man said, "Wait till I go to dinner." Didn't say, "Come to dinner," and didn't say nothin' 'bout, "Have dinner." Just said, "Wait till I go eat my dinner." When he come back, Abe Lincoln was up there looking over his books. He'd done changed his clothes and everything. He had guards with him but they didn't see 'em. That is the story I heard them tell.

Tom Hunley's (MS) "mammy" told him about a visit by Lincoln to her plantation. Slaves had a sense of the social and economic status of Southern whites, which depended mostly on one's wealth, and wealth in the antebellum South was typically associated with property (plantation) owners. At the bottom of the social ladder were the so-called white trash. This referred to whites who were rural, uneducated, poor, and usually nonslaveholders. Slaves may have applied this socioeconomic interpretation in some ways to Lincoln. In many of the narratives mentioning Lincoln, characteristics of "poor white trash" were often used to depict the president. Although they did not specifically use the term "white trash" in reference to him, for some it was implied. For example, references to his ragged clothing and being from the backwoods are features that Southerners often used in referring to one as being at the bottom rung of the social strata. Typical of many accounts of Lincoln's alleged visits to the South, he was characterized as an ordinary person who was dressed in modest clothing.

Bob Maynard (OK) shared a story about a visit by Lincoln before his election:

'Fore the election he traveled all over the South and he come to our house and slept in old Mistress' bed. Didn't nobody know who he was. It was a custom to take strangers in and put them up for one night or longer, so he come to our house and he watched close. He seen how the niggers come in on Saturday and drawed four pounds of meat and a peck of meal for a week's rations. He also saw 'em whipped and sold. When he got back up north he writ old Master a letter and told him he was going to have to free his slaves, that everybody was going to have to, that the North was going to see to it. He also told him that he had visited at his house and if he doubted it to go in the room he slept in and look on the bedstead at the heed and he'd see where he'd writ his name. Sho' nuff, there was his name: A. Lincoln.

Elizabeth Thomas, a free black woman more commonly known in her later years as Aunt Betty (DC), said she had a very personal encounter with Lincoln. Thomas and her husband, James, owned nearly 11 acres of farmland just north of Washington, now a part of the Brightwood section in the District of Columbia. In 1861 the Union Army appropriated part of Thomas's land to build Fort Stevens, which would become one of a network of 68 forts built around Washington during the Civil War to protect the nation's capital from Confederate attack. Fort Stevens was built to defend the main thoroughfare from the north into Washington. As Thomas later told a reporter, one day soldiers "began taking out my furniture and tearing down our house" to build the fort. During July 11–12, 1864, General Jubal Early attacked the fort approaching from Silver Spring, Maryland, hoping to divert Grant's attention from Richmond. Although Maryland never seceded, it was a slave state and had many Southern sympathizers, offering General Early an access to approach the capital. Aunt Betty's account described how after she had lost her houses, she sought shelter in a stable. "I was crying with my six-months-old child in my arms when a tall man dressed in black came out from the city," she said. "He tried to comfort me and said, 'It is hard, but you shall reap a great reward.'" She believed the man to be President Lincoln. Aunt Betty's encounter with the president was later recounted in John E. Washington's 1942 book *They Knew Lincoln*, a part folklore, part memoir, and part historical account of the African American men and women who worked for or came in contact with Lincoln.

Elizabeth Russell (IN) spoke of a similar direct encounter with Lincoln. She recalled that she was a child playing in the yard when her master and a man dressed in overalls "with a red handkerchief tied around his neck" approached her. She believed the man to be Abe Lincoln. She indicated that he picked her up in his arms and said, "Child, I hope you and your people will be free pretty soon." She also recalled that he secretly stayed with her master for three days without Southern people knowing about it because he would have been killed.

Rose Mercer (OK) claimed to have seen presidential candidate Lincoln and shook his hand. Mercer shared that he came through "Alabama riding on a grey mule." Again, the theme of Lincoln as a Northern spy surfaces in Mercer's narrative. After noting that the people of Alabama would have killed him, she recalled that he "came through spying as to the conditions of the slaves." In addition to Mercer's narrative, others such as that of Sarah Waggoner (MO) portray him as a spy.

Lincoln was characterized as being dressed in ragged clothes or being a tramp. Charity Austin (NC) said that when Lincoln came through town, no one knew who he was because he had lost everything and was looking for his people. Later Austin and others "heard" that he was in the White House, and then they knew that he was Lincoln. Alice Douglass (OK) also saw a couple whom she believed to be Lincoln and Mary Todd dressed like tramps in a hotel tavern in Gallatin, Tennessee. Again, she claimed that no one knew who Lincoln and his wife were until he made it to the White House and "writ back and told 'em to look 'twixt the leaves in the table where he had set and they sho' nuff found out it was him." Presumably she was referring to the owners of the hotel. The narrative of Henry Gibbs (MS) characterized Lincoln as traveling around the South on a mule pretending to be "crippled" to avoid detection. Gibbs said, "I always have believed that man was Lincoln. I know why he was called a 'rail [real] candidate,' he was a rail splitter and lived in a log cabin."

LINCOLN AS LIBERATOR

Lincoln took on several personas in the minds of slaves. He had a long personal commitment against slavery (Quarles 1968), and although he signed the Emancipation Proclamation in 1862, Lincoln's first priority from the outset of the war was to save the Union. He later freed the slaves in Rebel territory out of military necessity. By doing so, he removed them from the plantation fields that supported the Confederacy and armed them as Union troops (Smith 2003). He took other steps to derogate slavery, such as refusing to pardon Captain Nathaniel Gordon, who was convicted under the Piracy Law of 1820 for engaging in the African slave trade and was later executed. Lincoln supported abolishing slavery in the District of Columbia and also established diplomatic relations with the black-controlled governments of Haiti and Liberia.

However, the political realities he faced in trying to hold the nation together forced his hand to deal with the issue of abolishing slavery sooner than he wanted but later than many would have hoped. Lincoln had to walk a tightrope between abolitionists who wanted an immediate cessation of slavery and those who feared that such a move would pull the country further apart. Initially Lincoln's generals, such as George McClellan, argued against freeing the slaves. They believed that such an action would fragment the Union and destroy the army. The military command was also concerned about arming African American soldiers. Facing this dilemma,

Entitled *Emancipation of the Slaves* this lithograph was published in 1862 by the little-known firm of J. Waeshle of Philadelphia. It depicts a slave family kissing the hand of their liberator. Lincoln is shown with his arm raised and his finger pointing to heaven to likely signify it is God's will that the slaves be free. A log cabin is shown in the background, possibly Lincoln's. In the foreground are broken shackles representing the slaves' freedom from bondage. As noted by Holzer, et. al., in *The Emancipation Proclamation: Three Views,* the authors' note, "To either . . . Currier and Ives . . . or the virtually unknown Philadelphia firm of J. Waeshle, belongs the credit for first imagining the ritualized unshackling that Lincoln failed to provide." One of these firms—it is unclear which—touched off what soon became an industry in emancipation graphics and, later, in public statuary. (Library of Congress)

the Emancipation Proclamation that Lincoln signed proposed that only slaves in Southern states then in rebellion would be freed but not those in border states. A problem facing the Union was that slaves could not replace the men who were taken from farms and factories to serve in the military. Thus, labor for agricultural and industrial production in the North became constrained.

Some African Americans wanting to join Union forces were unable to do so because of constraints by their owners, and some were made to serve in various capacities in the Confederate Army whether or not they wanted to. This lessened the number of free blacks in the Union Army. As a result, Lincoln decided to free all slaves. He cast the Emancipation Proclamation on moral grounds and in so doing increased the ranks of the Union Army, which by most estimates grew by more than 200,000 with the addition of African American troops, about half of whom were freedmen and half ex-slaves from the South. With the adoption of the Thirteenth Amendment on December 6, 1865, slaves would finally gain their guaranteed freedom under the U.S. Constitution.

Most African Americans supported Lincoln and his policies. Even though the president eventually became a champion for the elimination of slavery, some black leaders north and south of the Mason-Dixon Line were very critical of him, noting that during the beginning of his first term he did not publicly oppose slavery until well into the war (McPherson 1993). Reflecting back on his efforts, however, it is clear that he justifiably deserves much credit for his important role in the freeing of slaves (McPherson 1995). Some African Americans also attacked him for his conservative approach to Reconstruction and suffrage. He did not advocate for black voting rights, and critics noted that his Reconstruction efforts left Southern whites in power, with African Americans continuing to labor in the same fields of white owners. When Lincoln was assassinated on April 14, black Americans were generally left in despair (McPherson 1993).

For some African Americans, Lincoln represented their hope for not only freedom but also for equal rights. Given his central role in the emancipation of slaves, many would view him as the great liberator, which is reflected in the narratives. Maltilda Shepard (AR) thought of Lincoln as a true and honest man who believed that all men should be set free. Mary Barnes (MD) shared her feelings about freedom and her view of Lincoln. She also recalled how close she got to him and the impression he made:

> I am so glad that slavery end. I like Abe Lincoln better dan Jeff
> Davis, thou Marse Bob wasn't a Yankee. He was sho crazy about
> Jeff Davis. Uncle Abe made me a free agent. If you had yo hands
> tied and some one come and cut 'em aloose wouldn't you be glad?
> Dat's why I like Abe. Uncle Abe was tall, he had a furred hat, eagle
> in front of it, a great big lovely cape and he was on a big black
> horse. I was standing on the stand where I could almost touch him.

Will Sheets (GA) saw Lincoln as a "great man" and a liberator and saw Confederate president Davis as an oppressor:

> I think Mr. Lincoln was a great man, 'cause he sot us free. When I
> thinks back, it warn't no good feelin' to be bound down lak dat.
> Mr. President Davis wanted us to stay bound down. No Ma'am, I
> didn't lak dat Mr. Davis atter I knowed what he stood for. 'Course
> dere is plenty what needs to be bound down hard and fast so dey
> won't git in no trouble. But for me I trys to behave myself, and I sho'
> had ruther be free. I guess atter all it's best dat slavery days is over.

In a similar vein, Louisa Adams (NC) viewed Lincoln as an emancipator and said that "Abraham Lincoln freed us by the help of the Lawd, by his help." Billy Slaughter (IN) characterized Lincoln as a hero. Slaughter was so touched by Lincoln that he took pilgrimages to Lincoln's farm. Elisha Doc Garey (GA) framed Lincoln and his role in the liberation of slaves in a biblical context, stating that "When Mr. Abraham Lincoln come to dis passage in de Bible: 'My son, therefore shall ye be free indeed,' he went to wuk to sot us free." Charles H. Anderson (OH) also cast Lincoln in a biblical light. When asked about the president, Anderson said that he saw Lincoln as naturally born for the role of liberator, similar to other biblical figures:

> Well, they's people born in this world for every occupation and
> Lincoln was a natural born man for the job he completed. Just
> check it back to Pharoah' time: There was Moses born to deliver the
> children of Israel. And John Brown, he was born for a purpose. But
> they said he was cruel all the way th'ough, and they hung him in
> February, 1859. That created a great sensation. And he said, "Go
> ahead. Do your work. I done mine." Then they whipped around till
> they got the war started. And that was the start of the Civil War.

Louis Davis (MS) did not give President Lincoln credit for his liberation but instead credited his owner. This interpretation might have been because the actual liberation occurred on the local plantation, and the political reality of the proclamation was that while it declared freedom for slaves, it could not actually free them since the war was as yet undecided. Davis saw it quite differently than most in that he felt that Lincoln was less willing than President Davis to let the slaves go free. According to Louis Davis, Lincoln did not want slaves to go to the North, which in a sense was true but obviously for different reasons than Davis assumed. But Davis also indicated his preference for life under slavery in these comments:

> Old Miss was the one that set all of us free, and Mr. Lincoln didn't
> have nothing to do with it. All of us belonged to Old Miss and if
> she hadn't said we was free we would have still belonged to her
> regardless of what Mr. Lincoln said. There was another great man
> in what they called the rebel army, his name was Robert E. Lee.
> Some like him and some don't. Some says it was him that tried to

keep the niggers slaves. That wasn't what the war was about. That slavery didn't have nothing to do with it. You see it was this way Jefferson Davis wanted to let the slaves go up to the North, and Abraham Lincoln wouldn't allow it, cause he didn't want no slaves up there, and that's what the whole thing was about. The colored folks was a lot better off in slavery time than they is now. They needs teaching and caring for. They was made to look after their-self better. Slave holders cared more their slaves than the slaves cared for theirself.

Reverend Perry Sid Jamison (OH) saw Lincoln as the leader who "struck off de handcuffs and de ankle cuffs from de slaves." John C. Bectom (NC) felt that "Abraham Lincoln was one of the greatest men that ever lived" and attributed freedom of the slaves to him.

Others such as Hannah Crasson (NC) and Charles W. Dickens (NC) believed Lincoln to be the great liberator of the slaves. Still others questioned the consequences of liberation. Although Dellie Lewis (AL) viewed Lincoln as a liberator, she felt that the ex-slaves simply worked for the Yankees following the war.

Following emancipation and freedom, some ex-slaves came to view Lincoln as not only a liberator but also as a father figure. This perceived need for a father figure by some may have been reflective of them not knowing what to expect with freedom. One might speculate that they were looking for some sense of order in their lives beyond their families, and the image of a fatherly Lincoln would have provided some assurance of order and calm in what would prove to be a trying time. Ironically, shortly before his death, Lincoln was more concerned about compensating slave owners for the loss of their slave labor than in paying slaves for their years of unpaid servitude (Jordan 1995). Reverend Squire Dowd (NC) also viewed Lincoln as a father figure: "I feel that Abraham Lincoln was a father to us." A similar characterization was shared by Jefferson Franklin Henry (GA), who said that "Mr. Lincoln was to be a father to the slaves atter he had done freed 'em."

Another similar theme in the narratives is that Lincoln was a fine and noble man. William Henry Towns (AL) commented that "I thinks that Abe Lincoln was a mighty fine man even if he was tryin' to save their union. . . . Any man that tries to help humanity is a good man." John William Matheus (OH) thought of Lincoln as "the greatest man that ever lived." Mingo White (AL) saw him as "nobler man as ever walked."

MESSENGER FROM HEAVEN

For some slaves, emancipation was a gift from the heavens, and Lincoln was more than human—he was a messenger from heaven. Some slaves viewed him as being of biblical proportions for his role in their liberation. Some of the narratives make these connections between Lincoln and what they knew about Christianity. Doc Daniel Dowdy (OK) compared Lincoln's status as second only to the Apostle Paul: "I think Abraham Lincoln was the greatest human being ever been on earth 'cepting the Apostle Paul." Dowdy gave Lincoln credit for liberating 4 million slaves. Bob Maynard (OK) raised Lincoln's status even higher when he said, "I think Abe Lincoln was next to de Lewd. He done all he could for de slaves: he set 'em free." Sarah Waggoner (MO), who claimed with pride to have been born in the same county on almost the same day as Lincoln, placed him next to Jesus Christ for freeing the slaves: "Abe Lincoln was jes' next to Jesus Christ."

 Rezin Williams (MD) also noted that many slaves viewed Lincoln as a messenger from heaven. Jim Allen (MS) indicated that Lincoln used the Bible as a guide for his actions, including being against slavery. Frank Hughes (MS) believed that Lincoln was placed on Earth to carry out God's plan, similar to what Moses did in freeing his people. Hughes stated that "I think it was de will of de Lawd to talk to Abraham Lincoln through de spirit, to work out a plan to set the niggers free. . . . I think he carried out God's Plan." Julius Jones (TN) enlisted in the Union Army to gain his freedom. He observed that "Mr. Lincoln was sure a wonderful man. He did what God put him here to do. Took bondage off the colored people and set them free." In contrast, Jones added, "Mr. Lee sure didn't leave no such record behind him." William Nelson (OH) characterized Lincoln as a saint when he said, "I think Abraham Lincoln was a mighty fine man, he is de 'Saint of de colored race'." Robert Burns (OK) indicated that Lincoln was like a god to his people, but they could not reveal this to their owners. Rather, Burns revealed that slaves had to keep their feelings for Lincoln secret and instead publicly praised Jefferson Davis:

> We all thought Abraham Lincoln was our God, but we had to keep it a secret as our Master did not like him as he was trying to set us free. We had to pretend, to him, dat we liked Jefferson Davis, to our Master as he pretended to us dat Davis was de niggers friend, and dat he, Davis was going to set dem free and give each nigger family 40 acres and a mule.

LINCOLN AS A NEGATIVE FORCE

While many viewed Lincoln as a noble and kind man, others were not so positive. Some resented him because he failed to deliver on his promise of a better life. For many of his ex-slave critics, Lincoln's policies failed to follow up after the war with land, mules, and other things associated with emancipation. The end of the war did not bring the anticipated prosperity to many ex-slaves. The fact that Lincoln was assassinated almost immediately following surrender, which most historians believe at the least obfuscated and delayed intended transitional aid to slaves, did not register with some of the Works Progress Administration (WPA) respondents. For example, Harriet Ann Daves (NC) indicated that "I think Abraham Lincoln was a fine, conscientious man; my mother worshipped him, but he turned us out without anything to eat or live on." Jerry Eubanks (MS) viewed Lincoln as starting a lot of things that he did not finish:

> Abraham Lincoln started heap of things he didn't finish. Nobody ever went back where he left off. He wanted to brings all nations together.

John Smith (NC) thought that Lincoln sold out to the devil:

> I doan think Mr. Abraham Lincoln was a good man, no sir-ree, de debbil got him atter he whupped and won all de lan'. Ee wanted to gib it back agin. De debbil got de bes' o' him. Ee didn' lib long atter he whupped, did he?

Ed Barber (SC) felt that Lincoln should have left things the way they were because he did not know what he was doing:

> What I think of Abe Lincoln? I think he was a poor buckra white man, to de likes of me. Although, I 'spects Mr. Lincoln meant well but I can't help but wish him had continued splittin' them fence rails, which they say he knowed all 'bout, and never took a hand in runnin' de government of which he knowed nothin' 'bout. Marse Jeff Davis was all right, but him oughta got out and fought some, lak General Lee, General Jackson and 'Poleon Bonaparte. Us might have won de war if he had turned up at some of de big battles lak Gettysburg, 'Chickenmaroger' [sic] and 'Applemattox' [sic]. What you think 'bout dat?

Henry Bobbitt (NC), after being asked what he thought about President Lincoln, said that Lincoln was one of the worst things that could have happened to the slaves because of the consequences of being free:

> Well, I thinks dat he was doin' de wust thing dat he could ter turn
> all dem fool niggers loose when dey ain't got no place ter go an'
> nothin' ter eat. Who helped us out den? Hit wuzn't de Yankees,
> hit was de white folkses what was left wid deir craps in de fiel's, an'
> was robbed by dem Yankees, ter boot. My ole massa, fur instance,
> was robbed uv his fine hosses an' his feed stuff an' all dem kaigs o'
> liquor what he done make hisself, sides his money an' silver.

THOUGHTS ON LINCOLN'S LIFE

In his review of the narratives, Andrew Ward (2008) found many examples of former slaves viewing Lincoln as an undereducated, unsophisticated, and awkward man. In contrast, Ward found many references to Jefferson Davis being a sophisticated Southern gentleman and war hero. Some of the previous citations contained within this chapter characterize Lincoln as an ordinary and often poorly attired man.

Some of the narratives refer to different aspects of Lincoln's life, and some recalled when Lincoln was elected. His election was a major event that meant to many, both white and African American, that war was inevitable. At the beginning of his presidency, Lincoln was ridiculed in the press and by his many critics for the seemingly cowardly act of sneaking through Baltimore on his way to the inauguration. Under a perceived threat of assassination in Baltimore, he traveled under disguise to Washington. Lincoln vowed afterward that he would never again take extraordinary actions to protect himself from possible harm. Throughout his presidency and during the war, he would almost carelessly expose himself to great risk. Lincoln did in fact commandeer his army out of frustration with General McClelland's lack of action. Lincoln took command of Union forces and galvanized them into taking the port of Norfolk, Virginia. Jim Gillard (AL) summed up how many slaves viewed Lincoln: "Yassu'm, Mr. Abraham Lincoln died a warrior for dis country."

Lincoln's assassination came as a shock to many. Upon learning of his death, many African Americans took to the streets in despair (Quarles 1968). They had lost their champion and their great liberator, their Moses. The grief was overwhelming for many. Thousands passed by his body as it lay in state at the Capitol. The sense of security they had gained through his efforts was now shaken. The despair caused by the news of Lincoln's death is reflected in the narratives. Edgar Dinsmore, an African American soldier from New York, summarized the feelings of his people in a letter to his fiancée:

> We mourn the loss of our great and good President as a loss irrepa-
> rable. Humanity has lost a firm advocate, our race its patron Saint,
> and the good of all the world a fitting object to emulate. . . . The
> name Abraham Lincoln will ever be cherished in our hearts, and
> none will more delight to lisp his name in reverence than the future
> generations of our people.
>
> (McPherson 1993, 312)

Louis Meadows (AL) was not worried about going back to slavery but did believe that Lincoln's death had a negative impact:

> When Mr. Lincoln was kilt, us didn't think us would go back to slavery,
> 'cause us done been turned free. We had took de oath dat as long as
> dere was breath in de body or blood in de veins, dat never agin would
> we go back to slavery. But things was hurt by Mr. Lincoln gettin' kilt.

Sarah Harris (NC) saw Lincoln's death as destiny and saw him as a great man carrying out God's will: "The Lord put it into Abraham Lincoln to do as he done. . . . The Lord knowed he would be killed." George Conrad Jr. (OK) said, "Abraham Lincoln was a smart man, but he would have done more if he was not killed." John Finnley (TX) knew exactly where he was when he received the news of Lincoln's death:

> You knows when Abe Lincoln am shot? Well, I's in Nashville den
> and it am near de end of de war and I am standin' on Broadway
> Street talkin' with de sergeant when up walk a man and him shakes
> hands with me and says. "I's proud to meet a brave, young fellow
> like you." Dat man am Andrew Johnson and him come to be presi-
> dent after Abe's dead.

Charity Austin (NC) claims to have been lied to by her masters following Lincoln's death. She and the other slaves on her plantation believed every-thing they were told by the owners.

Boss tole us Abraham Lincoln wus dead and we were still slaves. Our boss man bought black cloth and made us wear it for mourning for Abraham Lincoln and tole us that there would not be freedom. We stayed there another year after freedom. A lot o' de niggers knowed nothin' 'cept what missus and marster tole us. What dey said wus just de same as de Lawd had spoken to us.

SLAVE SIGHTINGS AND PERCEPTIONS OF UNION GENERALS GRANT AND SHERMAN

The names of Generals Grant and Sherman were well known to the WPA respondents. Richard Johnson (TX) even asserted that he was present when Lee surrendered to Grant at Appomattox:

I was at Appomattox, and I seen General Lee and General Grant. General Grant didn't act high and mighty. He jes' rid up, an' got off his horse, and says to General Lee, "Howdy, General."

Anna Washington (AR) said that she saw General Grant in Little Rock, Arkansas. Hattie Gates (TX) may have also seen him:

One time a big General cum ter town wid de Yankee soljers, dey was all dressed up in de blue uniforms an' dey told us hit was General Grant, but I don't know fer sure who hit was, dey paraded up an down de street an he made a speech ter de crowd, den dey went away on de steamboat back ter de Missippi ribber.

William Kirk (AR) said, "I know General Grant looked fearful when he come by. After surrender he had a corps pass through and notify the people that the war was over." William Lattimore (AR) saw Grant: "I knowed General Grant when I seed him."

General Sherman was another major Union Army figure whom many claimed to have seen. Many ex-slaves recalled when Sherman and his troops passed through their region. Simon Walker (AL) said, "Nawsuh, Mass Jim an me ever did go to de wawh, but us seed de Yankees whin' Gen'l Sherman come marchin through our plantation." Mrs. Lydia Calhoun Starks (GA) claimed to have seen General Sherman accompanied by his bodyguards: "He came on our place with 'bout three body guards." She guessed that he wanted to get the lay of the land. Willis Williams (SC)

offered that he not only heard about him but also had seen him. Williams
described Sherman's appearance:

> He had a big name but he warn't such a big man; he was a little
> spars made man. I member now when I seed him the last time. He
> had two matched horses going down to Petersburg. Six guards
> riding by the side of his turnout. Oh my God, what clothes he had
> on! He was dressed down in finest uniform.

In another account, Frank A. Patterson (AR) claimed to have served dinner
to General Sherman and his officers in Georgia. He described Sherman:

> They got up from the dining table and Sherman ordered them to
> "Recover arms." He had on a big black hat full of eagles and he had
> stars and stripes all over him. That was Sherman's artillery.

Susan McIntosh (GA) did not see Sherman but did experience his assault
on Atlanta:

> I never saw no Yankees in Athens, but I was in Atlanta at Mrs. Winship's
> on Peachtree Street, when General Sherman come to that town
> 'parin' his men for to go home. There was about two thousand in
> all, white and black. They marched up and down Marietta Street
> from three o'clock in the evening 'til seven o'clock next morning.
> Then they left. I remember well that there warn't a house left stand-
> ing in Atlanta, what warn't riddled with shell holes. I was scared
> pretty nigh to death and I never want to leave home at no time like
> that again. But Pa saw 'em soon after that in Athens. They was a
> marching down Broad Street on their way to Macon, and Pa said it
> looked like a blue cloud going through.

William Ward (GA) also was there during Sherman's March to the Sea,
and the following is a description written by Ward's interviewer:

> Ward recalls vividly Sherman's march through Georgia. When
> Sherman reached the present site of Hapeville, he bombarded
> Atlanta with cannon, afterwards marching through and burning the
> city. The white residents made all sorts of frantic attempts to hide
> their money and other valuables. Some hiding places were under

stumps of trees and in sides of hills. Incidentally Sherman's army found quite a bit of the hidden wealth. Slaves were never allowed to talk over events and so very few, if any, knew about the war or its results for them before it actually happened. At the time that Sherman marched through Atlanta, Ward and other slaves were living in an old mansion at the present site of Peachtree and Baker Streets. He says that Sherman took him and his fellow slaves as far as Virginia to carry powder and shot to the soldiers. He states that he himself did not know whether Sherman intended to keep him in slavery or free him.

CONFEDERATE PRESIDENT JEFFERSON DAVIS

Aside from that which is well known about the life of Jefferson Davis, he was a man whom most historians believe was a very private and difficult man to know and was one of the most enigmatic figures of the Civil War. A slaveholder for most of his adult life, he was paternalistic, benevolent, and in some ways democratic in the way he conducted the governance of his own slaves, which was very enlightened for the time (Eaton 1977). Yet as president of the Confederacy, he was the public face of the fight to perpetuate a slave system in which many of its proponents practiced unrestrained mistreatment and deprivation of their slaves. He forbade the whipping of his own slaves (Johnson 2008) at a time when the whip's sting was considered by many as necessary discipline on the plantation. Davis denied that slavery as it existed in the South was a sin or an evil. Rather, he said that it was an "institution for the preparation of that race [Negroes] for civil liberty and social enjoyment" (Eaton 1977, 69). Although Davis treated African Americans with respect and received their respect in return, critics suggest that he also believed in white supremacy.

A devoted and agreeable family man in private, Davis was "cold and haughty" as a public figure (Eaton 1977, 32). He worked very hard to build his own plantation and yet earlier as a West Point cadet was an underachieving student and in his early military career was aristocratic and possessed of a troublesome pride that would later become problematic for him as president. Though he graduated from West Point in 1828 23rd out of a class of 32, he was nevertheless a refined Southern gentleman who didn't flinch when his wife, Varina, used money he gave her for a piano for the education of one of her brothers (Eaton 1977).

Though many of his slaves both before and after the war offered glowing testimonials about life under Davis, he was also plagued by some servants who turned on him as spies for the North. Historian James McPherson (1988) has said that Davis was incorruptible to a fault. Others have portrayed Davis as an overbearing, hot-tempered micromanager who insisted on having everything his way (Tate 1998).

One of the more curious personal relationships in Davis's life was the one he had with Jim Pemberton, the most faithful and trusted of his slaves. Davis and Pemberton grew up together as boys on Samuel Davis's plantation, and Jefferson's father awarded Pemberton to him when Jefferson was 15. Pemberton served young Davis as a body servant in the early 1830s when Davis was stationed in the Midwest and during the Black Hawk War. Later Pemberton helped Davis clear the land that became the Davis plantation, Brierfield, named for the tangled wilderness it was in 1835, and helped his owner build the 800 cultivated acres south of Vicksburg into a productive cotton plantation (Cooper 2000). The Slave Schedule of 1850 lists Davis as owning 53 slaves, and the Slave Schedule from 1860 counts his slaves at 115 (Bowman 2010, 163).

As time went by, Pemberton became more than just a faithful servant to Davis; Pemberton grew to become a trusted business associate and personal friend. In the early years of establishing Brierfield between 1835 and 1843, the two people with whom Davis had the most conversation were his older brother, Joseph, and Pemberton (Eaton 1977). Pemberton was made by Davis the overseer of Brierfield, a position seldom held by blacks in the antebellum South, and the plantation prospered under his wisdom and character. Varina Davis wrote of Pemberton's relationship with his master:

> They were devoted friends, and always observed the utmost courtesy and politeness in their intercourse, and at parting a cigar was always presented by Mr. Davis to him. James never sat down without being asked, although his master always invited him to be seated. James was a dignified, quiet man, of fine manly appearance, very silent, but what he said was always to the point.
>
> (Eaton 1977, 41)

Brother Joseph, from whom Jefferson acquired the land for Brierfield, believed in the British social reform philosophies of Robert Owen, preferring persuasion to compulsion and believing profits could be maximized through "rational" and humane labor practices (McMillen 2007). Slaves were referred to as "servants" or "the people," never as slaves. Although Jefferson Davis differed from Joseph in his views on the capability of slaves to be independent, both brothers used a slave-run judicial system to deal with miscreant slave behavior, which included the slaves themselves meting out any punishment. Joseph frequently would even reduce sentences of the slave jury or even pardon the convicted culprit, as did Jefferson (Eaton 1977). While Jefferson Davis was in Washington as a member of Congress, Pemberton managed the slaves at Brierfield on his own. Joseph never freed any of his slaves, since he believed that he was caught in the same dilemma as Thomas Jefferson: although they thought that slaves should be freed, they worried for their welfare and preparedness for freedom. Ironically, it was Jefferson Davis who offered manumission, or a gradual process toward freedom, to Pemberton in 1846, but Pemberton chose instead to look after the Davis family during their lifetime, after which he would accept his freedom. But since Pemberton predeceased both Jefferson and Varina (he died in 1850 from pneumonia), he was never freed, nor was any other Davis slave until after the war (Hermann 1999, 32). None of the white overseers who followed Pemberton would ever manage as well or reliably, and although Brierfield continued to generate a profit after Pemberton's death, its physical appearance declined considerably (Matrana 2009, 149).

There were at least two known incidents of African American servants who tended to the Davis family in Richmond during the war years and became spies for the North. Davis's house servant and personal coachman, William Jackson, after a few months in the Confederate White House escaped and turned over Confederate military details to Union major general Irvin McDowell (Rose 1999). Excerpts of a letter from McDowell to Secretary of War Edwin Stanton detailing Jackson's efforts were later reported in several newspapers of the day. The following account is reprinted from the June 7, 1862, edition of *Harper's Weekly*:

The coachman overheard a conversation between Davis and Dr. Gwin, formerly United States Senator from California. Davis said he had sent General J. R. Anderson from North Carolina to resist the march of the Nationals from Fredericksburg, and to delay them long enough for him to see the probable result of the contest before Yorktown, so that if that was likely to be unsuccessful he would have time to extricate his army from the peninsula and get

them into Richmond and out of Virginia; that otherwise they would
all be caught. . . . The coachman says that Mr. and Mrs. Davis have
all their books, clothing, and pictures packed up ready to move off;
that there is much outspoken Union feeling in Richmond; that, having been a waiter in a hotel there, he knows all the Union men of
the place, and that the Yankees are looked for with much pleasure,
more by the whites than even the colored people. Confederate
money is not taken when it can be avoided.

(Anon. 1862, 363)

Mary Elizabeth Bowser, a freed slave who was also placed as a servant in
the Confederate White House, became another who spied for the North,
releasing in great detail troop movements that had serious impact on the
Confederate war effort (Frank 2008). Bowser was working with Elizabeth
Van Lew, a white Richmond resident who so hated slavery that she began
operating a spy ring for the Union from Richmond when the war broke out
(Johnson 2008). While Bowser cleaned the house and waited on President
Davis and his military leaders, she read war dispatches and overheard conversations about Confederate troop strategy and movements. She memo-
rized details and passed them along to Union spies, who coded the
information and sent it to Generals Grant and Butler, "greatly enhancing
the Union's conduct of the war" according to the account assembled by the
U.S. Army Military Intelligence Corps Hall of Fame, into which Bowser
was inducted in 1995. Her induction citation said that she "succeeded in a
highly dangerous mission to the great benefit of the Union effort. She was
one of the highest-placed and most productive espionage agents of the
Civil War" (Frank 2008, 136).

Little is known about the lives of Jackson and Bowser, because after the
war the U.S. government destroyed records of many Southern spies and
their agents for their protection, fearing among other things retaliation
from lingering Confederate sympathizers. The characteristics that both
Jackson and Bowser possessed that made them so valuable to the Union
cause—besides, of course, their courage—were that both were literate and
were said to have nearly photographic memories. The Southern assumption that slaves were illiterate and not intelligent and the way slave servants
were trained to seem invisible played greatly to their advantage. Jackson
and Bowser were able to read dispatches and correspondence and overhear
strategic conversations, memorizing it all until they could get to their con-
tacts. Both posed as dull but hardworking slaves, and though both were

This is a post–Civil War photograph of the Jefferson Davis family taken by Edward L. Wilson sometime between 1884 and 1885. It shows the Davis Family at Beauvoir, Mississippi. From left are Varina Howell Davis Hayes [Webb] (1878–1934); Margaret Davis Hayes, who was Jefferson and Varina's daughter; Lucy White Hayes [Young] (1882–1966); Jefferson Davis; unidentified servant; Varina Howell Davis; and Jefferson Davis Hayes (1884–1975), whose name was legally changed to Jefferson Hayes-Davis in 1890. The children were three of five that Margaret and Addison Hayes had. It may or may not be significant that the photographer failed to name Davis's pictured servant, and may have been an indication of the continued low esteem held for African Americans following the war, or it may have been just an innocent oversight. Wilson was publisher of the photographic journal *The Philadelphia Photographer* and a founder of what later became the Photographers' Association of America. (Library of Congress)

free, both had formerly been slaves. In the three years that Bowser spied from the Davis White House, the president never suspected that the leaks were coming from her until very late, and she was able to escape in January 1865 (Williams 2008).

Similar to the case with Lincoln, some of the ex-slaves reported that they had seen or had involvement with Jefferson Davis. The odds of this occurring with Davis would have been greater than with Lincoln. For example, Dempsey Pitts (MS) said that he saw Davis in Vicksburg, although his narrative doesn't say when. John Wells (AR) also claimed to have seen Davis following the war, also in Vicksburg:

> I have seen Jeff Davis. I never seen Lincoln. They said it was Jeff Davis I seen. I seen him in Vicksburg. That was after the war was over.

John Majors (TX) said that he saw Davis when the Confederate president traveled to his brother's plantation:

> W'en we was down here hit was durin de war an' I has seen Massa Jeff Davis, dat was de President of de Confederacy, as he pass goin' to de old Hurricane House, but as de war got worse, den his young wife went away an' he did'nt cum any more. I 'members w'en de blockade was on at New Orleans an' how all de folks had to git out dey spinnin' wheels to make de cloth dey called de Homespun for dey clothes, for dey could'nt git anything shipped into New Orleans or up to Memphis for de blockade.

The mansion at the Joseph Davis plantation, Hurricane, was burned by Union soldiers in 1862, and after the war both Hurricane and Brierfield, Jefferson's plantation, were taken by the U.S. Army, which later tried to turn both over to the Freedmen's Bureau to operate (Cooper 2000, 572). Fearing that Brierfield would be confiscated because of Union sentiment toward his brother, Joseph was able to convince authorities that he owned Brierfield, since there was never any paperwork associated with the transfer of Brierfield to Jefferson. In an extraordinary turnabout in Southern history, Joseph sold both Hurricane and Brierfield to his favorite former slave, Isaiah Montgomery, and Montgomery's two sons in 1867 (Cooper 2000). After extensive legal battles, Jefferson Davis regained ownership in 1878 but rarely visited Brierfield between then and his death in 1889.

George Washington Ramsay (MS) offered this encounter with Jefferson Davis:

> But I can tell you about ole man Jeff Davis. He shook hands with me right there where the Confederate Home now is. I went to tell him about the Ramsays that was Confederate soldiers an' to recommend them. I guess I'm the only cullud man around here that ever seen Jeff Davis.

Nick Carter (MS) claimed that he "followed President Jefferson Davis throughout the War Between the States for the entire period." Nancy Gardner (OK) said that she knew Davis well and that he was a mean "old rascal":

> Why I was jest as close to him as I am to dat table. I've talked wid him too. I reckon I do know dat scoundrel! Why, he didn't want de niggers to be free! He was known as a mean old rascal all over de South.

William Dunwoody (AR) also claimed to have seen Davis:

> I saw Jeff Davis once. He was one-eyed. He had a glass eye. My old mistiss had three girls. They got into the buggy and went to see Jeff Davis when he came through Auburn, Alabama. We were living in Auburn then. I drove them. Jeff Davis came through first, and then the Confederate army, and then the Yankees. They didn't come on the same day but some days apart.

There is considerable folklore regarding the circumstances surrounding the capture of Jefferson Davis, much of which suggests that he was captured in women's clothing in a failed effort to escape Union troops. Many versions by many authors both North and South, including some of the participants in the May 10, 1865, capture, have left a battery of information, misinformation, half-truths, and outright lies about what really happened. After the fall of Richmond more than a month earlier, Davis, members of his cabinet, and a retinue of guards and family members took flight on a journey deeper into the South trying to reach the Trans-Mississippi West, where they hoped that the Confederacy might yet regroup. The group was awakened in the early morning hours at their camp near Irwinsville, Georgia, by two groups of Federals under the direction of Major General James H. Wilson, U.S. Cavalry Corps. In the confusion, Davis turned back into his tent and reached for his raglan (a type of raincoat popular in the 1860s worn by both men and women) but instead grabbed his wife's raglan, using it to hide his light-colored gray suit in the dark forest (Johnson 2008, 181). Varina threw a shawl over his head to protect him from the cold air; shawls were also worn in the 1860s by both men and women. Davis's story was that he put the raglan over his shoulders. Varina remembered that she threw the raglan over his shoulders. Both of them remembered that she threw the shawl over his head (Johnson 2008). Whether the intent of the raglan and the shawl was to protect Davis from the cold, damp morning or to adopt a disguise in hope of escape depends on which version of the story one believes.

At Varina's encouragement, Davis tried to run toward the creek away from his captors but was caught. James H. Jones, a Davis body servant who was with the presidential party at capture, told a slightly different story. In an interview with a *New York Times* correspondent in 1911 when he was 83 years old, Jones said that when the Federals ordered the president and Mrs. Davis out of the tent on the morning of the capture, it was Jones who

> grabbed up Mrs. Davis' raglan coat, thinking I had Mr. Davis' coat instead, and threw it around his shoulders. So when he stepped out of the tent he did have a woman's coat on for a moment, but it was only for a moment because I saw the mistake right away, and changed coats, putting Mr. Davis's on instead of the one belonging to Mrs. Davis that I had thrown on in the hurry and excitement of the time.
>
> (Jones 1911)

Wilson sent a telegram to Secretary of War Edwin Stanton on May 13 notifying the Secretary that Davis was in custody and mentioned that he had been found wearing his wife's dress (Johnson 2008). However, in his official battle report to Stanton, written after the telegram, Wilson makes no mention of Davis being in women's clothes or even in disguise. But the story was out of the gate, for shortly after the telegram was made public, *Harper's Weekly* and the *New York Times* both published the Wilson-to-Stanton telegram word for word. Newspapers across the country began running all sorts of variations of the story, and Stanton, to protect himself, ordered that Varina's hoopskirt, which had nothing to do with the capture, and the raglan and shawl that Davis wore be confiscated (Johnson 2008). Since at that time Stanton and others in the North believed that Davis was a conspirator in the assassination of Lincoln, there was little sympathy outside the South for getting the story right. Having the president of the Confederacy captured in such a manner of disguise helped fuel the Northern propaganda mill, a fact not lost on Secretary Stanton. Some of the slaves apparently heard this version of Davis's capture and mentioned it in their narratives. For example, WPA respondent Dilly Yellady (NC) told this account of Davis's capture:

> Ole Jeff Davis said he wus goin' to fight de Yankees till hell wus so full of 'em dat dere legs wus hangin' over de sides, but when dey got 'im in a close place he dres in 'omans clothes an' tried to git away frum 'em but dey seed his boots when he started to git in dat thing dey rode in den, a carriage. Yes dats what it wus a carriage. Dey seed his boots an' knowed who it wus. Dey jus laffed an' pointed at 'im an' said you hol' on dere we got you, we knows who you is an' den dey took 'im. He wus mighty brave till dey got 'im in a close place den he quit barkin' so loud. Mammy an' dad dey said dere wus a lot of de white folks didn't keer much 'bout Jeff Davis. Dey said he wus jus de bragginest man in de worl', always a-blowin'. Dat bird flew mighty high but he had to come back to de groun' an' course when he lit de Yankees wus waitin' for 'im an' ketched 'im.

In another narrative account of the capture of Davis, Elmo Steele (MS) described a wartime encounter with Davis. Steele, who was a volunteer in the Union Army, described how he identified Davis and was almost able to capture him. The account incorporates the folklore of Davis being dressed as a woman to avoid apprehension by Union forces:

> I wuz a volunteer private under Captain Tool. De war wuz a gittin' close to de end. Captain Tool got orders to be on de look out fer Jefferson Davis dat he had been to Washington D.C. an' dat it wuz important dat he wuz kept from gettin' to Virgiana to where de Southern Ammunition an' strongest forces wuz at. Captain Tool learned dat dey would stop at a way-side inn. Several wuz along in de crowd an' dey had a little boy attendent 'bout fifteen years ole. Captain Tool wuz sharp, he didn't want to cause no suspicion. He give me some money an tole me to go talk to dat nigger an' den offer him money to tell me if Jefferson Davis was one o' dem men which one. I axed dis boy if he wanted to see all de money I had. I showed it all to him an' axed him how he would like to hab some ob it. He grinned from ear to ear, he wanted dat money. I tole him I'd give him a five dollar bill if he would tell me if Jefferson Davis was deir, he wouldn't do it,

I offered him another five, he still wouldn't tell, I offered him another an' another 'till I showed him twenty, den he tole me yes, I hurried back an' tole Captain Tool. He sont me back wid another five to git de boy to tell me which one. He also tole me how to go 'bout dat; an' dis wuz how it. When dey sit down to eat de colored boy tucked de napkins under deir chins. He wuz to pull Jefferson Davis'es twice under his chin before tuckin' it in. I watched close den tole Captain Tool. When Jefferson Davis saw he wuz about to be kotched, he disguised as a woman an' got away but dey wuz so close on his trail. Him an' his men wuz kept from de ammunition an' forces in time to ward off deir plans.

John Rogers (GA) said that black Union soldiers told the Yankees that Davis was down by the spring and that this was where he was captured. Alice Battle (GA) said that she witnessed Davis pass by her owner's home. Henry Bland (GA) claimed to have seen Davis surrender his sword to General Sherman, which no historian has ever validated. Martha Everett (GA) said that she saw a captured Davis pass by the big house following his capture. The introduction to the WPA narrative of Florida Hewitt (MS) describes how she was a servant to Davis when he lived in seclusion on his plantation. The interviewer added that this servant woman saw Davis every day during his stay at Brierfield. She claimed to have not seen him during the war but did in the autumn of 1870 when he returned to Brierfield. She shared what happened during his return, which was summarized by the WPA interviewer:

It must have been during the autumn of 1870 that she stood at her cabin door, smiling upon some Negro boys who played around in their shirt tails. Suddenly they raised a shout, "Here comes Marse Jeff!" Aunt Florida stared at the approaching rider who no longer sat superbly erect, but drooped and sagged like a tired old man. Since he left Brierfield an empire had crumbled beneath him; his friends were slain on the field of battle; his beloved little son had fallen from a balcony in Richmond and died at his feet. He had suffered agonies at Fortress Monroe. The sight of one eye was gone and the dead orb glittered blindly. Yet Jefferson Davis didn't forget the little slave children at home, for he brought a bunch of shoes, dangling like fish strung on a cord. These shoes he dropped on Florida's porch and told each of the boys to pick a pair.

According to Hewitt, the slaves at Davis's Brierfield plantation were loyal to him. In another WPA narrative, a different respondent claimed to have ties to Davis. John Williams (MS) claimed to have parents who were sold to Davis and later served at his Beauvoir home. Williams recalled working for Davis after the war:

> When I was one year old my father and mother was sold to
> Mr. Jefferson Davis, President of de Confederacy, and dere was not
> much difference in mine and "Miss Winnie's" ages. I was too young
> to remember much that happened until we went to Beauvoir, atter
> de war was over and worked fer Mr. Davis. I kin remember Miss
> Winnie and me watching fer Mr. Davis's carriage, and running
> down to open de big gate fer him to drive in.
>
> De udder culled folks at Beauvoir besides my mama and daddy
> was de cook who was name "Laura Ramsay." She belonged to
> Mr. A. J. Ramsay's grandfather befo' de war. She had a son name,
> "Greene Ramsay," who died a few years ago at Beauvoir. Dey give
> him a "paper" at de Cotehouse, and he was saunt out to Beauvoir to
> be took keer of till he died. He claimed to be Jefferson Davis's
> body-guard, and always went with him on his trips to Jackson and
> ovah in Lou'sana. He drove his carriage fer him. Mr. Davis had a
> big black hoss and a big bay one. I kain't remember dere names, but
> I does remember de names of de mules dey hauled freight wid—
> dey was "Jack and Joe."

Other WPA respondents spoke about working as Davis's servant. Frank Loper (MS) recalled the day the master called his slaves together for his farewell address. According to Loper, Davis announced that "In case of trouble to the plantation, I depend upon you all to take care of the family, and if it becomes necessary, to fight for them" (Ward 2008, 18). Loper remembered that all the slaves cheered for him because he had been kind to them, at least his house slaves. "We all cheered him, and promised that we would, because Mr. Davis was a kind master, and never would allow us to be whipped," he said. But some of Davis's ex-slaves characterized him as cruel to his field slaves. However, Loper said that Davis would come to see his slaves when they were ill. "Whenever we were sick, he would come and see about us himself," he said. Loper did not question Davis's motives, which were likely tied more to them being seen as property rather than as human beings. Owners were known to visit ill slaves for a variety of reasons, including real concern, but more likely in most cases because slaves were viewed as property. Owners wanted to be sure that slaves were truly ill and not feigning illness to avoid work (Covey 2007). Idle slaves were not productive slaves. Clement Eaton (1977, 41), in his milestone biography of Davis, wrote that "Jefferson established such kindly relations with his slaves that, according to Varina, when he went to their quarters, the slaves, even the children, would greet him enthusiastically, and the master was in the habit of shaking hands with them."

When Union forces arrived at the Davis plantation, Loper indicated that the "people" were upset that they took Davis's things. Some historians indicate that Davis did not himself believe in selling slaves because it broke up families. In his research, Eaton found no available records indicating that Davis ever sold a slave, although he did buy some for plantation and domestic use (Eaton 1977, 41). However, other historians disagree with the notion that Davis would not sell slaves. In his narrative, James Lucas (MS) said that he was owned by several masters, including briefly by Jefferson Davis, and claims to have been sold by a "bank." Other historians say that Lucas was sold by Davis, who then later tried to trade Loper, Loper's mother, and four of his brothers "for some mules" (Ward 2008, 18). The Loper trade was never consummated, and Loper's loyalty continued following emancipation, as he stayed on as a servant with the Davis family following the war. He later moved to Colorado Springs, Colorado, at the request of Jefferson Hayes Davis, grandson of Jefferson Davis and vice president of a local bank there, lending further credence to the belief that Roper's loyalty to the Davis family never waivered.

Still other historians note that Davis sold two slaves on January 1, 1864, to raise money (Hattaway and Beringer 2002, 268). Davis was a man of contradictions, and while it may be true that his personal beliefs lessened his role in selling slaves, there appears at least some solid evidence that he did engage in the slave trade on occasion.

Another respondent, Edward Taylor (MO), said that he served Davis before he became president of the "United States [*sic*]":

> I took care of Jeff Davis for years, long fore he ever got president of des United States. Yes sir, I did. When de stars fell people all runin' and hollerin' judgment done come. I didn't see no need in all dat citement, as long as de white folks livin' I thought they could keep us niggers livin'.

Some of the narratives seem to praise and admire Davis. Unlike their characterizations of Lincoln, whom they portrayed as lower class, slaves' descriptions of Davis were of a man of culture and high status. For example, Mark Oliver (MS) did not question that Davis endorsed slavery and thought it the natural state for slaves. Rather, Oliver believed Davis to be a great man:

> There is Abraham Lincoln, he was talked of much, 'cause he set us all free, and Jefferson Davis, he was a great man. He done his part for what he thought was right. He didn't think they had a right to take the slaves away from their owners, when they had done bought them.

Charlie Davenport (MS) believed in Davis and thought that he did the only thing he could do, and that was to fight back. Davenport, typical of some narratives, cast Davis as a "gentleman":

> Pusonally, I 'bleeve in what Mr. Davis done. He done de only thing a gentleman could do. He tole Mr. Abe Lincoln to tend to his own business 'en he'd tend to hissen. But Lincoln was a fightin man en he come down here to run other folks plantations. Dat made Mr. Davis so all fired mad dat he spit hard between his teeth en say: "I'll whip de socks offen dem damn Yankees."

Simon Hare (MS) viewed Davis as a gentleman and never linked this perception with what he allegedly said to a crowd in Meridian, Mississippi. If Hare's account is accurate, Davis's comments were degrading to slaves and reaffirmed their place as being servile to whites:

> I met Jefferson Davis! We toted him, right here in Mer-ree-dian, toted him on our shoulders, didn' let him put he feets on de ground, toted him frum de train ter de courthouse. He was gonter make a speech. He was a old gent'mun, looked mild. He got off de train at de Ragsdale Hotel. I was greasin' cwars then. Dey had little small engines an' had smokers on top of 'em, great big things; de first little engines de A. & V. run; th'owed wood in there. An' my fo'man said, "Knock off an' go see our President." Had one lady wid him, Miss Winnie, say she was his daughter. He made a speech at de courthouse. Say, "You b'long ter us. You aint free." Say, "You can't

hurt a nigger; all he needs, keep him full of some'pin t'eat; work him hard; he show steal if he git hongry; he steal him a hog an' car'y hit home. Feed him an' work him, dat's all."

Davis spent two years at Fortress Monroe after his capture and was released in 1867. He was never tried, nor were any charges ever brought against him. A tired and broken man bedeviled by many chronic afflictions, he lived out the remainder of his life, from 1879 on, mostly at his home in Beauvoir, Mississippi, writing, occasionally speaking, and struggling to regain his beloved Brierfield. He never recanted his views of slavery. Davis wrote the two-volume *The Rise and Fall of the Confederate Government* (1881) and also wrote *A Short History of the Confederate States of America*, which was published two months before his death in 1889.

Davis's funeral was called "the South's Greatest Funeral," and a number of his former slaves made the journey to attend. One of them, William Simpson, wept openly at the funeral. When asked by a Northern reporter how he felt about Davis, Simpson replied, "That I loved him, this shows, and I can say that every colored man he ever owned loved him" (Sons of Confederate Veterans 2012, 1). In Varina's memoir, she wrote affectionately of "Old Bob" Brown, who was also called "Uncle Bob," a former servant of the Davis family. In 1893 Davis's body was moved from its burial site in New Orleans to its final resting place in Richmond via a 1,200-mile funeral train procession. Brown was a passenger on the train. When he saw the many flowers that children had laid on the side of the railroad tracks, he "was so moved that we wept uncontrollably" (Johnson 2003).

The year before Davis died, he received a letter from one of his former slaves, James H. Jones, who since emancipation had a successful career as an alderman and also a deputy sheriff. Jones told Davis that "I have always been as warmly attached to you as when I was your body servant" and went on to say that he always defended Davis from "any attack of malicious or envious people" (Cooper 2000, 644). Davis's relations with African Americans has been portrayed as follows:

Without question he respected individual African Americans and in turn received their respect. His dealings with his slave James Pemberton and with Ben Montgomery as both a slave and a freedman illustrate such a relationship. Inviting Davis to attend the Colored State Fair in

Vicksburg in 1886, Montgomery's son Isaiah said he knew Davis would have an interest "in any Enterprise tending to the welfare and development of the Colored people of Mississippi." "We would be highly pleased to have you here," Isaiah Montgomery asserted, and he closed "with best wishes for your continued preservation."

(Cooper 2000, 643)

Though Davis may have respected some individuals, he still viewed blacks as an inferior race.

SLAVE SIGHTINGS AND PERCEPTIONS OF CONFEDERATE GENERAL ROBERT E. LEE AND OTHERS

In the recollections of the WPA respondents, only one other Confederate seemed to take on a status equal to or surpassing that of President Davis, and that individual was General Robert E. Lee. There are examples of respondents having encounters with Lee. Mary Flagg (AR) said, "Why I waited on the table when General Lee stopped there for dinner on his way from Mobile to meet Sherman." William H. McCarty (MS) claimed to have served under various generals and had seen General Lee many times, shook his hand, and talked with him once in New Orleans.

Besides Lee, other narratives contain references to other Confederate generals such as Hood, by William Porter (AR); Wheeler, by Claiborne Moss (AR) and John Boyd (SC); and Thomas "Stonewall" Jackson, by Gus Brown (AL). Brown shared his memory of Stonewall Jackson and how impressive he was even in the glare of adversity:

> I remember Stonewall Jackson. He was a big man with long whiskers, and very brave. We all fought wid him until his death. We wa'n't beaten, we was starved out! Sometimes we had parched corn to eat and sometimes we didn't have a bite o' nothin', because the Union mens come and tuk all de food for theirselves. I can still remember part of my ninety years. I remembers dey fought all de way from Virginia and winded up in Manassah's Gap.

OBSERVATIONS

It is as true today as it was in their time that the major figures of the Civil War take on legendary status that is often surrounded by considerable folklore and legend. For those who lived through the Civil War, figures such as

Davis and Lincoln as well as their generals were, to borrow the cliché, larger than life. The folklore and hearsay surrounding these figures became reality for many ex-slaves.

In their narratives, ex-slaves looked for ways to connect with these individuals by reporting personal encounters and visits with Lincoln, Davis, and other historical figures of the time. What better way was there to connect with them than to have these figures of American history pay a personal visit? With few exceptions, these encounters were improbable if not impossible. Lincoln frequently visited the front lines of the war. However, he was a man with very recognizable features and would not have traveled incognito to visit slaves in the Deep South during the war.

Ex-slaves attributed a wide range of characteristics and motives to Lincoln, some of them positive and others negative. Slaves idolized Lincoln for bringing freedom and damned him for not following through on his promises. The same could be said of Davis, who ranged from being a brilliant leader to an obstinate fool, very similar to how many historians have characterized him. In Davis's case, his own slaves and those of his brother not surprisingly more often than not portrayed him as a kindly caretaker, while those slaves who didn't have personal contact with him displayed a wider range of emotions about him. Ex-slaves often characterized both Lincoln and Davis as riding either mules or horses. In the end, we are left with the conclusion that neither figure perfectly matched any of these perceptions, but some of the ex-slave recollections are particularly poignant and fit what we do know about these two leaders.

CHAPTER 9

Freedom and What Came After

Yessir, I thought master would divide his land with us and give us a mule. Instead of that we were turned out like a stray bunch of cattle without anything to eat or wear. Well if master hadnt been afraid of the Yankees, he never would have freed us cause he cursed every breath. He didnt give us the clothes that we had when the war was over, made us stay and work them out at twenty five cents a day. And after the war it was almost impossible for the negro to get anything to eat or wear. The white man sure was rough on us because he were mad cause the north freed us. It looked to us negroes like the north ought to have taken car of us, cause they first captured us brought us to this country and sold us in to slavery, then fought a war and freed the slaves, then turned us out to starve as the negro then was not anything but a brute like the cattle and horses of this day. He couldnt read and write, didnt know how to farm hisself. All he knew was what the white man made him do, and after the war all the negro knew was farm work. We most generally had to work for almost nothing. We received from $1.50 to $2.50 per month all the clothes we got was old clothes the white man wouldnt wear for long time after the war we never voted unless under compulsion to vote like our white man made us vote. If he could vote us like he wanted it was all right if not our grub was cut off, or we lost our job. I'se believe that since the negro has the same responsible that white man has we ought to have more voting privilige then the negro he has because we has become more educaed, in the ways of the world and free life if we can call life that now.

(Elige Davison, TX)

When the secessionist states withdrew from the Union, the new republic claimed its justification to be the protection of states' rights. In truth, a close reading of the states' secession proclamations and of the new Confederate Constitution reveals that it was primarily the right to preserve African American slavery within each state's borders. But the South's decision to secede proved to be the worst possible choice it could have made to preserve that right.

At the time there was antislavery sentiment in the North, but many Northerners had sentiments that were strongly antiblack. Northern whites sometimes shared their Southern counterparts' prejudicial attitudes toward African Americans. Northerners were antislavery and Southerners were proslavery, but most in both the North and the South were antiblack (Jordan 1995). White Northerners did not wish for slavery to expand into new areas of the nation, which they believed should be preserved for white nonslaveholding settlers. This was partly why Republicans pledged to protect slavery where it existed, because their constituencies did not want an influx of ex-slaves into exclusively white territories should slavery end abruptly.

THE FIGHT FOR FREEDOM

Initially the Northern goal in the Civil War was a quick restoration of the Union under the U.S. Constitution and laws in effect in 1861, both of which recognized slavery as legitimate. However, Northern opposition to slavery would make reunification of the country more difficult. Union forces were ordered not only to defeat the Confederate armies but also to prevent slave insurrections. In the early months of the war, slaves who escaped to Union lines were often returned to their masters in accordance with the Fugitive Slave Act of 1850, which was in contradiction to Northern abolitionist forces.

The movement for the abolition of slavery was troubling for all involved and was agonizingly slow. The Emancipation Proclamation freed some 4 million slaves in theory (Berlin et al. 1987). But the precise moment when a slave could think of himself or herself as a free person was not always clear (Litwack 1979). From the outset of the war, many slaves thought that they were free the moment Yankee soldiers came into their area. With the military situation so fluid in the early years of the war, any freedom predicated on troop support was precarious at best. Slaves often found it confusing as to whose authority prevailed. Additionally, the Emancipation Proclamation excluded numbers of slaves from its provisions, specifically those in border states. Some masters claimed to be unaware of the proclamation, others refused to acknowledge it while the war's outcome was in doubt, and some doubted its constitutionality after the hostilities concluded (Litwack 1979). Ambrose Douglass (FL), a former North Carolina slave, recalled the confusion surrounding emancipation:

> I guess we musta celebrated 'Mancipation about twelve times in Harnett County. Every time a bunch of No'thern sojers would come through they would tell us we was free and we'd begin celebratin'. Before we would get through somebody else would tell us to go back to work, and we would go. Some of us wanted to jine up with the army, but didn't know who was goin' to win and didn't take no chances.

Since there was not one single day when slaves became free, some referred to the period from emancipation until many months after the war as the days of Jubilee. Whenever slaves learned that they were free, that became their day of Jubilee, as noted by Patricia and Fredrick McKissack, authors of *Days of Jubilee*. In his narrative, William Cole (TN) said:

> For Mas' and his family, the Fourth Day [of July] was their Jubilee. That's when they all got free to be. Mas' give us the day off to celebrate 'long with them. And we did. But all the time we was wishin' for our own day of independence.
>
> (McKissack and McKissack 2003, 1)

For liberated slaves and whites there were many changes, such as race relations becoming less crystallized and boundaries becoming more unclear. For freed slaves education became a possibility, but freedom left some African Americans without work, and life was less certain than it had been under the oppression of slavery. Black Union troops were often assigned to liberated areas of the South to maintain order, guard against guerrilla attacks, and protect the helpless. Southern whites found this presence of recently liberated African American soldiers difficult to accept (Redkey 1992). The South had not only lost the war, but now Southern whites were subjected to the authority of black troops. Their armed presence caused much resentment and hostility among Southern whites, who viewed them as inferior victors. The South had long had an aversion to arming blacks; thus, having armed black soldiers in their communities was a major test. Racial tensions increased and reminded whites that they had not only lost the war but that their status had declined relative to African Americans.

Union solders sometimes wrote about their reception by Southern blacks. Ex-slave and preacher Garland H. White, Union Army chaplain, 28th U.S. Colored Infantry, was asked to speak upon entering Richmond on April 3, 1865. Black soldiers, who had besieged the city for months, were among the first to enter the city when Lee abandoned it on April 2. In a letter dated April 12, 1865, detailing his experiences on the day of Lee's abandonment of Richmond, White wrote:

> I have just returned from the city of Richmond; my regiment was among the first that entered the city. . . . A vast multitude assembled on Broad Street, and I was aroused amid the shouts of ten thousand voices, and proclaimed for the first time in that city freedom to all mankind. After which the doors of all of the slave pens were thrown open, and thousands came out shouting and praising God, and father, or master Abe, as they termed him. In this mighty consternation I became so overcome with tears that I could not stand up under the pressure of such fullness of joy in my own heart.
>
> (Redkey 1992, 175–176)

Tensions resulting from freedom remained high during and following the war. Freed slaves represented everything that the South had struggled for, sacrificed, and fought against. All of the passion and hatred that people held for each other were diminished compared to that targeted toward the ex-slaves (Quarles 1968). Southern sacrifices in terms of human life, property, and wealth had been great, and the loss of the war was not readily accepted. Carrie Hudson (GA) described one white Southerner's reaction this way:

> De day dey told us dat us was free dere was a white man named Mr. Bruce, what axed: "What you say?" Dey told him 'gain dat all de Niggers was free. He bent hisself over, and never did straighten his body no more. When he died, he was still all bent over. Mr. Bruce done dis to sho' de world how he hated to give his Niggers up atter dey done been sot free.

From the Southern perspective, the greed, inhumanity, and cruelty of slavery were not the blame for the tragic war; it was the slaves themselves who were at fault. The South would take many measures after the war to keep blacks under the yoke of oppression. So-called Black Codes, a series of state laws intended to define the freedmen's new rights and responsibilities, were

This Thomas Nast print, published in *Harper's Weekly* in 1866, is entitled *President Lincoln Entering Richmond, April 4, 1865.* It depicts Lincoln walking through the Confederate capital the day after Union forces occupied the city. Lincoln had committed to personally tour Richmond and was accompanied by Admiral Porter, Captain Bell, and a small unit of soldiers. The streets became crowded as residents tried to see the "Great Emancipator." Many in the crowd were recently emancipated slaves who wanted to pay homage to their liberator. The small boy holding Lincoln's hand is his son, Tad, whom the President brought with him to see the fallen city; it was the boy's 12th birthday. As Lincoln walked the streets of Richmond, one group of liberated slaves shouted, "Glory Hallelujah!" and fell to their knees before him. "Don't kneel to me," he told them. "You must kneel only to God, and thank him for your freedom. Liberty is your birthright. God gave it to you as he gave it to others, and it is a sin that you have been deprived of it for so many years." (Courtesy Picture Collection, The Branch Libraries, The New York Public Library, Astor, Lenox and Tilden Foundations. Image ID 813678.)

passed in many Southern states to adjust to their new status after slavery ended. But the Black Codes were also an attempt to stabilize the African American workforce and limit its economic options apart from plantation labor (Foner 1988). After the war, some Northern states also put restrictions on African Americans moving from state to state and on allowing them to vote. Louisiana enacted its Black Codes in 1865 and was soon followed by Mississippi later the same year. South Carolina defined white employers as "masters" and black employees as "servants" (McPherson 2001, 553). Mississippi required all African Americans to annually possess written evidence of employment for the coming year. Anyone leaving their jobs before the contract expired would forfeit wages already earned and be subject to arrest by any white citizen (Foner 1988). South Carolina's Black Code did not forbid blacks from renting land but did bar them from any occupation other than farmer or servant except by paying an annual tax ranging from $10 to $100, a severe blow to African Americans. However, the U.S. Army and the Freedmen's Bureau eventually suspended enforcement of the parts of the Black Codes that discriminated between the races. Jim Crow laws would soon follow but never fully restored the control that whites held over blacks.

FREEDOM FOR THE SLAVES

Freedom for the slaves began with the Emancipation Proclamation, which after the war culminated with the Thirteenth Amendment banning slavery in the United States. The amendment proclaimed that neither slavery nor involuntary bondage shall exist in the United States. Ironically, the emancipation of slaves was debated as a possibility very early during the war by Southern whites (Durden 1972; Levine 2006). Slaves learned of their freedom in a variety of ways. One common means was when owners called them to the big house and made the announcement. Pierce Cody (GA) learned of his freedom in this manner, as did other slaves on his plantation. He noted that upon receiving the word, slaves danced in jubilation:

When the Emancipation Proclamation was signed, the slaves were called to the "big house" in a group to receive the news that they were free. Both old and young danced and heered when this information was given out. Many of the families remained there for a year or two until they were able to find desirable locations elsewhere.

This illustration entitled *Emancipation of the Negroes*, January, 1863, was a Thomas Nast wood engraving published in *Harper's Weekly*, January 24, 1863. Nast's cartoons and illustrations helped the general population see slaves as people and not property. The center image is of what the future might hold for freed slaves, depicting an African American family with many characteristics of a white family of the day. Nast shows the family living in a nice home with other nice possessions, such as furniture and a cast iron stove. Family members are dressed in fine clothing. The print includes three generations of family members, including a seated senior and children in the foreground. The father is bouncing his child on his knee while the family is doing all the normal things a white family of the day might have been doing. The bordering images capture the cruelty of slavery showing whipping and other tortures, and escaped slaves being hunted down like dogs. Slaves are also shown being sold at auction. Thomas Nast was very supportive of the war effort and the preservation of the Union. (Library of Congress)

Charles Graham (AR) recalled a large celebration and acknowledgment of Lincoln as freeing the slaves:

> The first clear thing I remember was when everybody was rejoicing because they were free. The soldiers were playing and boxing and chucking watermelons at one another. They had great long guns called muskets. I heard em say that Abraham Lincoln had turned 'em loose. Where I was at, they turned 'em loose in '63. Lincoln was assassinated in '65. I heard that the morning after it was done. We was turned loose long before then. I was too young to pay much

attention, but they were cutting up and clapping their hands and carrying on something terrible, and shouting, "Free, free, old Abraham done turned us loose."

But some of the Works Progress Administration (WPA) respondents indicated that celebrations were guarded. George Lewis (GA) recalled that all of the slaves on his plantation were glad when they were told they were free, but there was no big demonstration, as they were somewhat fearful of retribution from the master.

THE ANNOUNCEMENT OF FREEDOM

The announcement of freedom and/or surrender was remembered in some of the narratives, some of which indicated that freed slaves held local rallies. Minnie Davis (GA) told of the day they learned about the surrender. African Americans rallied around the flagpole near city hall and sang the following tune: "We rally around the flag pole of liberty, the Union forever, Hurrah! Boys Hurrah!" Moble Hopson (VA) recalled a celebration among the slaves, who were "shoutin' fo' joy cause 'Marse Lincoln done set em free." Abe Livingston (TX) learned of his freedom from Union troops, even recalling the time: "News of the freedom come 'bout 9 or 10 o'clock on a Tuesday morning." Jeptha Choice (TX) learned from Yankee troops who visited her plantation:

After the War, some Federal provost officers on horseback, came to the plantation and told the old Missus to call everybody up to the house, and then read a proclamation saying that we niggers was as free as our masters; and not to work anymore unless we got paid for it—and that if we wanted to, we could have land free to farm.

Lindsey Moore (FL) witnessed a parade and a band marching through the area. The WPA interviewer summarized Mr. Moore's experience:

Lindsey's first knowledge of the approach of freedom came when he heard a loud brass band coming down the road toward the plantation playing a strange, lively tune while a number of soldiers in blue uniforms marched behind. He ran to the front gate and was ordered to take charge of the horse of one of the officers in such an abrupt tone until he "begin to shaking in my bare feet!" There followed much talk between the officers and Lindsey's mistress, with the soldiers finally going into encampment a short distance away from the plantation.

Mary Anderson (NC) told of the approaching Yankees and the announcement made by her master of freedom for the slaves:

> Then one day I heard something that sounded like thunder and missus and marster began to walk around and act queer. The row slaves were whisperin to each other. Sometimes they gathered in little canyons in the grove. Next day I heard it again, boom, boom, boom. I went and asked missus "is it going to rain?" She said, "Mary go to the ice house and bring go some pickles and preserves." I went and got them. She ate a little and gave me some. Then she said, "You run along and play." In a day or two everybody on the plantation seemed to be disturbed and marster and missus were crying. Marster ordered all the slaves to come to the great house at nine o'clock. Nobody was working and slaves were walking over the grove in every direction. At nine o'clock all the slaves gathered at the great house and marster and missus came out on the porch and stood side by side. You could hear a pin drap everything was so quiet. Then marster said, "Good morning," and missus said, "Good morning, children." They were both crying. Then marster said, "Men, women and children, your are free. You are no longer my slaves. The Yankees will soon be here."

Matilda Brooks (FL) characterized the announcement of freedom as being an exciting time for slaves, as the news traveled fast among them that the Yankees were coming and that the slaves would be set free:

> The coming of the Yankee soldiers created much excitement among the slaves on the Pickens plantation. The slaves were in ignorance of activities going on, and of their approach, but when the first one was sighted the news spread "just like dry grass burning up a hill." Despite the kindness of Governor Pickens the slaves were happy to claim their newfound freedom.

Mack Mullen (FL) recalled the day slaves learned of their emancipation. Mullen remembered the loud sound of Yankee guns echoing through the woods and the plantation, after which the Yankees appeared. The troops informed them that they were free. According to Mullen, the slaves when hearing of their freedom burst out in song and praises to God. It was a gala day. The emancipated slaves did not work for a full week afterward, as they were celebrating. Louis Napoleon (FL) provided a very similar depiction of the day of his liberation. The freed slaves put on their best clothes and headed to town to celebrate:

> It was in May, in the middle of the day, cotton and corn being planted, plowing going on, and slaves busily engaged in their usual activities, when suddenly the loud report of a gun resounded, then could be heard the slaves crying almost en-masse, "dems de Yankees." Straightway they dropped the plows, hoes and other farm implements and hurried to their cabins. They put on their best clothes "to go see the Yankees." Through the countryside to the town of Tallahassee they went. The roads were quickly filled with these happy souls. The streets of Tallahassee were clustered with these jubilant people going here and there to get a glimpse of the Yankees, their liberators. Napoleon says it was a joyous and un-forgettable occasion.

It was frequently the case that Yankee troops would gather all of the slaves together and read a proclamation of their freedom, typically on plantation grounds or in town centers with both troops and slaves gathered together. Victoria Perry (SC) described how this occurred on her South Carolina plantation:

> One day a Yankee come by the house and told my master to get all the colored people together; that a certain Yankee general would come by and would tell them that they were free. So one day the niggers gathered together at the house, and the Yankee general was there with some soldiers. They formed a circle around the niggers and the general stood in the middle and told us all we were free. My mother shouted, "The Lord be praised." There was a general rejoic-ing among the niggers and then we backed away and went home. My mother told me she knew the Lord would answer her prayers to set her free.

Another example of Yankee troops announcing the freedom is contained in the narrative of Mollie Edmonds (MS), who never forgot the day she was liberated. Although her liberation came at the hands of Union soldiers, it did not reduce her fear of them:

> I never shall forget the day we heared of freedom. The Yankees
> came riding in the place right up to the quarters, and told how we
> was all free. Them soldiers had shiny bayonetts and guns laying
> cross the saddles. I was so scared I ran to my pa and wouldn't turn
> loose of him for nothing. He tells me 'taint nothing to be scared
> 'bout it means that freedom done took place. I says "I don't care
> what done took place I is still scared them Yankees."

Typical of the accounts are memories of how masters and their families accepted the emancipation of their slaves. Mary Anderson recalled the master's family crying with the announcement. Henry Bobbitt's (NC) narrative reflected the anger expressed by his owner at losing his property:

> I 'members de day moughty well when de Yankees come. Massa Dick
> he walked de floor an' cussed sherman fer takin' his niggers away. All
> o' de niggers lef', of course, an' me, I walked clean ter Raleigh ter
> find out if I was really free, an' I couldn't unnerstan' half of it.

Jake Dawkins (MS) noted that his master was drunk when he made the announcement in the following manner:

> Fact was, he was drunk when Surrender came and he call us to de
> house and us not knowin' whether we's gwinter get whipped or what
> and he say, "Niggers, I hates to tell you but you is as free as I is."
> We all shouted, "Thank Gawd A'mighty, we's free at last." Dat's
> where dey got dat church song dey sing now dat goes like dat.

SLAVE RELUCTANCE TO BEING FREE

Masters were not sure what to do following the end of the war, and some were reluctant to let their slaves go free. Some owners did not inform their slaves that they were free, delayed telling them, or simply lied. For some slaves, it was years before they learned of their freedom. Fannie Berry (VA) said, "I wuz free a long time fo' I knew it." After working for years, she said that her mistress told her "Fannie, yo' ar' free an' I don't have to pay your master for you now." Then her mistress added, "You stay with me." Madison Bruin (TX) had a similar experience: "Nobody ever telt me I's free." Squire Dowd (NC) indicated that it was five years following the war before he learned of his freedom. Implied in his narrative is his attempt to survive independently of the plantation, but this proved difficult, and he eventually returned to the plantation:

> I did not know I was free until five years after the war. I could not realize I was free. Many of us stayed right on. If we had not been ruined right after the war by carpet baggers our race would have been, well,—better up by this time, because they turned us against our masters, when our masters had everything and we had nothing. The Freedmen's bureau helped us some, but we finally had to go back to the plantation in order to live.

Anderson and Minerva Edwards (TX) reported a similar experience with their owner, who according to their account waited until after the war to let his slaves know. "They didn't tell us we was free till a year after the war," said Minerva. John C. Bectom (NC) said that some masters lied about the freedom but that the slaves eventually figured it out and either quietly disappeared or slowed down their work:

> The marsters would tell the slaves to go to work that they were not free, that they still belonged to them, but one would drop out and leave, then another. There was little work done on the farm, and finally most of the slaves learned they were free.

Clara Brim (TX) found out about her freedom from Yankee soldiers following the war's end and not from her master:

> De Yankees didn' come 'till atter de war stop. Dey say, "Don't you know you free?" Us say, "No. Ol' master he neber tol' us." Dey tol' ol' master go give his han's part of eb'ryt'ing he got what dey help him raise. I got some co'n. I 'member I sol' my co'n at a dollar a barrel. Ol' master neber did tell us. De Yankee sojers tol' us. Ol' master he jis' cry and cry like a chile when dey tol' us dat.

Annie Row (TX) described her master's response to freeing the slaves and the death of his son, John. In response to this news, her master struck her mother and then grabbed a gun and headed toward the fields to "free" some slaves. Although nobody is mentioned as being killed, her narrative implies that some of the field slaves came close to being shot. Her narrative underscores the drama often experienced with the war and the pending freedom of slaves:

> One day aftah de wah am fightin' fo' mo' dan two yeahs, de Marster gits a letter f'om Marster Billy. Dat letter says, De nigger sho am gwine to be free, de wah am 'bout over, dat hims will be home soon, an' dat John am killed. W'en de Missy heahs dat letter read, she stahts a cryin' an' says, "My poor boy, my poor boy, my Johnny. Ise not see him any mo'." She keeps dat up 'til she am 'zausted. Den she lay down an' was mo'nin'. De Marster says nothin', jus' sits an' stares. Den suddenly him jumps up an' stahts cussin' de wah, de nigger, Abe Lincoln an' ever'body. He goes to de fish place, picks up de hot pokah an' says, "Free de nigger, will dey? I'se free dem." Den he hit my mammy on de neck. Dat lick bu'ns a scah dat mammy carries to her grave. My mammy stahts mo'nin' an' screamin' an' draps on de flooah. Dere 'twas, de Missy a mo'nin', my mammy a mo'nin', an' de Marster am a cussin' loud as him can. He was a sayin', "Ise free de nigger f'om slavery." Den him takes his gun off de rack an' stahts fo' de field whar de niggers am a wo'kin'. My sistah an' Ise in de house an' w'en weuns see dat, weuns stahts runnin' an' screamin', 'cause weuns have sistahs an' brudders in de field an' weuns don' wants 'em shoot. Lawd a Massie! Dat was a crazy place an' nobody knows w'at to do. It looks lak dem niggers in de field sho will be killed.

Jefferson Franklin Henry (GA) told of his master not telling his slaves that they were free:

> When freedom come I was down in the lower end of Clarke County on Marse George Veal's plantation whar Marse Robert had done sont Miss Martha and the chillun and part of the slaves too. My white folks was fleein' from the Yankees. Marse Robert couldn't come 'long 'cause he had done been wounded in battle and when they sont him home from the war he couldn't walk. I don't know what he said to the slaves that was left thar to 'tend him, but I heared tell that he didn't tell 'em nothin' 'bout freedom, leastwise not for sometime. Pretty soon the Yankees come through and had the slaves come

together in town whar they had a speakin' and told them Negroes
they was free, and that they didn't belong to nobody no more.

WHAT TO MAKE OF THE NEW DISORDER

Some slaves did not know what to do when they were liberated. Apart from
the initial celebrations and jubilation, for some slaves the prospect of freedom was imposing and filled with fear of the unknown. Having lived their
entire lives under the rules and restrictions of slavery, with freedom came
a degree of anomie or normlessness that many had never experienced.
Freedom meant uncertainty. In William Curtis's (OK) narrative, he implies
that the sense of order was gone and describes the comfort of seeing his
father return to the family. Curtis seems to be longing for the way things
were before the war:

> Course, after the war nothing was right no more. Yes, we was free
> but we didn't know what to do. We didn't want to leave our old
> Master and our old home. We stayed on and after a while my pappy
> come home to us. Dat was de best thing about de war setting us
> free, he could come back to us.

In a similar vein, John Smith (NC) did not know what to do with his newfound freedom:

> I seed many Yankees during de war in Alabama. When de war ended
> dey tole me I was free. I was so glad I didn' know whut to do. De
> Yankees tole me I was free. I went wid 'em. I stayed wid 'em from
> May till August. Den I slipped away from 'em.

Some years after the war, an Alabama ex-slave recalled the return home of
Confederate soldiers, another sign of how the old way of life had been
turned upside down:

> I seen our 'Federates go off laughin' an' gay; full of life an' health.
> Dey was big an' strong, asingin' Dixie an' dey jus knowed dey was
> agoin' to win. I seen 'em come back skin an' bone, dere eyes all sad
> an' hollow, an dere clothes all ragged. Dey was all lookin' sick. De
> sperrit dey lef' wid jus' been done whupped outten dem.
>
> (McPherson 2001, 535)

Aunt Adeline (AR) indicated that she wanted to stay on the plantation because it was the only world she had ever known. She had established a way of life that at least was familiar to her. Even under threat, she "stayed on":

> After the War many soldiers came to my mistress, Mrs. Blakely, trying to make her free me. I told them I was free but I did not want to go anywhere, that I wanted to stay in the only home that I had ever known. In a way that placed me in a wrong attitude. I was pointed out as different. Sometimes I was threatened for not leaving but I stayed on.

John Glover (SC) also indicated that slaves did not initially know what to do following emancipation. "Slaves didn' know what to do de first year after freedom on den de Yankees tell do white folks to give de slaves one-third of dey crops."

FOR SOME THERE WAS NOT MUCH DIFFERENCE

Some slaves reported that they did not see much difference in their lives following the war and liberation. For some, the WPA narratives indicate that they were better off under slavery. While this point of view was clearly made in the narratives, it must always be kept in mind that some of the WPA respondents remained cautious when responding to their white interviewers, a point made by some researchers who have worked to interpret the narratives. While this is an important point, some of the respondents probably believed that they were better off under slavery and were not trying to impress or mislead their white interviewers. It has been noted that the Fisk University narratives were conducted with African American interviewers and thus are a more realistic and honest depiction of life under slavery and the thoughts of those interviewed. This is likely the case for some but not necessarily all of the WPA respondents, many of whom were brutally honest much of the time. There are numerous examples of the brutality of slavery expressed in the WPA narratives. The best way to think about these positive comments about life under slavery is to take them at face value. Only the respondents knew for sure whether they were being honest.

With the proclamation of freedom, some ex-slaves held high expectations that things would be different. Elizabeth Finley (MS) recalled the broken promises that her family experienced: "Dem Yankee mens tole us

This wood engraving entitled *Celebration of the Abolition of Slavery in the District of Columbia by the Colored People, in Washington, April 19, 1866* by Frederick Dielman appeared in *Harper's Weekly* dated May 12, 1866, v. 10, no. 489, p. 300. It captures the spirit of celebration expressed by many African Americans following the Emancipation Proclamation. Dressed in their best finery, the large gathering of people, including what appears to be African American soldiers in the center of the print, typifies the joy that many were feeling. Dielman was a draftsman and painter of genre pictures. He later contributed illustrations for the works of such writers as Longfellow, Hawthorne, and George Eliot. (Library of Congress)

de guvment would give us some land and a mule or some hosses to work wid, but we never did git nothing frum dem." Isaac Stier (MS) captured some of the anticipation that slaves held for freedom and the disappointments that they instead endured:

> De slaves spected a heap from freedom dey didn' git. Dey was led to b'lieve dey would have a easy time—go places widout passes— an have plenty o' spendin' money. But dey sho' got fooled. Mos' of 'em didn' fin' deyse'ves no better off. Pussonally, I had a harder time after de war dan I did endurin' slav'ry.
>
> De Yankees passed as us frien's. Dey made big promises, but dey was poor reliance. Some of 'em meant well towards us, but dey was mistol' 'bout a heap o' things. Dey promised us a mule an' forty

acres o' lan'. Us aint seen no mule yet. Us got de lan' all right, but twant no service. Fac' is, 'twas way over in a territory where nothin' 'ud grow. I didn' know nothin' 'bout farmin', nowhow, I'd always been a coachman an' play companion to de white chillun.

The promise of 40 acres and a mule was widespread among the recently liberated slaves. This promise and other promises would go unfulfilled for most (Alexander 2004).

Some ex-slaves welcomed freedom with great expectations but would soon discover that their dreams and hopes would be unrealized. Felix Haywood (TX) shared that he and other slaves believed that they would fare well following emancipation:

We knowed freedom was on us but we didn't know what was to come with it. We thought we was goin' to get rich like the white folks. We thought we was goin' to be richer than the white folks, 'cause we was stronger and knowed how to work, and the whites didn't and they didn't have us to work for them any more. But it didn't turn out that way. We soon found out that freedom could make folks proud but it didn't make them rich.

For ex-slaves whose lives changed little, some remained in their same location doing the same work under slightly different conditions. Arey Lamar (AR) did not see much difference since becoming free: "I went back and stayed 45 years on the Lambert place." Lewis Bonner (OK) spoke of how after freedom his family stayed on for 3 years. He recalled that "We got little money, but we got room and board and didn't have to work too hard." Then he added a comment that little had changed: "It was 'nough difference to tell you was no slaves any more." Nancy East (OH) character-ized what happened as being pretty much the same. She made the point that in her view, those whites who announced their freedom seemed to be off base with their comment that ex-slaves did not have to work for whites anymore, but in fact they did in most cases. East also implied a preference for slavery in that they were taken care of during bondage:

After de wah, everybody jist went on working same as ever. Than one day a white mens come riding through the county and tole us we was free. Free! Honey, did yo' hear that? Why we always had been free. He didn't know what he was talking 'bout. He kept telling us we was free and dat we oughtn't to work for no white folks 'less'n we got paid for it. Well Miss Nancy took care of us then. We got our cabin and a piece of ground for a garden and a share of de crops. Daddy worked in de mill. Miss Nancy saw to it that we always had nice clothes too.

Wylie Miller (MO), who suggested that little had changed, made a similar report:

When de war was ober, Ole Massa call us all up to de fron' porch and tell us now de war is ober an we is free, but it don' make much diffrence. We stays dar jes de same for few year.

Felix Haywood (TX) said, "But the War didn't change nothin'." Robert Wilson (AR) mentioned that he "didn't care whether I was free or not." Carrie Hudson (GA) echoed Wilson's view: "I tell 'em I already free! Didn't mek no diffrunce to me, freedom!" Clara C. Young (MS) went into more detail about what freedom meant to her:

De Yankees came 'round af'er de war an tol' us we's free an we shouted an san' an hed a big cel'bration fer a few days. Den we got to wonderin' 'bout what good it did us. It didn' feel no diff'ent; we all loved our marster an missus an stayed on wid dem jest lak nothin' had happened. De Yankees tried to get some of de men to vote, too, but not many did 'cause dey was scared of de Ku Kluxers. Dey wud cum at night all dressed up lak ghosts an scare us all. We didn' lak de Yankees anyway.

Parker Pool (NC) also did not welcome freedom, stating that he was better off under slavery. For Pool, it came down to who paid the expenses:

I dunno what ter think o' Abraham Lincoln. Dey said he was all right. I guess he was a man God loved, or all right man. I think some o' de slaves was better off when dey had owners and was in slavery den dey is now. De colored people are slaves now more den dey was den. I can show you wherein de nigger's got all his expenses ter bear now. He gits his pay out'en de white man and de white man don't pay him much. De nigger in de South is jest as much a slave as ever. De nigger now is a better slave den when dey owned him, 'cause he has his own expenses to bear. If you works a horse an' doan have him ter feed, you is better off, dan if you had ter feed and care fer him. Dat is de way dat thing is now.

Jane Cotton (TX) had higher expectations from the Yankees than what she felt they delivered, and she thought that her ex-master gave the liberated slaves nothing but a "hard deal." Her narrative depicts life after freedom as being harsh, as the ex-slaves had next to nothing other than worthless ragged clothing:

> I expected a better treatment from the Yankees and the south than we got in place of giving us a home they turned us a loose like a bunch of stray cats, only cat have better way of making living then we had; they ought to have give us a home as we didnt know any-thing at all. Didnt know how to make a crop or anything. All we knew was to hop when master said hop. Master he never give us anything but a hard deal, some few old cast off clothes that wasnt any good. We liked to have starved to death after the war. If that was to be gone over son, they wouldnt be any negro cause the woods was full of wild game and we could plant acre or two corn and it would make 50 or 60 bushel of corn to acre.

Of course, most slaves welcomed freedom. Comments are abundant in the narratives about valuing freedom, such as the one made by Victoria Adams (SC), who thought that freedom was better than slavery when she said that "I like being free more better" and then added that "Any niggers what like slavery time better, is lazy people dat don't want to do nothing."

STAYING ON

With no specific place to go or any other options, liberated slaves often stayed with their ex-masters and worked as sharecroppers or tenant work-ers. A very common response to emancipation and the war's end was to simply stay on the plantation and continue to do what they had always done: work the fields and be servants. It was typical that owners would let them continue to work as low-paid tenant farmers or sharecroppers, almost as if they were doing them a favor. Hattie Jefferson (MS) succinctly dis-closed what a common occurrence this was for many slaves:

I neber seed any soldiers but heard em talkin' bout dem. An' one day Marse Hillery run dat big bell an' had all de slaves come to de house; he tole us all we wus free an' sed we cud stay dar an' finish de crop an' he wud pay dem all. Some uf dem stayed an' some uf dem left. Dem dat stayed neber got any pay. He sed dey et it all up.

Thomas McMillan (OH) said:

I saw de blue jackets, dat's what we called de Yankee soldiers. When we heard of our freedom we hated it because we did not know what it was for and did not know where to go. De massa say we could stay as long as we pleased. De Yankee soldier asked my father what dey wuz all doing around der and that day were free. But we did not know where to go. We stayed on wid de massa for a long time after de war wuz over.

Mariah Calloway (GA) made a similar statement regarding staying on: "After the war some of the slaves left the plantation to seek their fortune; others remained, renting land from the Willis family or working with them on a share crop basis." Isaac Adams (OK) said that ex-slaves stayed on because "They wasn't no place to go, anyway, so they all stayed on." Julia Stubbs (MS) recalled that "After de war was over we wont give no land nor nothing dat dey promised fo' de war." She then added that "Mos' all de slaves didn't know what to do," so her family stayed on "till we learn how to git out an' look out fer ourselves."

Bell McChristian (MS) indicated that her master told the slaves that they were free and could work for whomever they wanted. She said, "Me an' my sisters stayed on 'till de crops was gathered an' then we went to live with my mammy what had been sold to another fellow who lived close." Ann May (MS) recalled that "After the War, I stayed with Mr. Alford and worked in the field. I had a mighty hard time trying to raise my children and make a living for them." Simon Gallman (SC) mentioned sharecropping following the war: "When freedom come, de slaves hired out mostly as sharecroppers." He also said that freed slaves "worked at most anything dey could get to do" and added that "De ones dat moved to town worked at odd jobs, some at carpenter work, janitor work or street work; but most of dem worked in fields around town."

Parilee Daniels (TX) provided more detail about staying on. Her master proceeded to manipulate his ex-slaves into remaining completely dependent on him, just like they had been in the past. He coerced them into essentially the life they had under slavery, only they were theoretically free. In Daniel's narrative, she notes that he did not provide medical care as he had when they were slaves. This statement underscores the theme that under slavery, slaves were seen as valued property, and it was important for owners to take care of property by providing adequate (often minimal) food, shelter, and medical care (Covey 2007; Covey and Eisnach 2009). Under the tenant system that developed following the war, ex-slaves were not property and thus were less likely in the eyes of their ex-owners to need and receive assistance. Daniel's comments reflect that she was well aware of this altered relationship between ex-slaves and their ex-owners:

> When that war was over Maser heard that the south had lost and we was freed, he called us all to his back door and told us that we was free. We all begin to cry and ask Maser what we was going to do and he said he did not know, they had freed us and he did not have any more to do with us, but he said this much, I still have the teams, tolls and the quarters and we could go on living there in the quarters and he would pay us fo the work that we did. So we made a trade with Maser to work for him there for 20 cents a day.
>
> The year after the war he was to furnish our groceries and clothes but no sir, he would not get us a doctor when we got sick, we then had to depend all together on old black mammy as we did not have the money to get a doctor with, and Maser he would not get us a doctor, if we died then Maser would not lose anything because we was free and was not worth anything to him. We sure did live hard after we went to work for Maser because he would not let us get in debt to him at all, the clothes we wore old cast off clothes of the white people, as it took everything we could make to get something to eat with and nothing left to buy clothes with, so we had to do the hest [best] we could.

Frank A. Patterson (AR) stayed on and eventually realized that his previous owners were still exploiting him:

> Right after the War, I stayed with the people that owned me and worked. They give me two dollars a month and my food and clothes. I stayed with them five years and then I quit. I had sense enough to quit and I went to work for wages. I got five dollars a

month. And I thought that was a big salary. I didn't know no better.
I learnt better by experience.

For some ex-slaves, their former masters made them offers of patches of
land and other incentives to stay on and basically work for little or nothing.
Amos Clark (TX) mentioned how his former owner enticed his ex-slaves
into working for him by giving them a little plot of land:

> Atter freedom, Marse tole us to kill a yearlin' an' hab a big dinner
> an' dance. De young ones he tole to scatter out an' hunt em work.
> He tole us to not steal, to pay what us owed an' wukk hard. Some of
> de olest ones he gibed a cabin an' a patch ob lan'. By now de big
> house was finer an' larger an' had a lot ob store bought fernichure.
> Marse Ed brought looms an' spinnin' wheels long fore dis an' he
> built him a mill. He said all de niggers dat want to stay on an' help
> him work can do so effen he can make enough to feed em. I stayed
> wid Marse Ed even tho he had gib me a patch of twenty acres an' a
> sorghum mill to make a livin' on.

A similar rumor of an offer of incentives was circulated among the slaves
on the plantation where Andrew Boone (NC) served. However, in Boone's
case, his former masters never provided much:

> Den a story went round an' round dat de marster would have to give
> de slaves a rule an' a year's provisions an' some lan', about forty
> acres, but dat wus not so. Dey nebber did give us anything. When
> de war ended an' we wus tole we wus free, we stayed on wid
> marster cause we had nothin' an' nowhere to go.

Lucinda Elder (TX) and her family stayed on not only because of the
incentive of land offered but also because she and the other ex-slaves
"loved" her former master. This "love" occurred despite being exploited
by her master:

> Well, things was jes' 'bout de same all de time till jes' 'fore free-
> dom. Course, I hears some talk 'bout bluebellies, what dey call de
> Yanks, fightin' out folks, but dey wasn't fightin' round us. Den one
> dey mamma took sich and she had hear talk and call me to de bed
> and say, "Lucinda, we all gwine be free soon and not work 'leas we

git paid for it." She sho' was right, 'cause Marse John calls all us to
de cookhouse and reads de freedom papers to us and tells us we is
all free, but iffen we wants to stay he'll give us land to make a crop
and he'll feed us. Now I tells you de truth, dey wasn't no one leaves,
'cause we all loves Marse John.

In a similar vein, Hilliard Yellerday (NC) noted that very little was left for
those ex-slaves who decided to stay on. Yellerday said that ex-slaves moved
from plantation to plantation, and "The landlords got all we made except
what we ate and wore." Ben Brown's (OH) narrative described how ex-
slaves were paid in pennies because they did not really understand the
differences in money and could not read or write. Brown said that ex-
slaves on his plantation were not allowed to have much money. If they were
caught with extra money, they were whipped because having money meant
less dependency on Southern plantation society. Plantation owners generally wanted cheap and poor laborers to work their fields and otherwise
serve their needs. Brown said:

When de wah was ovah, de missie nevah tell me dat I was free an' I
kep' on workin' same as befoh. I couldn't read or write an' to me all
money coins was a cent, big copper cents, dey was all alike to me.
De slaves was not allowed any learnin an' if any books, papers or
pictures was foun' among us we was whipped if we couldn't explain
where dey cum from. Mah sistah an' brother cum foh me an tell me
I an free and take me with them to Mastah Maxies' place where day
workin. Dey had a big dinnah ready foh me, but I was too excited to
eat. I worked foh Mastah Maxie too, helpin' with de horses an'
doin' chores. Mammy cum' an was de cook. I got some clothes and
a few cents an' travelers give me small coins foh tending dere
horses an' I done odd jobs here an dere.

Albert Hill (TX) stayed on initially but eventually left when he turned
21. He mentioned that the master died and that there was a "powerful sorrow." Hill described his compensation for staying on:

When freedom am here, massa call all us together and tells us 'bout
de difference 'tween freedom and hustlin' for ourselves and depen-
din' on someone else. Most of de slaves stays, and massa pays them
for de work, and I stays till I's 21 year old, and I gits $7.00 de month

and de clothes and de house and all I kin eat. De massa have died
'fore dat, and dere am powerful sorrow.

As the narratives reveal, a number of factors contributed to ex-slaves
staying on following emancipation, including the lack of opportunity
available to emancipated slaves, racism, threats, coercion, manipulation,
deception, promises of rewards, lack of experience with the outside world,
and fear of the unknown.

ANNOUNCEMENT OF FREEDOM NOT ALWAYS WELCOMED

Ellen King (AL) recalled that when the Yankees came through and told all
the slaves that they were free, some of them went with the Yankees but others did not. Ellen's father and others were scared and hid in a big cave until
the soldiers left. Many slaves were taught to fear the Yankees. Alice Baugh
(NC) noted that her mother said that the slaves "cried when the Yankees
came" and also said that her mother was not forced to work under slavery
but did so because she "wanted to do it an not' cause dey make her." She
said that slaves marched behind Yankee soldiers singing anti-Lincoln
songs. Finally, she mentioned, "Yes mam, dey was sorry dat dey was free,
an' dey ain't got no reason tu be glad, case dey was happier den dan now."
Even the abolitionist writer Harriet Beecher Stowe's motives were questioned by Thomas Hall (NC), who felt that she wrote *Uncle Tom's Cabin*
"for her own good." Hall said that "She had her own interests at heart and
I don't like her, Lincoln, or none of the crowd." Hall likened freedom to
being put back into slavery again. "The Yankees helped free us, so they say,
but they let us be put . . . back in slavery again." A similar observation was
made by Lizzie Grant (TX), who said that the transition for many ex-slaves
after the war was from being a slave to being a peon:

When that war was over lots of money had been spent, nothing won,
but a lot of new graves, widows and orphan children suffering—their
homes all wrecked. Slavery had not ended, no we just went from
slaves to peons, and they are worse off than slaves ever were. In slavery time the poor negro was taken good care of, now after they were
supposed to free the negroes, they did free them in one sense of the
word, but put them in a whole lot worse shape as they turned them
loose to make their own way with nothing to make it with. They took
the Negro from under good care of the slave owners to where if the

white man, who was Lord and Maser over the Negro race, did not care for killing a Negro or if the Negro became sick that was no loss to the white man anymore if he should die. Then the man was not responsible for us and he could not or would not see that we had good medicine given us, or any care taken of us.

In the case of Rosa Pollard (TX), the announcement of freedom was not something that she wished for. She vividly described the return of her master following the end of the war and her subsequent freedom. Freedom for Pollard was uncharted territory and did not offer suitable health care; thus, ill ex-slaves just "died":

Maser he was in that war and he was wounded. Had a leg broken and when he came home was the awfullest sight you ever saw. His beard was half-inch long, clothes all ragged and dirty. He was wounded and blood had dried on his clothes and they were stiff. He told Mistress, "we went through hell and still we lost." He was on the side of South and I never want to see or hear of another war. Then he turned to me as I was helping Mistress there in her kitchen and said, "you are free, you can go where you please, do as you please, I am not your Maser any more." I was glad in a way to hear that I was free, but still I didn't want to be free because we never had nothing and nowhere to go. If we got sick we just died, nothing to get doctor with. You know we was worse off after freedom that we was during slavery time.

HARD TIMES FOLLOWING EMANCIPATION

Emancipation and freedom did not guarantee that life would automatically improve. Some ex-slaves recalled that hard times followed the war's end. Fannie Berry (VA) said that following freedom, "Baby, all us wuz helpless an' ain't had nothing." Samuel Sutton (OH) remembered that "Some ways I recollect times was lots harder after de War. Some ways dey was better. But now a culled man ain't so much better off 'bout votin' an such some places yet, ah hears dat." Patsy Moore (AR) recalled the initial jubilation and celebration that came with freedom but then came a sudden decline, as folks looked for work and were famished. Her father served in the military and was mustered out, only to find little work.

When freedom come, folks left home, out in the streets, crying, praying, singing, shouting, yelling, and knocking down everything. Some shot off big guns. Den come the calm. It was sad then. So many folks done dead, things tore up and nowheres to go and nothing to eat, nothing to do. It got squally. Folks got sick, so hungry. Some folks starved nearly to death. Times got hard. We went to the washtub onliest way we all could live. Ma was a cripple woman. Pa couldn't find work for so long when he mustered out.

Waters McIntosh (AR) noted that following the war, there was a great scarcity of food for both whites and blacks. According to McIntosh, if anybody had food, they did not let others know. McIntosh's grandmother, who was well respected, went out to find food. McIntosh said, "A white woman named Mrs. Burton gave her a sack of meal and told her not to tell anybody where she got it."

Others viewed the war's end as a period of hard times and broken promises. W. L. Bost (NC) vividly described how tough it was for slaves in his area:

Most of the people get everything jes ready to run when the Yankee sojers come through the town. This was toward the las' of the war. Cose the niggers knew what all the fightin' was about, but they didn't dare say anything. The man who owned the slaves was too mad as it was, and if the niggers say anything they get shot right then and thar. The sojers tell us after the war that we get food, clothes, and wages from our Massas else we leave. But they was very few that ever got anything. Our ole Massa say he not gwine pay us anything. Corse his money was no good, but he wouldn't pay us if it had been.

Martha Ann Dixon (AR), using the Great Depression as a way to frame her response, remembered that the postwar times were like the Depression:

Money scarce and prices high, and you had to start all over new. Pigs was hard to start, mules and horses was mighty scarce. Seed was scarce. Everything had to be started from the stump. Something to eat was mighty plain and scarce and one or two dresses a year had to do.

Sarah Debro (NC) acknowledged that following the war, the Yankees provided liberated slaves with housing but that it was far from adequate. Her account illustrates how harsh living conditions were for some emancipated slaves:

> When de war was over de Yankees was all 'roun' de place tellin' de niggers what to do. Dey tole dem dey was free, dat dey didn' have to slave for de white folks no more. My folks all left Marse Cain an' went to live in houses dat de Yankees built. Dey wuz like poor white folks houses, little shacks made out of sticks an' mud wid stick an' mud chimneys. Dey wuzn' like Marse Cain's cabins, planked up an' warm, dey was full of cracks, an' dey wuzn no lamps an' oil. All de light come from de lightwood knots burnin' in de fireplace.
>
> Mammy took me to de stick an' mud house de Yankees done give her. It was smoky an' dark kaze dey wuzn' no windows. We didn' have no sheets an' no towels, so when I cried an' said I didn' want to live on no Yankee house, Mammy beat me an' made me go to bed. I laid on de straw tick lookin' up through de cracks in de roof. I could see de stars, an' de sky shinin' through de cracks looked like long blue splinters stretched 'cross de rafters. I lay dare an' cried kaze I wanted to go back to Mis' Polly.
>
> Dem was bad days. I'd rather been a slave den to been hired out like I was. Kaze I wuzn' no fiel' hand, I was a hand maid, trained to wait on de ladies. Den too, I was hungry most of de time an' had to keep fightin' off dem Yankee mens. Dem Yankees was mean folks.

Just as times were hard for some, for others life became better. A. M. Moore (TX) painted a positive picture of what happened after the war and spoke of how young Rebel soldiers returned and divided things up with the exslaves. Moore and his brother were able to eventually purchase some land:

> After Emancipation and the war subsided, the young white men that returned from the war treated the slaves nice in this part of the country. Down in Louisiana lots of the owners divided syrup, meat, and other things with the slaves. Through here, the industrious ones learned to save money and buy homes. It was their own fault if they never had anything. My brother and me bought and paid for 500 acres of land after emancipation.

SOME TAKE THE OFFENSIVE

Lest the impression be left that a majority of ex-slaves were timid and afraid of freedom or were happier under slavery or were victims of the postwar confusion, there were also thousands in the years after the war who "shouldered the responsibilities" of freedom to take advantage of what the hard fight for peace had delivered to them (Foner 2005, 128). This occurred in many ways including political leadership, as in the example of James K. Green, a former slave in Hale County, Alabama. During Reconstruction, Green became an active Republican Party speaker in central Alabama; served as an officer of the Alabama Labor Union, an effort to organize black agricultural workers; helped organize an African American militia after a freedman was shot; and also was a voter registrar. He was elected to the Alabama state constitutional convention and served eight years in the Alabama legislature (Foner 2005). John Roy Lynch was another former slave who "shouldered the responsibilities" of freedom. Lynch was elected to the Mississippi legislature in the first election after African American suffrage was granted in that state, working hard to raise funds for the reconstruction of schools and government, both of which had been decimated during the war (Franklin 1970). In fact, no development in the years after the war marked so dramatic a break with tradition or aroused such bitter hostility from Reconstruction opponents than the rise of large numbers of African Americans to positions of political power just a few short years after the demise of slavery. Before the Civil War, African Americans could vote in only a handful of Northern states, and blacks holding office was unprecedented. However, during Reconstruction as many as 2,000 African Americans held public office, from justice of the peace to governor and U.S. senator (Foner 2005). Thousands more headed Union Leagues and local branches of the Republican Party, edited newspapers, and influenced the political process in other ways.

The so-called Reconstruction Amendments—the Thirteenth Amendment abolishing slavery, the Fourteenth Amendment overturning the *Dred Scott* decision and making African Americans citizens, and the Fifteenth Amendment giving blacks the right to vote—were all adopted in the first five years after the Civil War and represented a fundamental shift in power in Southern life. By the early 1870s, biracial democracy, something unknown in American history, was working effectively in many parts of the South (Foner 1987, 2005). Men only recently released from bondage had access to and were exercising real political power. Many whites who could not let go of the status quo of racial hatred and white domination turned to the Ku Klux Klan and other terrorist organizations as a way to hold on to their dominance.

The Bureau of Refugees, Freedmen, and Abandoned Lands, popularly known as the Freedmen's Bureau, was established by Congress in March 1865 because lawmakers believed that freed African Americans would have difficulty adapting to freedom. The bureau operated between 1865 and 1872 and assisted in protecting African American farmers and laborers, helped to establish schools for freedmen, and aided in the search for family members who had been sold throughout the South. Free blacks and whites—women, children, soldiers, and contrabands—dispossessed by the war all needed food and shelter, and all received assistance from the bureau to procure these necessities (Ham 1993). As an example of the inquiries that the bureau received, freedman Hawkins Wilson on May 11, 1867, wrote to the head of the bureau at Richmond: "I am anxious to learn about my sisters, from whom I have been separated many years. . . . I have never heard from them since I left Virginia twenty four years ago. . . . I am in hopes that they are still living and I am anxious to hear how they are getting on" (National Archives 2012). Historical records do not indicate whether Wilson ever found any of his relatives, though it is doubtful that he did.

Another piece of Freedmen's Bureau correspondence illustrates the difficulties in organizing the bureau and the coming flashpoint of relations between former masters and former slaves. On September 1, 1865, the superintendent of the bureau's Sixth District in Virginia (Augusta County), W. Storer How, wrote to his boss in Richmond:

I have stationed civilians as Assist Superintendents at the principle points, Winchester, Staunton, and Lexington, and have thus been enabled to [unclear: convey] the impression throughout this region that the freedmen are being cared for, and that they may not be ill-treated with impunity.

The freedmen are generally at work but whether or not for their former masters cannot be determined in the absence of census returns. The feelings of the former masters are now [unclear: adverse] to the interests of the Freedmen whose newly acquired rights they are not disposed to respect although they verbally acknowledge their freedmen as "free persons of color."

If left to themselves by the withdrawal of the military, the former masters would generally resume the old mastership, and the condition of the freedmen [*unclear: becomes*] worse than when they were slaves.

(Valley of the Shadow Project 2012)

The slogan "40 acres and a mule" evolved from a promise by Republicans to break up plantations and give each freed slave 40 acres and a mule. The idea energized former slaves for two reasons: it represented a way for them to make a living and satisfied their need for revenge against their oppressors. The "40 acres and a mule" concept had its origins in Field Order No. 15 issued in January 1865 by General William Tecumseh Sherman, whose intent was to relieve his army of the burden of caring for thousands of African American refugees after his March to the Sea, not to begin a social revolution (Foner 2005). In South Carolina, Georgia, and Mississippi, more than 40,000 freedmen benefited briefly from the policy, which had the backing of Secretary of War Edwin Stanton, and received their 40 acres, occupying 300,000 acres of land (Smith 1996). However, after Abraham Lincoln's assassination, President Andrew Johnson, a Tennessean and Jacksonian Democrat with Southern sympathies, rescinded Field Order No. 15 in March 1866 and ordered the return of property to the former white owners. Ironically, it was the Freedmen's Bureau that instructed the freed slaves to sign labor contracts with their former masters or be evicted. Federal troops forcibly removed those African Americans who believed they had a right to the land. By late 1866, only about 1,500 of the 40,000 freed people who had occupied land retained possession of their acreage (Smith 1996). The slogan "40 acres and a mule" became the cynical catchphrase for the failures of Reconstruction and the symbol of reparations that never materialized. When sharecropping became the reality instead of land ownership, many freed slaves began voting Democratic when the party that freed them could not deliver on their "acres." The memory of this injustice would linger, and a Mississippi African American would later recall that "De slaves spected a heap from freedom dey didn't git. . . . Dey promised us a mule an' forty acres o' lan'" (Foner 2005, 64).

While the country had the incredible good fortune to have Abraham Lincoln guide it through the Civil War, it had the staggering misfortune of having Andrew Johnson guide it through Reconstruction. Johnson was probably the worst possible person to have been president following the Civil War because of his incompetence, his racist views, and his gross miscalculation of public support for his policies, all of which resulted in a peace that was neither adequate nor just. He did more to extend the national discord over race than to heal the wounds of the war (Miller Center 2012).

After the cumulative effect of Reconstruction policies began to shape the extended dissension of race relations, many freedmen began to despair that they would ever achieve equality in the land of their birth. Some even went so far as to entertain the notion of migrating back to Africa from whence their ancestors came. In September 1877 a freedman named Henry Adams, who was born a slave in Georgia in 1843, wrote a letter to the American Colonization Society saying that he had put together 60,000 "hard laboring people" who were anxious to leave the South (Foner 2005, 189). The society was founded in 1816 with the express purpose of resettling blacks in Africa. "This is a horrible part of the country," Adams wrote, "and our race cannot get money for our labor. . . . It is impossible for us to live with these slaveholders of the South and enjoy the right as they enjoy it." Living in Louisiana at the time, Adams formed a group that called itself the Colonization Council and tried to obtain for African Americans "a territory to ourselves," preferably in Africa "where our forefathers came from." No one knows if Adams succeeded in immigrating to Africa. The last historical record of him was that he was working in New Orleans in 1884, after which he disappears from history. No one knows if he really had gathered 60,000 blacks willing to move to Africa, although it was probably an exaggerated number. His efforts, though, underscored the frustration that many African Americans were having with freedom in an unequal world.

OBSERVATIONS

The liberation of slaves took place in many venues, under many different circumstances, and over an extended period of time. For some, the message of freedom was borne by Yankee troops or freedmen, but for others it was communicated by reluctant masters with varying degrees of civility. No single generalization can be made in the variety of ways in which freedom came. Thousands became contrabands when their masters fled before invading Union troops, and many slaves who stayed behind would welcome the Yankees as liberators. Tens of thousands followed after Sherman's army as it cut through Georgia and the Carolinas. Some slaves helped Yankee soldiers loot the big house; others helped the mistress bury the silver (McPherson 2001). Some of the most trusted slaves, among them house servants and drivers, were often the first to flee the plantation for protection amid the ranks of Union soldiers; others remained faithful to their masters until the end. Many contrabands and freedmen served as guides and scouts for Yankee soldiers, while others pretended to be ignorant or outright refused to give information to Northern armies.

One safe generalization is that the overwhelming majority of slaves welcomed freedom no matter how confusing or dispiriting it proved to be, though some seemed to prefer the way of life they had known for generations no matter how oppressive. It did not take long after the end of the war, however, before ex-slaves realized that being legally free did not mean that they were equal in a white society. In the South, racial hatred erupted almost immediately after the cessation of hostilities, and in the North, though most Northerners opposed slavery, most nevertheless had little use for blacks and feared their competition in the labor force. In one way or another, the news of emancipation had penetrated to the most remote corners of the South by the autumn of 1865 (McPherson 2001). Regardless of how the message of freedom was communicated, it was delivered in a climate of uncertainty for both whites and freedmen. The peculiar institution of slavery had been in place for more than 200 years in North America, and its legacy would be difficult to shed. Many could not envision what freedom really meant, and it took the Reconstruction Amendments to the U.S. Constitution over the next several years after the war to help define the meaning of freedom. For most former slaves it was major change, but for others the change seemed insignificant because they simply continued to do what they had always done, work hard in the fields for white people to eke out a subsistence living.

Historians have long vacillated over the course that history might have taken had Lincoln survived to complete his presidency. Many have theorized that Reconstruction would have been a gentler and more just reunification of the country and that blacks might have benefited from a fuller and more rapid rise to equality. But the hand that fate dealt shaped the course of events for the next century, which saw African Americans assuming menial jobs as sharecroppers, tenant farmers, servants, and porters while at the same time fighting for equality in education and other areas of civil rights and striving to take their place as equals in a multiracial America.

References

Aaron, Daniel. 1973. *The Unwritten War: American Writers and the Civil War.* New York: Knopf.

Adams, Dennis, and Grace Morris Cordial. 2007. "Robert Smalls: War Hero and Legislator." http://www.beaufortcountylibrary.org/htdocs-sirsi/smalls.htm.

Alexander, Danielle. 2004. "Forty Acres and a Mule: The Ruined Hope of Reconstruction." http://www.neh.gov/humanities/2004/januaryfebruary/feature/forty-acres-and-mule.

Anon. 1862. "Jeff Davis's Coachman." *Harper's Weekly: A Journal of Civilization*, June 7, 1862, 363.

Anon. 1864. "The Black Flag." *New York Times*, April 16, 1.

Aptheker, Herbert. 1938. *The Negro in the Civil War.* New York: International Publishers.

Archer, Jermaine O. 2009. *Antebellum Slave Narratives: Cultural and Political Expressions of Africa.* New York: Routledge.

Armstrong, Hannibal. 1924. "How I Hid a Union Spy." *Journal of Negro History* 9(1): 34–40.

Austerman, Wayne R. 2004. "The Black Confederates." In *Black Confederates*, edited by Charles Kelly Barrow, J. H. Segars, and R. B. Rosenburg, 37–49. Gretna, LA: Pelican.

Bailey, Anne J. 2002. "The USCT in the Confederate Heartland, 1864." In *Black Soldiers in Blue: African American Troops in the Civil War Era*, edited by John David Smith, 227–248. Chapel Hill: University of North Carolina Press.

Bailey, Anne J. 2006. *Invisible Southerners: Ethnicity in the Civil War.* Athens: University of Georgia Press.

Bailey, David Thomas. 1980. "A Divided Prism: Two Sources of Black Testimony on Slavery." *Journal of Southern History* 46: 381–404.

Baker, Ronald L. 2000. *Homeless, Friendless, and Penniless: The WPA Interviews with Former Slaves in Indiana.* Bloomington: Indiana University Press.

Ball, Charles. 1859. *Fifty Years in Chains: Or the Life of an American Slave.* Detroit: Negro History Press.

Bankole, Katherine K. 1998. *Slavery and Medicine: Enslavement and Medical Practices in Antebellum Louisiana.* New York: Garland.

Barnickel, Linda. 2010. "'No Federal Prisoners among Them': The Execution of Black Union Soldiers at Jackson, Louisiana." *North and South* 12(1): 59–62.

Barrett, Joseph H. 1865. *Life of Abraham Lincoln.* Cincinnati: Moore, Wilstach and Baldwin.

Barrow, Charles Kelly, J. H. Segars, and R. B. Rosenburg, eds. 2004. *Black Confederates.* Gretna, LA: Pelican.

Bellard, Alfred. 1975. *Gone for a Soldier: The Civil War Memoirs of Private Alfred Bellard.* Boston: Little, Brown.

Berlin, Ira. 1998. *Many Thousands Gone: The First Two Centuries of Slavery in North America.* Cambridge, MA: Belknap.

Berlin, Ira, Francine C. Cary, Steven F. Miller, and Leslie S. Rowland. 1987. "Family and Freedom: Black Families in the American Civil War." *History Today* 37: 8–15.

Berlin, Ira, Marc Favreau, and Steven F. Miller. 2007. *Remembering Slavery: African Americans Talk of Slavery and Emancipation.* New York: New Press.

Berlin, Ira, Barbara J. Fields, Steven F. Miller, Joseph P. Reidy, and Leslie S. Rowland. 1992. *Slaves No More: Three Essays on Emancipation and the Civil War.* New York: Cambridge University Press.

Berlin, Ira, Joseph P. Reidy, and Leslie S. Rowland, eds. 1998. *Freedom's Soldiers: The Black Military Experience in the Civil War.* Cambridge: Cambridge University Press.

Berry, Harrison. 1969. *Slavery and Abolitionism, as Viewed by a Georgia Slave.* 1861; reprint, Philadelphia: Historic Publishers.

Blassingame, John W. 1975. "Using the Testimony of Ex-slaves: Approaches and Problems." *Journal of Southern History* 41: 473–492.

Blassingame, John W., ed. 1977. *Slave Testimony: Two Centuries of Letters, Speeches, Interviews and Autobiographies.* Baton Rouge: Louisiana State University Press.

Blassingame, John W. 1979. *The Slave Community: Plantation Life in the Antebellum South.* New York: Oxford University Press.

Blight, David W. 2001. *Race and Reunion: The Civil War in American Memory.* Cambridge, MA: Harvard University Press.

Botkin, B. A., ed. 1945. *Lay My Burden Down: A Folk History of Slavery.* Chicago: University of Chicago Press.

Bowman, Shearer Davis. 2010. *At the Precipice: Americans North and South during the Secession Crisis.* Chapel Hill: University of North Carolina Press.

Brasher, Glenn David. 2012. *The Peninsula Campaign and the Necessity of Emancipation.* Chapel Hill: University of North Carolina Press.

Brewer, James H. 1969. *The Confederate Negro: Virginia's Craftsmen and Military Laborers, 1861–1865.* Durham, NC: Duke University Press.

Brown, Christopher Leslie, and Philip D. Morgan, eds. 2006. *Arming Slaves: From Classical Times to the Modern Age.* New Haven, CT, and London: Yale University Press.

Brown, William Wells. 2003. *The Negro in the American Rebellion: His Heroism and His Fidelity.* 1867; reprint, Athens: Ohio University Press.

Burton, Brian K. 2001. *Extraordinary Circumstances: The Seven Days Battles.* Bloomington: Indiana University Press.

Cain, Marvin R. 1982. "A 'Face of Battle' Needed: An Assessment of Motives and Men in Civil War Historiography." *Civil War History* 28: 5–27.

Castel, Albert. 2004. "The Fort Pillow Massacre: An Examination of the Evidence." In *Black Flag over Dixie: Racial Atrocities and Reprisals in the Civil War*, edited by Gregory J. W. Urwin, 89–103. Carbondale: Southern Illinois University Press.

Cimprich, John. 2002. "The Fort Pillow Massacre." In *Black Soldiers in Blue: African American Troops in the Civil War Era*, edited by John David Smith, 50–168. Chapel Hill: University of North Carolina Press.

Clark, Peter H. 1969. *The Black Brigade of Cincinnati.* New York: Arno.

Clayton, Ronnie W. 1990. *Mother Wit: The Ex-Slave Narratives of the Louisiana Writer's Project.* New York: Peter Lang.

Close, Stacey K. 1997. *Elderly Slaves of the Plantation South.* New York: Garland.

Cook, Artemas. 1864. Letter to Curtis Babbott, dated January 3, 1864, Rutherford B. Hayes Memorial Library, Fremont, Ohio.

Cooper, William J., Jr. 2000. *Jefferson Davis, American.* New York: Knopf.

Cornish, Dudley Taylor. 1956. *The Sable Arm: Negro Troops in the Union Army, 1861–1865.* New York: Longmans, Green.

Covey, Herbert C. 2007. *African American Slave Medicine: Herbal and Non-Herbal Treatments.* Lanham, MA: Lexington.

Covey, Herbert C., and Dwight Eisnach. 2009. *What the Slaves Ate: Recollections of African American Foods and Foodways from the Slave Narratives.* Santa Barbara, CA: Greenwood.

Covey, Herbert C., and Paul Lockman. 1996. "Narrative References to Older African Americans Living under Slavery." *Social Science Journal* 33: 23–37.

Crawford, Martin. 2000. "Jefferson Davis and the Confederacy." In *The American Civil War*, edited by Susan-Mary Grant and Brian Holden Reid, 98–117. Harlow, UK: Longman.

Davenport, A. 1861. Letter to his family, dated June 19, 1861. New York Historical Society, New York.

Davis, Jefferson. 1881. *The Rise and Fall of the Confederate Government*, Vols. 1–2. Richmond, VA: Garret and Massie.

Davis, Jefferson. 1889. *A Short History of the Confederate States of America.* New York: Belford.

Davis, Robert Scott. 2007. "'Near Andersonville': An Historical Note on Civil War Legend and Reality." *African American History* 92(1): 96–105.

Delaware Valley Rhythm & Blues Society. 2011. "Heroes of Camden, New Jersey: Landsman John Lawson." http://www.dvrbs.com/CW/CamdenCountyHeroes-JohnLawson.htm.

Dollard, John. 1957. *Caste and Class in a Southern Town.* Garden City, NY: Doubleday.

Douglas, Robert L. 1989. "Myth or Truth: A White and Black View of Slavery." *Journal of Black Studies* 19(3): 343–360.

Douglass, Frederick. 1845. *Narrative of the Life of Frederick Douglass, an American Slave, Written by Himself.* Boston: Anti-Slavery Office.

Douglass, Frederick. 1855. *My Bondage and My Freedom.* Chicago: University of Illinois Press. Reprinted in 1987 and edited by William L. Andrews.

Douglass, Frederick. 1863. "Why a Colored Man Should Enlist." The Frederick Douglass Papers at the Library of Congress, http://memory .loc.gov/cgi-bin/ampage?collId=mfd&fileName=22/22006/22006page .db&recNum=0.

Durden, Robert F. 1972. *The Gray and the Black: The Confederate Debate on Emancipation.* Baton Rouge: Louisiana State University Press.

Eaton, Clement. 1977. *Jefferson Davis.* New York: Free Press.

E.D.W. 1864. "Letter to the Editor." *Christian Recorder*, April 2, 1864, http://battleofolustee.org/letters/edw_54th_mass_cr.html.

Engs, Robert Francis. 2002. "Slavery in the Civil War Era." http://www .civilwarhome.com/slavery.htm.

Equiano, Olaudah. 1995. *The Interesting Narrative of the Life of Olaudah Equiano, or Gustavus Vassa, Written by Himself.* Edited by Robert J. Allison. 1789; reprint, Boston: Bedford Books.

Escott, Paul D. 1979. *Slavery Remembered.* Chapel Hill: University of North Carolina Press.

Faust, Drew Gilpin. 1980. "Culture, Conflict and Community: The Meaning of Power on an Ante-bellum Plantation." *Journal of Southern History* 14(1): 83–96.

Faust, Drew Gilpin. 2008. *This Republic of Suffering: Death and the American Civil War.* New York: Vintage.

Finkelman, Paul, and Joseph C. Miller, eds. 1998. *Macmillan Encyclopedia of World Slavery*, Vols. 1–2. New York: Macmillan.

Fisk University. 1945. *Unwritten History of Slavery: Autobiographical Account of Negro Ex-Slaves.* Nashville: Social Science Institute.

Fold3. 2012. "Confederate African Americans: Civil War." U.S. Military Records, Division of Archives, Lindon, UT, http://www.fold3.com/ page/1201_confederate_african_americanscivil_war/.

Foner, Eric. 1987. "Rights and the Constitution in Black Life during the Civil War and Reconstruction." *Journal of American History* 74(3): 863–883.

Foner, Eric. 1988. *Reconstruction: America's Unfinished Revolution, 1863–1877.* New York: Harper and Row.

Foner, Eric. 2005. *Forever Free: The Story of Emancipation and Reconstruction.* New York: Knopf.

Forbes, Ella. 1998. *African American Women during the Civil War.* New York: Garland.

Forrest, Nathan Bedford. 1872. "Testimony before the Joint Select Committee to Inquire into the Condition of Affairs in the Late Insurrectionary States, 42nd Congress, 2nd Session." *Senate Report 41*, Vol. 13. Washington, D.C.

Frank, Lisa Tendrich. 2008. *Women in the American Civil War*, Vol. 1. Santa Barbara, CA: ABC-CLIO.

Franklin, John Hope. 1965. *From Slavery to Freedom: A History of American Negroes.* 2nd ed. New York: Knopf.

Franklin, John Hope. 1967. *The Negro in Twentieth Century America: A Reader on the Struggle for Civil Rights.* New York: Random House.

Franklin, John Hope, ed. 1970. *Reminiscences of an Active Life: The Autobiography of John Roy Lynch.* Chicago: University of Chicago Press.

Franklin, John Hope, and Alfred A. Moss Jr. 2000. *From Slavery to Freedom: A History of American Negroes.* 8th ed. New York: Knopf.

Genovese, Eugene V. 1965. *The Political Economy of Slavery.* New York: Vintage.

Genovese, Eugene V. 1976. *Roll, Jordon, Roll: The World the Slaves Made.* New York: Vintage.

Goodson, Martha Graham. 1979. "The Slave Narrative Collection: A Tool for Reconstructing Afro-American Women's History." *Western Journal of Black Studies* 3: 116–122.

Gordon, Lawrence. 1979. "A Brief Look at Blacks in Depression Mississippi, 1929–1934: Eyewitness Accounts." *Journal of Negro History* 64: 377–390.

Grant, Susan-Mary. 2000. "Fighting for Freedom: African-American Soldiers in the Civil War." In *The American Civil War*, edited by Susan-Mary Grant and Brian Holden Reid, 191–213. Harlow, UK: Longman.

Ham, Debra Newman, ed. 1993. *The African-American Mosaic: A Library of Congress Resource Guide for the Study of Black History and Culture.* Washington, DC: Library of Congress.

Hammond, Thomas. 2007. "William H. Carney: 54th Massachusetts Soldier and First Black U.S. Medal of Honor Recipient." *America's Civil War,* January 29, http://www.historynet.com/william-h-carney-54th-massachusetts-soldier-and-first-black-us-medal-of-honor-recipient.htm.

Hanna, Charles W. 2002. *African American Recipients of the Medal of Honor: A Biographical Dictionary, Civil War through Vietnam War.* Jefferson, NC: McFarland.

Hannon, Helen. 2004. "African Americans in the Navy during the Civil War: Interview with Steven J. Ramold and William B. Gould IV." *Journal of African American History* 89: 358–361.

Harper, Charles W. 2004. "Black Loyalty under the Confederacy." In *Black Confederates*, edited by Charles Kelly Barrow, J. H. Segars, and R. B. Rosenburg, 7–29. Gretna, LA: Pelican.

Harrison, James L. 2004. "A Tribute to Loyal Confederates." In *Black Confederates*, edited by Charles Kelly Barrow, J. H. Segars, and R. B. Rosenburg, 61–70. Gretna, LA: Pelican.

Hattaway, Herman, and Richard E. Beringer. 2002. *Jefferson Davis, Confederate President.* Lawrence: University of Kansas Press.

Hermann, Janet Sharp. 1999. *The Pursuit of a Dream.* Jackson: University Press of Mississippi.

Hewitt, Lawrence Lee. 2002. "An Ironic Route to Glory: Louisiana's Native Guards at Port Hudson." In *Black Soldiers in Blue: African American Troops in the Civil War Era*, edited by John David Smith, 78–106. Chapel Hill: University of North Carolina Press.

Hilliard, Sam Bowers. 1972. *Hogmeat and Hoecake: Food Supply in the Old South, 1840–1860.* Carbondale: Southern Illinois University Press.

Hoar, Jay S. 2004. "Aged Body Servants among the Last Survivors of the Confederate Army." In *Black Confederates*, edited by Charles Kelly Barrow, J. H. Segars, and R. B. Rosenburg, 71–91. Gretna, LA: Pelican.

Hollandsworth, James G., Jr. 1995. *The Louisiana Native Guards: The Black Military Experience during the Civil War.* Baton Rouge: Louisiana State University Press.

Hollandsworth, James G., Jr. 2004. "The Execution of White Officers from Black Units by Confederate Forces during the Civil War." In *Black Flag over Dixie: Racial Atrocities and Reprisals in the Civil War*, edited by Gregory J. W. Urwin, 52–64. Carbondale: Southern Illinois University Press.

Hurmence, Belinda. 1990. *Before Freedom: 48 Oral Histories Former North and South Carolina Slaves.* New York: Mentor.

Jacobs, Harriet A. 1987. *Incidents in the Life of a Slave Girl Written by Herself.* 1857; reprint, Cambridge, MA: Harvard University Press.

Jameson, John Franklin, Henry Eldridge Bourne, and Robert Livingston Schuyler, eds. 1896. *The American Historical Review,* Vol. 1. New York: Macmillan.

Johnson, Calvin E., Jr. 2003. "The Jefferson Davis Funeral Train Story," June 3, http://www.freerepublic.com/focus/f-news/924431/posts.

Johnson, Clifton H. 1969. *God Struck Me Dead.* Philadelphia: United Church Press.

Johnson, Clint. 2008. *Pursuit: The Chase, Capture, Persecution and Surprising Release of Confederate President Jefferson Davis.* New York: Citadel.

Jones, James Henry. 1911. "Jefferson Davis as His Negro Servant Saw Him." *New York Times,* June 11.

Jordan, Ervin L., Jr. 1995. *Black Confederates and Afro-Yankees in Civil War Virginia.* Charlottesville: University of Virginia Press.

Joyner, Charles W. 1971. "Soul Food and the Sambo Stereotype: Foodlore from the Slave Narrative Collection." *Keystone Folklore Quarterly* 16 (Winter): 171–177.

Joyner, Charles W. 1984. *Down by the Riverside: A South Carolina Slave Community.* Urbana: University of Illinois Press.

Joyner, Charles W. 1991. "The World of the Plantation Slaves." In *Before Freedom Came: African-American Life in the Antebellum South,* edited by Edward D. C. Campbell Jr. and Kym S. Rice, 51–99. Charlottesville: University Press of Virginia.

Kennedy, Randall. 2002. *Nigger: The Strange Career of a Troublesome Word.* New York: Random House.

Kennedy, Randall. n.d. "A Note on the Word 'Nigger.'" HarpWeek, http://blackhistory.harpweek.com/1Introduction/RandallKennedy Essay.htm.

Killion, Ronald, and Charles Waller. 1973. *Slavery Time When I Was Chillun down on Marster's Plantation.* Savannah, GA: Beehive.

King, Wilma. 1995. *Stolen Childhood: Slave Youth in Nineteenth-Century America.* Bloomington: Indiana University Press.

Kiple, Kenneth F., and Virginia Himmelsteib King. 1981. *Another Dimension to the Black Diaspora: Diet, Disease, and Racism.* Cambridge, MA: Cambridge University Press.

Kiple, Kenneth F., and Virginia Himmelsteib Kiple. 1977. "Slave Child Mortality: Some Nutritional Answers to a Perennial Puzzle." *Journal of Social History* 10: 284–309.

Levin, Kevin M. 2010. "Until Every Negro Has Been Slaughtered." *Civil War Times* 49(5): 32–37.

Levine, Bruce. 2006. *Confederate Emancipation: Southern Plans to Free and Arm Slaves during the Civil War.* Oxford: Oxford University Press.

Lincoln, Abraham. 1862. "Executive Order Authorizing Employment of 'Contrabands.'" The American Presidency Project, July 22, http://www.presidency.ucsb.edu/ws/?pid=69815.

Litwack, Leon F. 1979. *Been in the Storm So Long: The Aftermath of Slavery.* New York: Knopf.

Lofton, Williston H. 1949. "Labor and the Negro during the Civil War." *Journal of Negro History* 34(3): 251–273.

Louisiana State Legislature. 1862. "Official Copy of the Militia Law of Louisiana, Adopted by the State Legislature, Jan. 23, 1862." http://openlibrary.org/books/OL24597062M/Official_copy_of_the_militia_ law_of_Louisiana.

Lovett, Bobby L. 1976. "The Negro's Civil War in Tennessee, 1861–1865." *Journal of Negro History* 61(1): 36–50.

Lowe, Richard. 2002. "Battle on the Levee." In *Black Soldiers in Blue: African American Troops in the Civil War Era*, edited by John David Smith, 107–135. Chapel Hill: University of North Carolina Press.

Lowry, Thomas P., and Albert H. Ledoux. 2009. "More Black Confederates?" *North and South* 11(3): 58–60.

Lunsford, P. Charles. 2004. "The Forgotten Confederates." In *Black Confederates*, edited by Charles Kelly Barrow, J. H. Segars, and R. B. Rosenburg, 97–102. Gretna, LA: Pelican.

MacDonald, John. 2011. *The Historical Atlas of the Civil War.* New York: Chartwell Books.

MacKethan, Lucinda H. 1998. "Looking for Marlboro Jones." *Southern Review* 34(1): 140–141.

Martin, Joan M. 2000. *More than Chains and Toil: A Christian Work Ethic of Enslaved Women.* Louisville, KY: John Knox.

Matrana, Marc A. 2009. *Lost Plantations of the South.* Jackson: University of Mississippi Press.

Mays, Joe H. 1984. *Black Americans and Their Contributions toward Union Victory in the American Civil War, 1861–1865.* New York: Lanham.

McConnell, Roland C. 1950. "Concerning the Procurement of Negro Troops in the South during the Civil War." *Journal of Negro History* 35(3): 315–319.

McKissack, Patricia C., and Fredrick L. McKissack. 2003. *Days of Jubilee: The End of Slavery in the United States.* New York: Scholastic Press.

McMillen, Neil R. 2007. "Isaiah T. Montgomery, 1847–1924" (in two parts). History Now, http://mshistory.k12.ms.us/articles/55/isaiah-t -montgomery -1847–1924-Part-I and http://mshistory.k12.ms.us/articles/ 55/index.php?id=57.

McPherson, James M. 1965. *The Negro's Civil War: How American Negroes Felt and Acted during the War for the Union.* New York: Pantheon Books.

McPherson, James M. 1967. *Marching toward Freedom: The Negro in the Civil War, 1861–1865.* New York: Knopf.

McPherson, James M. 1988. *Battle Cry of Freedom: The Civil War Era.* Oxford: Oxford University Press.

McPherson, James M. 1993. *The Negro's Civil War.* New York: Vintage.

McPherson, James M. 1995. "Who Freed the Slaves?" *Proceedings of the American Philosophical Society* 139(1): 1–10.

McPherson, James M. 2001. *Ordeal by Fire: The Civil War and Reconstruction.* New York: McGraw-Hill.

Miller Center. 2012. "American President Andrew Johnson: A Life in Brief." http://millercenter.org/president/johnson/essays/biography/1.

Mohr, Clarence L. 1986. *On the Threshold of Freedom: Masters and Slaves in Civil War Georgia.* Athens: University of Georgia Press.

Moore, Stacy Gibbons. 1989. "Established and Well Cultivated: Afro-American Foodways in Early Virginia." *Virginia Cavalcade* 39:70–83.

Musick, Mike. 2012. "Is There Archival Proof of Black Confederates?" *Civil War Times* 51(1): 35.

Myrdal, Gunyar. 1962. *An American Dilemma: The Negro Problem.* New York: Harper and Row.

National Archives. 2012. "African American Heritage: Select Images from Freedmen's Bureau Records." http://www.archives.gov/research/african-americans/freedmens-bureau/highlights.html.

National Humanities Center Resource Toolbox. 2013. "The Making of African American Identity: Vol. I, 1500–1865." http://nationalhumanitiescenter.org/pds/maai/emancipation/text6/warsoldierswpa.pdf.

National Underground Railroad Freedom Center. 2012. "The Underground Railroad." http://freedomcenter.org/underground-railroad-0.

Nichols, Charles H. 1963. *Many Thousands Gone: The Ex-Slaves Account of Their Bondage and Freedom.* Leiden, Netherlands: E. J. Brill.

Northup, Solomon. 1968. *Twelve Years a Slave.* 1853; reprint, Baton Rouge: Louisiana State University Press.

Obatala, J. K., and Rebecca Maksel. 1979. "The Unlikely Story of Blacks Who Were Loyal to Dixie." *Smithsonian Magazine* 9: 94–101.

Perdue, Charles L., Jr., Thomas E. Barden, and Robert K. Phillips, eds. 1976. *Weevils in the Wheat: Interviews with Virginia Ex-Slaves.* Charlottesville: University Press of Virginia.

Phillips, Ulrich Bonnell. 1918. *American Negro Slavery: A Survey of Supply, Employment and Control of Negro Labor as Determined by the Plantation Regime.* New York: D. Appleton.

Pillai, Prabhakar. 2008. "Slavery during the Civil War." http://www.buzzle.com/articles/slavery-during-the-civil-war.html.

Public Broadcast System. 2012. "The Underground Railroad, c. 1780–1862." http://www.pbs.org/wgbh/aia/part4/4p2944.html.

Quarles, Benjamin. 1968. *The Negro in the Civil War.* New York: Russell and Russell.

Ramold, Steven J. 2002. *Slaves, Sailors, Citizens: African Americans in the Union Navy.* DeKalb: Northern Illinois University Press.

Ransom, Roger, and Richard Sutch. 1975. "The Impact of the Civil War and of Emancipation on Southern Agriculture." *Explorations in Economic History* 12: 1–28.

Rawick, George P., ed. 1972. *The American Slave: A Composite Autobiography*, Vols. 1–19. Westport, CT: Greenwood.

Redkey, Edwin S., ed. 1992. *A Grand Army of Black Men: Letters from African-American Soldiers in the Union Army, 1861–1865.* New York: Cambridge University Press.

Reed, John A., and Luther Samuel Dickey. 1910. *History of 101st Pennsylvania Veteran Volunteer Infantry, 1861–1865*. Chicago: L. S. Dickey.

Reid, Robert D. 1950. "The Negro in Alabama during the Civil War." *Journal of Negro History* 35(3): 265–288.

Rose, P. K. [aka Ken Daigler]. 1999. *Black Dispatches: Black American Contributions to Union Intelligence during the Civil War.* McLean, VA: Central Intelligence Agency, Center for the Study of Intelligence.

Salmon, John S. 2001. *The Official Virginia Civil War Battlefield Guide.* Mechanicsburg, PA: Stackpole.

Savitt, Todd L. 1978. *Medicine and Slavery: The Diseases and Health Care of Blacks in Antebellum Virginia.* Urbana: University of Illinois Press.

Sears, Stephen W. 1992. *To the Gates of Richmond: The Peninsula Campaign.* New York: Ticknor and Fields.

Segars, J. H., and Charles Kelly Barrow, eds. 2007. *Black Southerners in Confederate Armies: A Collection of Historical Accounts.* Gretna, LA: Pelican.

Shackel, Paul A. 2001. "Public Memory and the Search for Power in American Historical Archaeology." *American Anthropologist* 103(3): 655–670.

Shaffer, Donald R. 2004. *After the Glory: The Struggles of Black Civil War Veterans.* Lawrence: University of Kansas Press.

Shannon, Fred Albert. 1965. *The Organization and Administration of the Union Army, 1861–1865.* 2 vols. 1928; reprint, Cleveland, OH: Arthur H. Clark.

Smith, John David. 1996. *Black Voices from Reconstruction, 1865–1877.* Brookfield, CT: Millbrook.

Smith, John David, ed. 2002. *Black Soldiers in Blue: African American Troops in the Civil War Era.* Chapel Hill: University of North Carolina Press.

Smith, John David. 2003. "Introduction." In *The Negro in the American Rebellion: His Heroism and His Fidelity*, by William Wells Brown, xv–xl. Athens: Ohio University Press.

Sons of Confederate Veterans. 2012. "History of Beauvoir." http://beauvoir .org/history.html#top.

Stampp, Kenneth. 1956. *The Peculiar Institution: Slavery in the Antebellum South.* New York: Knopf.

Steckel, Richard H. 1986a. "A Dreadful Childhood: The Excess Mortality of American Slaves." *Social Science History* 10: 427–465.

Steckel, Richard H. 1986b. "A Peculiar Population: The Nutrition, Health, and Mortality of American Slaves from Childhood to Maturity." *Journal of Economic History* 46: 721–741.

Sunderland, Jonathan, D. 2004. *African Americans at War: An Encyclopedia.* Santa Barbara, CA: ABC-CLIO.

Sutch, Richard. 1975. "The Treatment Received by American Slaves: A Critical Review of the Evidence Presented in Time on the Cross." *Explorations in Economic History* 12: 386–394.

Sutch, Richard. 1976. "The Care and Feeding of Slaves." In *Reckoning with Slavery: A Critical Study in the Quantitative History of American Negro Slavery*, edited by Paul A. David, Herbert G. Gutman, Richard Sutch, Peter Temin, and Gavin Wright, 231–301. New York: Oxford University Press.

Tate, Allen. 1998. *Jefferson Davis: His Rise and Fall.* 1929; reprint, Nashville: J. S. Sanders.

Taylor, Joe Gray. 1982. *Eating, Drinking, and Visiting in the South: An Informal History.* Baton Rouge: Louisiana State University Press.

Taylor, Susie King. 1902. *Reminiscences of My Life in Camp.* Boston: Self-published.

Texas State Historical Association. 2013. "Buchel, Augustus Carl." http://www.tshaonline.org/handbook/online/articles/fbu03.

Thomas, Brian W. 1995. "Source Criticism and the Interpretation of African-American Sites." *Southeastern Archaeology* 14(2): 149–157.

Tomblin, Barbara Brooks. 2009. *Bluejackets and Contrabands: African Americans and the Union Navy.* Lexington: University Press of Kentucky.

Trinkley, Michael. 2006. "South Carolina—African-Americans—Hunger and Other Hardships." http://www.sciway.net/afam/slavery/food.html.

Turner, Maxine. 1988. *Navy Gray: Story of the Confederate Navy on the Chattahoochee and Apalachicola Rivers.* Tuscaloosa: University of Alabama Press.

Urwin, Gregory J. W., ed. 2004. *Black Flag over Dixie: Racial Atrocities and Reprisals in the Civil War.* Carbondale: Southern Illinois University Press.

U.S. Army Center of Military History. 2011. "Medal of Honor Recipients." http://www.history.army.mil/html/moh/civwaral.html.

U.S. Bureau of the Census. 1923. *Fourteenth Census of the United States, 1920.* Washington, DC: U.S. Government Printing Office.

U.S. Bureau of the Census. 1933. *Fifteenth Census of the United States, 1930.* Washington, DC: U.S. Government Printing Office.

U.S. Bureau of the Census. 1975. *Historical Statistics of the United States: Colonial Times to 1970, Part 1.* Washington, DC: U.S. Bureau of the Census.

U.S. Gen Web Project. 2012. "36th U.S. Colored Infantry Medal of Honor Winners." www.ncgenweb.us/ncusct/medals.htm.

Valley of the Shadow Project. 2012. "Freedmen's Bureau Records: W. Storer How to Orlando Brown, September 1, 1865." The Valley of the Shadow Project, Virginia Center for Digital History, http://valley.lib .virginia.edu/papers/B1113.

Valuska, David L. 1993. *The African American in the Union Navy, 1861–1865.* New York: Garland.

Varhola, Michael O. 2011. *Life in Civil War America.* Cincinnati: Family Tree Books.

Virginia Writers' Project. 1940. *The Negro in Virginia.* New York: Hastings House.

Wade, Richard C. 1964. *Slavery in the Cities: The South, 1820–1860.* New York: Oxford University Press.

Wagner, Margaret E., Gary W. Gallagher, and Paul Finkelman, eds. 2002. *The Library of Congress Civil War Desk Reference.* New York: Simon and Schuster.

Wallenstein, Peter. 1998. "Slave Narratives." In *Macmillan Encyclopedia of World Slavery*, Vol. 2, edited by Paul Finkelman and Joseph C. Miller, 803–805. New York: Simon and Schuster.

Ward, Andrew. 2008. *The Slaves' War: The Civil War in the Words of Former Slaves.* Boston: Houghton Mifflin.

Warfield, Carolyn. 1925. "For Freedom and Citizenship." *Grand Army Scout*, Newsletter of the GAR Civil War Museum & Library, Philadelphia, PA, http://pasuvcw19.homestead.com/Dispatches/Grand_Army_Scout _Newsletter_Winter_2011a.pdf.

Washington, Booker T. 1901. *Up from Slavery: An Autobiography.* New York: Doubleday.

Washington, John E. 1942. *They Knew Lincoln.* New York: E. P. Dutton.

Weider History Group. 2012. "Civil War Soldiers." http://www.historynet .com/civil-war-soldiers.

Weinberg, Carl R. 2012. "Judith Henry Carter at the Crossroads." *OAH Magazine of History* 26(2), http://magazine.oah.org/issues/262/ weinberg.html.

Wesley, Charles H. 1919. "The Employment of Negroes as Soldiers in the Confederate Army." *Journal of Negro History* 4(3): 239–253.

Wesley, Charles H. 1962. "The Civil War and the Negro-American." *Journal of Negro History* 47(2): 77–96.

Westwood, Howard C. 1992. *Black Troops, White Commanders, and Freedmen during the Civil War.* Carbondale: Southern Illinois University Press.

Wiley, Bell Irvin. 1938. *Southern Negroes, 1861–1865.* New Haven, CT: Yale University Press.

Wiley, Bell Irvin. 1952. "Billy Yank and the Black Folk." *Journal of Negro History* 36(1): 35–52.

Williams, David. 2005. *A People's History of the Civil War: Struggles for the Meaning of Freedom.* New York: New Press.

Williams, David. 2008. *Bitterly Divided: The South's Inner Civil War.* New York: New Press.

Williams, George Washington. 1968. *A History of the Negro Troops in the War of the Rebellion, 1861–65.* New York: Bergman.

Wilson, Keith P. 2002. *Campfires of Freedom: The Camp Life of Black Soldiers during the Civil War.* Kent, OH: Kent State University Press.

Winsboro, Irvin D. S. 2007. "Give Them Their Due: A Reassessment of African Americans and Union Army Services in Florida during the Civil War." *Journal of African American History* 92: 327–346.

Wish, Harvey. 1938. "Slave Disloyalty under the Confederacy." *Journal of Negro History* 23(4): 435–450.

Wolters, Raymond. 1975. "The New Deal and the Negro." In *The New Deal: The National Level*, Vol. 1, edited by John Braeman, Robert H. Bremmer, and David Brody, 170–217. Columbus: Ohio State University Press.

Woodward, C. Vann. 1974. "History of Slave Sources." *American Historical Review* 79: 470–481.

Woolley, John T., and Gerhard Peters. 1999. "Abraham Lincoln: Executive Order Authorizing Employment of 'Contrabands,' July 22, 1862." The American Presidency Project, University of California, Santa Barbara, http://www.presidency.ucsb.edu/ws/?pid=69815.

Yee, Gary. 2007. "The Black Confederate Sharpshooter." *Military Collector and Historian* 59(2): 144–146.

Yentsch, Anne E. 2007. "Excavating the South's African American Food History." In *African American Foodways: Explorations of History and Culture*, edited by Anne L. Bower, 59–98. Urbana: University of Illinois Press.

Yetman, Norman R. 1967. "The Background of the Slave Narrative Collection." *American Quarterly* 19: 534–553.

Yetman, Norman R. 1984. "Ex-Slave Interviews and the Historiography of Slavery." *American Quarterly* 36: 181–210.

Index

About the Authors

HERBERT C. COVEY has worked extensively with the Works Progress Administration narratives that form the basis of this book. He has authored or coauthored *What the Slaves Ate: Recollections of African American Foods and Foodways from the Slave Narratives* (Greenwood, 2009), *African American Slave Medicine: Herbal and Non-Herbal Treatments* (Lexington Books, 2007), *Helping People Addicted to Methamphetamine* (Praeger, 2008), *The Methamphetamine Crisis* (Praeger, 2006), *Youth Gangs* (Charles C. Thomas, 2006), *Street Gangs throughout the World* (Charles C. Thomas, 2003 and 2009), *A History of the Social Perceptions of People with Disabilities* (Charles C. Thomas, 1998), *Juvenile Gangs,* 2nd ed. (Charles C. Thomas, 1997), *Images of Older People in Western Art and Society* (Praeger, 1991), and *Theoretical Frameworks in the Sociology of Education* (Shenkman, 1980).

DWIGHT EISNACH has had a lengthy career in newspaper reporting and public relations. He is the coauthor of *What the Slaves Ate: Recollections from the Slave Narratives* (Greenwood, 2009) and has edited several other books and periodicals. Early in his newspaper years, he won several national awards for investigative reporting and feature writing.